Uncommon Sense

Building Lives of Love, Faith and Freedom

Carroll Rose Coplin, M.Ed., M.S., LPC

Uncommon Sense

ISBN 978-0-9916392-0-5

Published by:
Uncommon Sense, LLC

Uncommon
Sense

CONTENTS

PROLOGUE

HERE'S WHERE I WAS. I had two master's degrees and was managing a successful private practice as a licensed counselor and corporate consultant. I loved my work and had a second career as a wife and mother. Then one day, I had a realization. I was sitting at a lake near our home pondering life and asking God where to put my energies when a message silently swept through my head and startled me out of daydreaming.

"You only have 10 more years to live."

When that happened, I felt sad and more than a little panicked. I realized there were many things I would want my daughters to know if they lost their mommy at the ages of eleven and thirteen, so I began writing journals to tell them about our lives together and to share what I knew about living life as a Christian.

Fast-forward several years. I had given up corporate suits for blue jeans and become a full-time teacher and nurturer to my own family. Most of the time, I was busy creating a stimulating, child-friendly world for my now *three* little girls. I also took the time to attend a three-year Bible study. I had read God's Word front to back and was instructed by some great teachers. They explained many things about Old and New Testament I had not understood before, such as how infinitely good and wise God is. They taught me how, for a Christian, the Old Testament (the sacred writings of the Jews) and the New Testament (the sacred writings of the Christians) are considered to be Scripture. They also helped me understand that Christ, the human presence of God on Earth, was a Jewish rabbi (teacher) who taught us new (Christian) ways of relating to and understanding God.

So why did I lay face down on my living room floor one day, crying and pleading with my incredible God? Because life at home was harder than life at work had been. It was far less predictable. My parenting included haphazard decisions based on my moods. Too often, this was followed by insistent enforcement because I didn't want my authority to be undermined. I believed I had to let my children know who was running the show—raise my voice, send them to time out, even spank them at times, and lecture, lecture, lecture. I told my husband I felt like a trashcan for everything that went wrong in our family life.

"Mom, she called me stupid!"

"Mom, she took my doll."

"Mom, she won't stop talking, and I'm trying to watch…!"

By the end of the day, I was like an overflowing dumpster, and trash was coming out of my mouth. I was repulsed by the pretty-on-the-outside but ugly-on-the-inside person I had become. I needed help—the kind no human could give me.

As far as my marriage was concerned, things looked good from the outside. While most of my time was dedicated to nurturing my three little girls, I also worked at having an orderly and beautiful home for my husband. I cleaned up the house (and myself) before he came home, and had his dinner waiting for him. So why did he drink beer and watch sports and ignore his family? I remember complaining to a friend, Dr. William Van Horn, a brilliant counselor with laser-sharp insights. I told him that my loving husband had become dull and insensitive. Dr. Van Horn responded, "He's been married to *you* for ten years."

Ouch.

Most marriages are undermined by things like gambling, sexual misconduct by one or both spouses, rampant workaholism, alcoholism, finances, or apathy. Sometimes we simply become "dull" after being together for years. These are all hard battlegrounds that require the couple to work together if they are going to win the war and reignite passion and love. In order to rebuild our marriage, Jim and I consulted Dr. Van Horn, and he gave us a weekly to-do list. We had attended his healing seminar and were in the midst of follow-up meetings. We had been introduced to a love for humans that was so profound that it changed us forever. We wanted more and for our marriage to survive, so every Wednesday night, we came together with 50 to 70 other couples. If, and only if we had done our homework every day that week, Dr. Van Horn would talk with us in front of the group. We did our homework. Look at this list of passion-builders on the following page Jim and I worked into our lives each day. (Don't close the book when you read them. They are wonderful, but they are not required activities.)

COUPLES - DAILY GOALS

DAILY - each person	SUN	MON	TUE	WED	THU	FRI	SAT
KISSES and Verbally Affirm - Initiate 2 Kisses per day lasting 5 seconds per kiss outside of the bed and separate from hugs							
HUGS and Verbally Affirm - Initiate 2 hugs per day lasting 5 seconds per hug outside of the bed and separate from kisses							
AFFIRMATION CARD - 25 times per day, including affirmation of partner							
FLOW GRADING - each person is to give an overall grade for the day (if not an A, list 3 things that person did well, 3 things you didn't like and 3 ways they could raise the grade							

DAILY - lead person (male - odd days / female - even days)	SUN	MON	TUE	WED	THU	FRI	SAT
POSITIVE COMMUNICATION - 15 minutes or more per day - Hold hands 9 Things: 3 things you liked about the other, 3 ways they blessed you, and 3 ways God blessed you							
HOLDING - 15 minutes each in cradle position, listen to Christian music and focus on flowing in God's love							
ISSUE TIME - must hold hands, maximum of 15 minutes per day							
MEALS Together - 2 per day							
BIBLE Reading Together - Minimum of two minutes per day							
PRAYER Together - Minimum of two minutes per day with prayer list with 10 things on list							

WEEKLY - each person	HIS		HERS	
RELATIONSHIPS - 2 hours per week with other IHR (can be four 30 min. times)				

WEEKLY

FUN Together - activity we do for minimum of 2 hours per week (can be four 30 min. times)				
ASSEMBLY - attend church once per week together				
LETTER READING or SAD MOVIE - goal is to be able to cry together - may read sad letter or watch a sad movie together once per week				
CASUAL DATE- 3 hours (min.) can do double date, movies or public place *Or (one date per week, alternating casual/romantic and who plans)* **ROMANTIC DATE -** 3 hours (min.) must be alone so can talk intimately, no movies/crowds				

MARRIED COUPLES only

MAKING LOVE - minimum of three times per week (scheduled or spontaneous)				

I'm embarrassed to confess it, but I was angry with Jim and wanted to expose his faults in front of everyone. I also knew I needed all of the help I could get with my own out-of-control emotions. So, yes, we did everything on the list, and we spilled our guts each week. You know what came out of that? *Passion*. For one another. For our children and friends. And, most of all, for God. But this book is not about the list, it's about the strategies God gave me for living into this list. The hardest thing to do was to express positive communications all day and save my complaints for an isolated fifteen-minute window. At that time, I was a hurting, angry, depressed woman who was not accustomed to life being out of control. I was used to being a professional who was the paragon of virtue for her clients. And now here I stood, an intolerant and inconsolable mother to three needy children and a wife to a man I didn't like.

I didn't want to have an affair. I didn't want to resort to alcohol or to go back to work and stay too busy to notice that my home life needed mending. But I also didn't want to continue to live the way I had been, so I determined that I would lie face down on my living room rug and plead with God for a change—and that I wouldn't stand up until I had finished asking.

Now here is the neat thing that happened after my session with my loving God: He answered. I stood up, washed my face, and went to my kitchen table to journal. And what I received from Him was nothing short of miraculous. I had attended wonderful seminars, read great books, and realized some important things about my own qualities and needs. But what God gave me that day was more valuable than any of the wisdom I had gained from former experiences. This thing that God gave me was tangible. It's called a "character ticket." It is something I can use when I am angry or disappointed that won't take a toll on my relationships with others. More importantly, it aligns with Scripture. Essentially, it allowed me to give others feedback without expressing anger. (See Prov. 15:1.)

Over time, the Character Tickets developed into an entire lifestyle characterized not by my moods or attitudes, but by the simple teachings and philosophies of my faith. My entire family has had a more soothing and healing life because of it. *Uncommon Sense*, as I eventually came to call it, made parental leadership more respectful, interactive, predictable, affectionate, and likely. It made the children aware that they were loved, valuable, and accountable. More importantly, it helped us all to experience God every day.

By the way, I don't know why I heard what I did at the lake because I have lived more than ten years since that day. Or maybe I just missed a phrase and God told me, "*Live as though* you only have ten more years to live." I'm just thankful I responded the way I did: I have some great journals to hand down to my daughters and am infinitely happier for it.

If you make it through this book and implement some of its concepts and strategies you will:

- Learn to walk a thoughtful Christian path and leave the consequences to God.
- Make sure that your actions and your philosophies embrace loving Scriptures and exemplify Christ's teachings.
- Create simple, scriptural, predictable responses to life under the roof—at home and at work.
- Simplify your home environment.
- Simplify your relational environment.
- Understand features of human capacity and human limitations.
- Create a team to hold you accountable for your desires to honor Christ and to build you up when you get discouraged.
- Live an extraordinary life rather than a mediocre one.

INTRODUCTION

WHY IS IT THAT SO many professing Christians have so little knowledge of their faith? How can people go to church for years and not have a clue where the books of the Bible are located or what the contents of those books teach us about the management of our everyday lives? How is it that we are content to live by a philosophical phrase like "Do unto others as you would have them do unto you" without questioning it? The answers are actually rather simple: We are not being taught sufficiently, we are not content, and we often don't follow through on the wonderful wisdoms we *do* know.

In recent years books, such as *7 Habits of Highly Successful People* by Stephen Covey and The *Purpose Driven Life* by Rick Warren, have sky-rocketed in popularity as we strive to find significance and to live in ways that bring joy to our souls and peace to our world. Why do we seek these things? Because our Creator placed those needs within us. Humans inherently sense that we are made to live forever, to have purpose, and to know love, joy, and peace, throughout our lives on earth. Although we fight it, we know that good can come from tests, trials, and trauma. Inside each of us is something that, when we hear this truth expressed, causes us to nod our heads and say, "That's right."

My hope is that this book will invite Christians and any others who seek truth to consider the words and wisdom of Christ and His apostles anew as they expound upon the teachings of God, our Creator and great Lover. Christ is extraordinary. There is no debate on that. His teachings are of astonishing love, and He tells us we are capable of living it.

Uncommon Sense found its title one day as I was going over my eleven-year-old's history assignment with her. We were reading *Common Sense*, the pamphlet by Thomas Paine that inspired the American Revolution. I said to her, "That's what I want my book to do. I want it to start a revolution in the Christian community. I want people to learn the teachings of Christ, fall in love with Him, and celebrate Him because they realize they *can* live each day in accordance with His encouragements. When people experience how extraordinarily loving and wise and wonderful this faith is, they'll want to know more and to live it themselves."

The reason *uncommon* was chosen is because the teachings of Christ are known by many but applied by few. For instance, take our human tendency to berate our children when we don't get our way. This is common. However, this is *not* what Christ taught. Paul tells us "love does not insist on its own way" (1 Cor. 13:5, NLT). We are never told in any place in the Bible that it is acceptable to yell or to berate them, especially in front of others. On the contrary, the book of Proverbs tells us "only a fool gives vent to his anger" (Prov. 29:11). Christ said that when a person "sins against you, go and show him his fault, just between the two of you" (Matt. 18:15). We should settle our problems privately and respectfully.

Uncommon Sense is separated into five parts. Families often tell me during my seminars that the insights they gain about their faith and human nature (Parts 1 and 2) are critical. They believe these insights allow them to take on new attitudes and create new patterns in their homes (Part 3). Then, a sense of belonging and order begin to emerge from those attitudes and inspire them to try new ways of coping with life (Part 4). That is where the freedom comes in — freedom from old ways that didn't work and from ways that conflict with the loving, faithful beings we are designed to be. Life can be lived more simply if we cling to Christian truths (Part 5).

I invite you to experience the beauty of Christianity. You will learn about the One to whom you belong, who you can be in Him, and how you can live a life filled with more joy than you ever dreamed possible.

Identity Work

"Trust in the Lord with all your heart and lean not on your own understanding"

—Proverbs 3:5

"God is not the author of confusion but of peace."

—1 Corinthians 14:33 (KJV)

YOU'RE GOING TO LEARN WHAT a character ticket is and how to use it to change your life, but first, let's look at your beliefs. You may have chosen Christianity as your faith but may not be living a holy life because you have some old thoughts and habits that need to change. This first exercise will help you recall where you got some of your initial impressions of life and how old you might have been when you settled on them.

Have you ever realized that one of the deepest longings of the human heart is to know and be known? It is an inherent aspect of human nature given to us by our Creator, the almighty God who knows us and desires to be known by us. When I started teaching the Uncommon Sense lifestyle, the women and men who attended said that the most important thing they did was identity work. That is, they took a good look at themselves and the lives they had lived and were living. They had some realizations in a safe environment, which was conducive to growth and honesty.

Honesty means giving of yourself at a deep level so you can be loved at a deep level. What are the aspects of your life that grieve your heart or that cheer you?

You are a complex mix of the person God created you to be and the person humans convinced you to be. Sometimes, when those are in conflict, you can make mountains out of molehills. An exercise called "Highs and Lows"—taught to me by Dr. Van Horn—will help you to see why you respond so strongly to some stressors and are able to let others go. Pull out a few pieces of paper and, in three pages or fewer, write a letter about the highs and lows of your life. If you write it chronologically, it may help you to cover each important stage of your life. For example:

> *I was born in Indianapolis and moved to Colorado when I was five. Those years were chock full of highs. I made snow tunnels in the winter with my dad. We made and flew model airplanes in the spring. My mom worked at the bowling alley café and gave us cookies after school when we came to see her. We had a boat, and I learned to ski. We had a very Mayberry life. Another high was moving to Illinois and then to Iowa. I made friends quickly and was popular. I was a cheerleader and student council officer, and I fell in love with Jason Kitzer when I was a sophomore in high school.*
>
> *But I've had lows too. When I was fourteen, I went to a party with a girlfriend and her sister who was in college. We were camping out at a big event, and I got tired after dancing for hours on end. So I let a boy walk me back to my tent because I was scared to walk back alone and maybe get lost. I was glad he was there to guide and protect me. The boy walked me to my tent. Then he invited himself in and raped me. I didn't even know I had a place in my body for him to do that....*

PONDER

IDENTITY WORK

Stressors that confounded you as a child may still confuse or upset you because you think about and respond to them the way you did in the past. Our brains have a way of saving energy by repeating the same patterns over and over again, which can be beneficial for mundane tasks like running a copy machine, but not for reacting to pain or heartache.

- Ask yourself if you got the love and approval you needed. What were the strengths and weaknesses of the people who mattered to you?
- Are you repeating their failures in spite of yourself?
- Can you believe that you did not get all of the love that God wanted for you because humans are only as capable to give and receive affection as they have learned to be?
- Do you agree that we all have a lot more to learn? If so, you have just made your first step in the right direction. Humility is the key to surrender.

PART I

The Uncommon Sense Philosophy

MAKE ROOM FOR GOD

Make Room for God

"There is no fear in love. But perfect love drives away fear..."

—1 John 4:18

MY INTENTION FOR THIS BOOK is that it will teach you an undeniable (but often unrealized) truth—God is in our midst. His Kingdom is ours for the asking. We don't notice this because our lives don't revolve around His loving ways. Do you want to believe this? Do you have good teachers?

Let the first thing you do each day revolve around thankfulness to God for the good things you do have and the tragedies you don't. Throughout the day, communicate openly, honestly, and lovingly to people who want to hear you. This is God's way. Practice love. If you have lost something, trust that you don't need it to live fully and that, if you do need it, God will give it back. Don't worry. Have courage. Make Him your constant companion. Go to Christian bookstores or websites and find uplifting books and music written by loving, authentic people. Remember that you are a beautiful, wonderful, precious child of a wise, good and available God. End every night with a prayer. Use negative emotions to build positive character.

This is about you and lessons God is teaching you. He is pleased when you grow, so seek the lessons. Memorize this list of attitudes: love, joy, peace, patience, kindness, generosity, faithfulness, gentleness, self-control, compassion, hope, and humility (Gal. 5:22; Col. 3:12). When a negative emotion rises in you due to an unpleasant circumstance, ask God to tell you which one of these positive attitudes you need to exercise, and use it to resolve the difficulty. Attitudes, like muscles, grow strong with practice. Each time life is painful or frustrating, run through this list. God will point out the best attitude for that situation if you ask Him. Immediately, you'll feel relief as you replace the negative emotion with the positive attitude, and the situation will resolve itself more quickly than it would have if you had barreled ahead with your ways instead of His.

This and more I have to tell you about God, humans, and miracles. With God in your midst, read on.

CHAPTER 1

WHO WE ARE

"Before I formed you in the womb I knew you."

—JEREMIAH 1:5

"And even the very hairs of your head are all numbered."

—MATTHEW 10:30

N O HUMAN BEING IS COMMON. Each of us is a precious creation of God, which makes us wonderful and valuable. We are all His children, and we are created to have a rich relationship with Him. We are free to live as we wish, but we cannot live for long without realizing we are limited. We can't *do* everything or *be* everything we want. These limitations are good. They eventually cause many of us to look outside ourselves for strength and wisdom, and if we are especially blessed, we find ourselves matched with some very good teachers.

COMMON CHRISTIANS

In a nutshell, common Christians are the people who go to church occasionally and know about God and Christ because they have been taught some things by believers around them. They think about Christ if they are in church or have a need. But they seldom pray and may not know that Christianity means behaving like Christ, which means making your relationship with God a priority and loving others your primary purpose in life. I know all this because I used to be one.

I was raised in a number of small, American towns. You know the type—you could walk to town in ten minutes. There were four or five churches of different denominations, and at school, you didn't have a clue who went to which one except on Fridays because the lunchroom served fish for the Catholic kids.

When I was little, I and everyone I knew went to Sunday school and learned that even if you're small like David you can still beat up a big guy like Goliath if you have enough courage.

We sang "Jesus Loves Me," which is something for which I am eternally grateful. And we sang, "Joshua Fought the Battle of Jericho," which never explained exactly who Joshua was or why he was fighting, but it was a snappy tune.

Later, we had to memorize some things about the church and recite them to be accepted as members. It seemed to make the adults really happy. During the church services, we wrote and passed notes to our friends.

In college, we did some seeking and maybe even some professing (outside the walls of the church) but never changed our lifestyles because of it.

As a single adult, church was pretty much limited to the holidays of Easter and Christmas. However, once we married, we did the right thing and started attending church regularly again for our children's sakes.

Some of us came out of all of this with a shadowy faith and a weak relationship with Christ. Perhaps because of "Jesus Loves Me" and a little prayer that starts, "Now I lay me down to sleep, I pray the Lord my soul to keep..." some of us realized that when we were scared or just sad and feeling lost, we could turn to this person, Christ, who was bigger and wiser and capable of helping us. And if some of us got ourselves into trouble we could ask God to change things for us.

Uncommon Christians

An uncommon Christian is someone who realizes that life without the experience and support of God is not enough. They are people who are in the process of being transformed into His image, and they are thankful for it. They long to become more kind, gentle, hopeful, courageous, steadfast, and wise in Christ's ways and are willing to change their lives to accomplish that goal. They want to know Christ and wish His influence on their daily lives was more powerful and more apparent. They want to act on Christ's teachings and draw others into relationship with their sacrificial, protective God.

A couple of years ago, I went to Savannah to hear my daughters perform. I stayed at a hotel on the river and spent my free time reading and journaling. At the time, I was wondering how to define "believer" to an audience of individuals who might have been raised as Christians yet were confused or offended by terms like "born again." I wondered how I could let people know their faith life was common but that it could be extraordinary. About that time, a maid came by my room, so I decided to ask her my question.

"May I ask, are you a Christian?"

"Well," she replied, "I was raised in the church, but I don't know if I'm really a very good example. My mom and aunt and some of my other family are though."

"How do you define the difference between them and you?"

"They seem to *want* to try harder to do the right things. It matters to them because they really love God."

That's a perfect description of an uncommon Christian: someone who tries hard to live life Christ's way because they believe in Him and are in love with Him. How does that happen? Desire. Some of us are blessed because we become acquainted with the person of Christ as young children and fall in love with and accept Him. Often, this is because we had wonderful teachers or at least one person who displayed many of His loving qualities to us. Something made us want to know Him. He alone knows the longings of our hearts. It is the heart that matters to Him. He has told us that if we seek Him with all of our heart, mind, and soul—our invisible qualities—we will find Him.

Upping the Ante

Why don't all Christians have an uncommon relationship with God? Many Christians have not experienced the enormity of our awesome God. Some Christians stay too focused on humans to make time for their Creator. Others don't feel worthy of a relationship of that magnitude. Whatever the reason, God's unfathomable creation, protection, provision are meant for all of us, and He has a desire for an ongoing, intimate relationship with each one of His children. This is why James tells us, "Draw near to Him and He will draw near to you" (James 4:8 NKJV).

Have Christ's stories been read to you with passion, awe, and excitement? Have there been "ah ha!" moments? What have you done with them? Many of Christ's potential followers haven't come to realize the love, excitement, and adventure a relationship with Christ brings. Instead, all they understand of God is that He acted in the past and is distant in the present. Consequently, they mostly turn to Him when they fear humans aren't enough to fulfill their wants and needs. They have little awareness that Christ experienced every emotion they have experienced.

Jesus wept, He overturned tables at a temple, and He implored the Pharisees to consider the misconceptions of their faith and their hypocritical lifestyles (John 11:35; Matt. 21:12; Matt. 23). He endured the liabilities and He relished the joys of being human. I have no doubt there were quite a few people who jumped on Him like they had been called down on *The Price is Right* when He healed them of a lifelong disease! I bet He hit the ground laughing with them more than once. It wouldn't have been a somber moment. Christ knows how fun life can be, and He knows how challenging human emotions and limitations are. That's why He gave us strategies for success, healing, growth, and deep love.

Let the journey begin! I invite you to "be still" (Ps. 46:10) long enough to hear the quiet voice of God say, "I am the way, the truth, and the life…"(John 14:6) "Follow Me and let Me show you a better way." Let your heart be moved by Christ's longing for you. Say right out loud, "I accept your proposal, Christ. Teach me to love You." Christ's followers are described as His bride. They have been invited into a never-ending love relationship and have said, "I do."

Some Christians have done all of this, yet the journey doesn't seem like it has begun. They haven't fallen in love. They have the relationship without *experiencing* it because they never fill their lives with Christ's teachings and ways.

PONDER

COMMON AND UNCOMMON CHRISTIANS

Common Christians are people who lable themselves Christians because they think:[1]

1. I was reared by people who classified themselves as Christians, so I continue to think of myself as one.
2. I attend a Christian church.
3. I celebrate Christmas and Easter.
4. I believe in Christ, at least as a very wise person, so I let His philosophies guide my life.

Uncommon Christians are people who do not want to live life without God's input. They have humbled themselves at some point and admitted to God that they need and want Him to guide their lives. They long to understand God, Christ, and the Holy Spirit (the Holy Trinity) and to believe in Him with all their heart. They do not long to be god, they long to be God's.

Are you a common or uncommon Christian? What makes you common or uncommon?

---

1 No one is common. We are rich, complex, wonderful creations—each of us. This is simply a term I am using to describe the difference in *the relationship with God*: common (typical) or uncommon (active, devoted, daily).

When Christ performed miracles, He listened to the person to hear what he or she wanted before He acted. What do you want? How are you making it known? Are you asking Him for help?

Most people do not pray because they have little or no relationship with God or Christ

Do you interact with God?

Christ changed the world forever with three years of ministry. Why? Miracles. People witnessed them. They are still witnessing them. He is not just a man who had some incredible wisdom and philosophies. The co-creator of the universe longs to have an intimate relationship with you. He will help you navigate and change your life. He wants to participate in your transformation.

In everyday life, when you want to manipulate a situation (and you shouldn't or can't), pray instead. Ask God to inspire, support, and deliver a good result. As you humbly take notice of the miracles, your faith in Him will grow, and you will be inspired to interact more and more.

CHAPTER 2

GOD'S SIMPLICITY

"There are three things that will last forever—faith, hope and love—and the greatest of these is love."

—1 CORINTHIANS 13:13 (NLT)

IT DOESN'T HAVE TO BE that hard. Life, that is. In fact, the human condition can be summed up in a few, honest statements:

- We're confused. We sometimes make bad decisions. We need love.
- I'm confused. I sometimes make bad decisions. I need love.
- You're confused. You sometimes make bad decisions. You need love.

Christianity has been described as narrow-minded and condemning when it is actually the opposite. But confused followers of Christ have used Biblical terms and phrases in ways that have given us the reputation for being judgmental, negative, hypocritical, and a host of other unbecoming characteristics. Welcome to the human race. All humans are like that at times.

Here's the good news. The more real love we receive, the less confused we become. God is love as well as wisdom, strength, discipline. All at once. Not divided. Not dissected. It is His love we need because it is His love that restores. His qualities clear up our thinking so we can make good decisions—healing, soothing, life-giving, Christian decisions.

Moving away from our old way of living and thinking is very similar to the transformation a caterpillar undergoes. We move along with what seems like a logical perspective until something causes us to struggle. When that occurs, we enter a cocoon stage. The struggle can result in healthy growth, a new, broader perspective and a more productive life. After all, the caterpillar becomes a butterfly!

Many Christians move along like caterpillars, go through big life struggles, turn to God, and are blessed with fresh and freeing perspectives. What they make of that freedom depends on their choices and their teachers. Like the butterfly, we can become something more if we're willing to go through the process and lift ourselves above the fray to view life from better angles.

"Fear of the Lord is the beginning of understanding" (Prov. 9:10). Does that verse sound familiar? The word "fear" doesn't mean exactly what you might expect. Sometimes the Hebrew word *yirah* is used in the Bible for the *anticipation* of some danger or pain. Often, however, it translates to "amazement, respect, adoration, or trust." In this case, scholars interpret it to mean both. Stay on your toes, so that you don't hurt yourself or others. Practice the presence of the Lord. Respect Him. The reason we can respect, trust, adore, and seek God is because He is omniscient, good, and fair. The more we come to know Him, the more we understand the fear of Him from a healthy perspective.

Scripture tells us that God will not be mocked. We will be thankful for that when people are cruel and thoughtless and misuse their lives uncaringly. You might not think these things are true of God. You may not have lived long enough or experienced enough of life to know these things about Him. I didn't learn much of this until my late thirties.

Are you willing to look at, try on, and experience Christianity as you never have before? Did you grow up as a Christian and something in you knows that you want to experience God more intimately? Do you want to understand why some people trust God and you don't? These conditions suggest that God has your heart, but your mind needs training.

PONDER

WHERE ARE YOU?

Where are you spiritually as you begin this book?

Acquiring		Establishing		Reaping
1. No holy beliefs	→	No holy actions	→	???
2. Holy beliefs	→	No holy actions	→	Discomfort or despair
3. Holy beliefs	→	Holy actions	→	Life, peace, thankfulness

*Holy here means that which is good: God's wisdom and gifts used for God's good purposes

If you circled number one, you are probably not intentionally studying under those who understand loving Christian ways. If you don't know what God wants for you, you may just be doing whatever the culture around you is doing. That may make life easy, but it can be destructive.

If you know what God wants for you, but you aren't acting on it, it results in guilt, shame, and despair. That is not what your loving Father wants for you. He doesn't expect you to tackle everything at once, but if you are feeling convicted to change some things about your life, those could be the cocoons He wants to use in order to help you grow. Determine to come out healthy. Ask Him for His help. Look for it. Respond to it.

With God's unending grace, this book will help you build on option three, which ends with the joy and peace that only God can provide.

Most of the people who ended up at my kitchen table over the past ten years were vacillating between options two and three. They had begun to learn about God and Christ in a way that left them hungry for more. They, like the apostle Paul, wanted to trade out some of the unattractive elements of their lifestyles for those that were more soul-soothing. You know what elements I mean, the ones that cause you to look at yourself and say, *What have I become?* or *How did I get here and how can I improve things?* It is called introspection. Add a little humility, and you're right where God wants you so He can work in your life.

Christ's teachings are so simple and beautiful, yet they are challenging as well. Take 1 Corinthians 10:13 for example. It says, "The temptations that come into your life are no different from those that others experience. And God is faithful. He will keep the temptation from becoming so strong that you can't stand up against it. When you are tempted, he will show you a way out so that you will not give in to it." Three chapters later, in 1 Corinthians 13:4, we are told, "Love is patient and kind. Love is not jealous or boastful or proud or rude." So, according to chapter ten, God will give you a way to be patient and kind, even when everything in you wants to be rude. How?

By reading this book, you are moving down the path to honest, healing beliefs and attitudes. Those set you up for effective life strategies and coping skills. These are all parts of "the way out so you will not give in to temptations." Learn who you are and what your purpose is.

CHAPTER 3

A SIMPLE LESSON IN IDENTITY

"Remain in Me, and I will remain in You. For a branch cannot bear fruit if it is severed from the vine, and you cannot be fruitful unless you remain in me."

—JOHN 15:4 (NLT)

S EVERAL YEARS AGO, A FRIEND of mine came to my house to pick up her daughter's "blankie" that had been left after a slumber party. When it failed to show up, my friend began to cry and say, "We need to find it!" It didn't take a trained counselor to see that all was not right in paradise.

"Kay, what's wrong?" I asked. "This isn't about the blanket, is it?"

"No," she conceded. "Bob is leaving us...."

We met later that day and had coffee. Kay is a beautiful, popular woman who definitely knows how to have fun. She is bright and witty and has everything you would think a man would seek in a woman. On this day, however, she looked tired and defeated. After she revealed the shambles she and her husband had made of their lives, I admitted to her that Jim and I had gone through our own marital hell and that it had taught us some wonderful things. I asked her, "Kay, are you a Christian?" I wanted to know if I could talk honestly about my means of making order out of chaos, finding kindness in the midst of cruelty, and putting love back into a relationship that appears to have lost track of it.

"We go to church," Kay responded.

"Kay, when you were a little girl or an adult was there ever a time when either you truthfully said, 'I accept Jesus Christ as my Lord and Savior' or 'God, I'm sick of the way I live my life. I want You to live it for me.' Anything like that? Did you ever repeat the prayer to accept Christ at the end of a service and *mean it?*"

"Yes."

"Then you need to spend some time learning who you've become and what that means to you in terms of how you should be responding to life if you want to live it richly. Would you be willing to let me teach you? I guarantee it will make you feel better, and it may even help you heal your marriage."

The day when Kay responded to the invitation to become a Christian, she became a member of a very large family. She entered a spiritual realm that is mostly invisible and does not play by human rules. The kingdoms of earth are reliant on the ways of man: endlessly talking to attempt to agree on things, rejecting one another when we disagree, manipulating people, doing nice things for others so they will like us and we will like ourselves. It's a combination of good-looking behaviors and very unattractive behaviors designed to make individuals more comfortable living in an earthly realm. The kingdom of God, however, relies on the principles and strategies taught by Christ, which include principles taught throughout the Bible. It's all about *relationships.*

What Kay didn't realize is that when she chose Christ to be her guide and helper, she became a citizen of God's kingdom and was therefore accountable to a new set of standards. The old ways will not result in a gain for her; she has asked Christ to help her change. Earth is her classroom. Her circumstances are her lessons. Her goal is to become more loving to the people who cross her path here. Her most important relationship is with God, and her teachers are those who have studied and understand the loving ways of God and Christ. Actually, she can learn from those who haven't studied or embraced Christ's teachings. God uses those who have simply chosen the ways of love because something in them knows it is right. Other times, he uses foolish failures to teach us what not to do.

CULTURAL COMPLEXITY

Kay, like so many of us, was so blessed that she really didn't have to think about God on a daily basis to get through life. Since she and her husband did many of the culturally accepted things that "good parents" do, they thought they were doing well. You know what I mean: bake cookies, go to sporting events, go to work every day, stay sober at night, spend the weekends having fun with friends, and take the children to church on Sunday. Behind the closed doors of their home, however, the picture was disappointing and even destructive at times. Eventually one of them, tired of this obvious mediocrity, decided to leave.

If you're thinking, "Poor them," think again. Most of us live lives chock full of mediocrity that God never intended. Want an example? When a child or spouse fails to live up to another family member's expectations, don't most of us choose to nag and lecture? When someone hurts us, don't we either pout or fight? Oh, yes, we do this in increasingly sophisticated ways, but that is how we respond. We joke about it with friends, but most of us reach a point when we wish we could "get off the train" of our lives and board one headed the opposite direction.

Believe it or not, God wants us to live with one another in such a simple way that each of us can mess up *repeatedly* and still be treated like the beautiful, wonderful, precious creations we are. We have taught ourselves to believe that the path to improvement must be filled with scolding, but this is actually complicating our lives! In order to nag, you must say things people don't want to hear, and they eventually stop listening when you start talking. Furthermore, haranguing is insufficient, so you must add punishment to the mix. Have you ever heard someone say, "I've tried everything, and nothing works." How about "I spank and yell and send them to timeout, and they still…" or "I've talked and talked about this, and I still don't have a sense that they get it." To all of these comments, I say, "Good! I'm glad that isn't working, and I'm glad you don't like yourself while you are doing it." Biblically, it's all wrong.

God's Simplicity

God's system for helping one another change is much simpler. It is also more sensible, kind, effective, and joyful. He tells us that it takes love, and He is very specific about the qualities of love. Look at these simple, kind instructions from the Old and New Testaments. Notice that they are not metaphorical. You don't have to be a scholar to get this.

- "Fathers, do not exasperate your children, instead bring them up in the training and instruction of the Lord." (Eph. 6:4)
- "Let everything you say be good and helpful…." (Eph.4:29-32 NLT)
- "Fix your eyes on what is true and honorable and right." (Phil. 4:8 NLT)
- "Be angry but do not act on it…." (Eph.4:26 NLT)

As we begin to learn about Christianity, we are called to learn the simplest of all instructions. Remember, Christ said that unless you become as little children you cannot enter the kingdom of Heaven (Matt.18:3). Little children are uncomplicated. Think about it.

Scientists have discovered that most of us do not do well with abstract thinking until we're preteens or older. That means God gave us over a decade to come to understand His teachings in a very simple way that can be experienced in everyday life. Heaven may be a destination, but "the kingdom of God is in our midst" (Luke 17:20-21). Let's combine some of God's simple truths and some things we know about humanity and use that to guide our lifestyles. As we do this, we will become more amazed by and enamored with God, our Abba Father, and less disappointed with the lives He has given us to live on earth.

PONDER

What Is My Identity in Christ?

You are a vessel, one that is meant to be filled with God's love by the other vessels around you. The amount of God's love you receive in your life determines your spiritual maturity. Spiritual maturity is your ability to realize who you are and how to respond to life accordingly. In this case, reception includes not only being offered love, but also accepting it. God's love is available incessantly, but it is often not recognized when invisible. That's where we come in. God will express His love through us if we want Him to.

- Are you noticing the endless flow of God's love to you every day? What are some examples of that?
- To whom do you pass on the love?
- Do they receive it? If not, what do you think stops them from doing so?

CHAPTER 4

TWO KINGDOMS

"Pilate then went back inside the palace, summoned Jesus and asked him, 'Are you the king of the Jews?' Jesus said, 'My kingdom is not of this world...my kingdom is from another place.'"

—JOHN 18:33, 36

As I STUDIED THE BIBLE more intently, I became convinced that God knows what is best for us, that God's Word is absolute truth whether we understand it or not, and that I wasn't following Christ's instructions.

The Bible tells us we are made in God's image. Many of us think of an image as a visible thing, but we are meant to understand that He created us with His inherent qualities. For example, God is free. And humans love freedom. It is a need. God is so loving that He cannot enslave us even to Himself, so He gave us the freedom to disobey, ignore, and even deny Him. We have a choice. God allows this, "Come or go. Love me or leave me. Practice the habits of your wisdom or of mine."

There are two basic identities. You can believe that you are simply human and subject to human truths, or you can believe that the innermost part of you is a spiritual being subject to spiritual truths. Whichever one you think yourself to be is the one you'll lean on for understanding. If you think of yourself as a human, you will tend to look to humans for answers. If you think of yourself as God's child and Christ's teachings as your source for what makes life work, you have to throw away a lot of what you learn from humans and cling to spiritual truths. Now, here's the common sense question—Who do you think is wiser about what works in human relationships, humans or the God who created all that is seen and unseen?

Understanding your identity doesn't have to be that hard. Humans have created cultural dos and don'ts, philosophies, and "truths" that make life complicated and unsatisfying. Your children probably don't need to change schools, a divorce is probably not your best option, and you don't have to tolerate mediocrity. In fact, this book is not about tolerance; it's about transformation. Don't put it down, and don't be discouraged. You have a loving, encouraging, devoted God. He is your Father. Perhaps you just need a fresh look at how He can help you change. With this in mind, let's look at the two kingdoms.

The human kingdom is visible, fallible, and often confused, yet, because we are created in God's image, we strive for excellence and love. We may never be taught about God or that our essence, our core, is an invisible spirit who will leave the human body at death and move on. It is the spirit that has life. Did you know that scientific theory tells us that energy cannot be destroyed? If you have ever been in the presence of a dead body, one thing that is undeniably clear is that the spirit, the energy, is gone from the human form. Where did it go? Since God has allowed human scientists to realize that energy cannot be destroyed, we know that the energy (the spiritual being) that resided in the body (the flesh) has moved on. When you realize this, you can joyfully embrace the Scripture in the book of Luke: Christ reassures the man on the cross next to Him who believed in Him, "today [when you die] you will be with me in paradise" (Luke 23:43). Assuredly, Christ meant, "You, the spiritual being, will be with me in paradise. Only your physical body and physical brain will still be here on earth."

The kingdom of God is mostly invisible. It is the essence of love. In life. Throughout life. Everywhere. All of the time. Life is drenched in love. We can perceive it or ignore it because love is invisible. But if you pour love into a human heart and that human chooses to act on it, it becomes visible. You can see order, beauty, and power in God's creations. You can even study them. But He has told you that until you meet Him eye to eye, you will "see dimly" here (1 Cor. 13:12). In the kingdom of God, you are not expected to completely understand Him while you are on earth. In fact, you are told that you will be given this understanding in heaven. Here, on earth, you are only asked to seek Him and learn the lessons that come to you every day of your life. Are you noticing? To which kingdom do you aspire?

The goal of the human kingdom is to be happy. The goal of the kingdom of God is to become increasingly loving. The wisdom of the human kingdom changes and is corrected from generation to generation while the wisdom of the kingdom of God is unchanging and always correct. If you don't understand something in the human kingdom, you challenge it and study human answers. If you don't understand something in the kingdom of God, you pray, study His Word, and converse with those who know Him well. Then, you choose to be still, ask for wisdom, and listen for the Holy Spirit. If the answer you think you hear contradicts the definition of love, you wait until you hear an answer that doesn't. The kingdom of God is love and wisdom, alive and active.

One way to think of these two kingdoms is to consider them identical. They are both filled with God's beauty, but if we limit ourselves to the human kingdom, we crawl around like caterpillars. We have a limited way of navigating around this world and inadequate vision. We are willing to do whatever it takes to be happy. And we have some unbecoming ways of going about it, including punishment, fear, and manipulation. Eventually, some of us tire of the human kingdom and may even find ourselves dissatisfied or repulsed by it at times. That is good! We are not meant to be satisfied with it. We were created for higher purposes, and we know it. God wants to give us wings and to bless us with the ability to see things from His perspective. We were created for God.

In my thirties, I had begun to learn, at a deeper level than ever before about Christ and Christianity but was not really employing the teachings. When things didn't go my way, I used common human strategies to accomplish my goals. But when life became quiet, when I lay awake at night or was alone during the day with nothing to distract me, I realized that I was breaking my own heart by not demonstrating the qualities I most admired. My life was beautiful on the outside and hungry on the inside. Is that ever true for you?

The life principles of the two kingdoms are very different. All of God's life principles agree with who He is. One of the first things He wants us to know is that life in His kingdom is all about love. Not money. Not position. Not admiration. Not possessions. Those things may be used to serve His purposes, but He wants them to come to us as means, not as goals.

To aspire to the kingdom of God is to be dedicated to the pursuit of *holiness*: deep joy, peace that passes understanding, wisdom, compassion, patience, kindness, generosity, courage, and a host of other wonderful qualities of life. As you acquire these qualities, you will long to share them with the world. To aspire to the kingdom of God is to take note of the Almighty, to allow His love to pour out of you. When your heart is ready for the transformation, you can walk hand in hand with Christ into your new homeland.

God knows if your heart is ready. When it is, you desire to know His ways, hear His Word, serve His purpose for your life, and recognize and listen to His still small voice. You are ready to live as He asks because you finally *get it*. The uncommon truths of life become obvious: He knows what is best, not you. His kingdom is ultimately more beautiful than yours, and you are finally allowing your heart to realize it.

PONDER

Where Do You Live?

- Reading this book demonstrates that you are aspiring to something beyond the human kingdom. What feelings did you experience as you read this chapter?

- What thoughts ran through your head as you read about these two kingdoms?

- How might life look different for you if you lifted yourself above the fray a little more often and looked at life from God's perspective?

- Do you understand that you can be a butterfly and still limit yourself to walking like a caterpillar? We all do it.

CHAPTER 5

A DARK PLACE

"The joy of the Lord is your strength."

—NEHEMIAH 8:10

I WANT TO MAKE THIS CHAPTER simple and concise because many humans hate to look at things that are dark, ugly, and beyond their realm of belief. This is what happened according to the Bible. God created a magnificently beautiful and incredibly capable angel, Lucifer, who He loved—because God is love. Eventually, Lucifer became confused, as many of us do, and he contended with God for power and prominence, which few of us do. (Have you seen the movie *Bruce Almighty*? Yeah, you don't want the job.)

Lucifer's heart turned against God, so the Almighty gave him what God gives all of us: limited freedom. God gave Lucifer his own domain, commonly referred to as hell. And Lucifer, who also goes by the name of Satan, the devil, or the evil one, took a legion of confused angels with him to hell as part of his angry rebellion. God not only gave him his own domain, but also limited power on Earth for the time being. *Limited power.* We are told in the Bible that Satan "prowls around" among us, tempting us away from the good life God wants for us and working to destroy our relationship with God and with one another. (See John 10:10; 1Peter 5:8-9.)

If you read through the entire book of Job, you will notice that each time a tragedy is about to happen to Job, Satan asks God for permission to wreak havoc in Job's life. Then God responds to him, "You can do this, but not that." You see, God keeps everyone—even Satan—in relationship with Him. God is in control at all times, only allowing things to happen on earth that will result in eventual good for all of us. It is an enormous tapestry He is weaving. Sometimes we forget that. God does care deeply for each of us but also loves and is concerned for mankind as a whole. It's an unthinkably complex life condition. We are told that God's thoughts are not our thoughts; they are higher, indescribably more magnificent and expansive than our own (Isa. 55:8).

Now here is the amazing thing about God and why He allows darkness to disturb and discourage us: We have already won the war. God is not limited by time as we are. Two thousand years ago, Christ came. He gave us hope, was not deterred by confusion or death, and left us with a book of wisdom that cannot be destroyed. He offered His pure life for our messy ones. These actions are unheard of in the human justice system. A mother with a clean driving record cannot spend time in jail for a child who drove under the influence and killed others. But that is what God allowed Christ to do for us. He spent time in hell for us and then He left that place. Forever. It's over. He won the war for all of us and none of us have to succumb to darkness. All that is left is for each of us to understand Christ's gift and accept it.

Satan's beef is not with us; we are hardly worth pursuing. Satan simply uses us to try to prove that the only reason we love God is because He gives us good things. So, get this—when we are in dire straits and we love God anyway, it is like saying to darkness, "Don't mess with me. I'm in love with God no matter what. Whenever I am afraid, I will trust in Him" (see Ps. 56:3).

If we handle life as God has asked us to, it makes us stronger. When disturbances come from darkness, they can eventually lead to hope. Here is how we make that happen: move toward light. God told us to be aware of the evil one and his attempts to broadside us, but He also told us to focus on whatever is good, right, and honorable. Do not spend another moment focused on the darkness. It's like turning your head to look behind you for cars while you are changing lanes. If you focus on the potential danger for too long, you will certainly crash. Therefore, be aware of but not focused on darkness. Turn immediately toward the light. If you can't find it, ask someone to tell you about it. It's there. You belong to the kingdom of heaven; notice it in your midst and stay there as much as possible. If you ask God for help and listen, you'll find something good to put your energies into. It will give you endurance and patience when things are tough, which will lead to character which leads to hope (Rom. 5:3-5).

I can't think of a better story to illustrate light conquering darkness than something I saw during an episode of *Touched by an Angel*. If you've seen that show, you'll recall that the main characters are a young angel, Monica, and her mentor angel, Tess. One episode featured Lucifer. After Lucifer wreaked havoc, Tess turned to him and began to tell him how disgusting he was. She was raking him over the coals, which only made him smile. In that moment, another angel appeared and said to Tess, "I've been sent by God to replace you. You're going about this all wrong." So Tess left, and her replacement took a long, hard look at Lucifer and basically said, "God still loves you." And Lucifer melted away.

If you are ever afraid or feel that the darkness has completely encroached upon you, say something like, "In the name of Jesus Christ, be gone." Say it and mean it. You have supernatural power over the darkness because Christ is in God, you are in Christ, and Christ is in you if you have made Him your life. (See John 14:20.) You are hemmed in by the kingdom of light, and light always overcomes the darkness.

PONDER AND ACT

DARKNESS

The Bible tells us that we are not fighting against humans when we squabble and fuss about one another's daily choices; we are fighting against "spiritual forces" (Eph. 6:12-18). Many of us have seen cartoons or shows that depict an angel on one shoulder and a demon on the other. This is a pretty good illustration of how the invisible realm of darkness challenges that of light. Darkness makes life mediocre. It is part of your nature to give in to these downers, but God wants you to learn and practice a new way. He has given you strategies for getting right back on your feet when you fall down.

Say this prayer every day and mean it. Watch what God will do to help you fight the darkness and to bring you into the light.

> *Search me, O God, and know my heart;*
> *Test me and know my anxious thoughts.*
> *See if there is any offensive way in me,*
> *and lead me in the way everlasting.*
>
> – PSALM 139:23-24

CHAPTER 6

ONLY GOD IS AWESOME

"In the beginning, God created the heavens and the earth."

—GENESIS 1:1

S EVERAL YEARS AGO, OUR FAMILY went on vacation in Sunset Beach, North Carolina. On Sunday morning, Jim and I went to a small church and heard one of the most beautiful and memorable sermons of our lives. At that time, the word "awesome" was used to describe almost everything. "Hey, dude, that shirt is *awesome*... The movie was *awesome*... Their chicken nuggets are *awesome*...." So, on this Sunday at Sunset Beach, the pastor began his sermon by reminding us of some of the silly little things we described as awesome, and then he began to describe some things that really *were* awesome: a newborn baby, mountains and gorges, a thunderstorm, and human fortitude. After pausing, he said, "These things are miraculous, fascinating, unbelievable, indescribable, overwhelming, magnificent, stupendous! But awesome? No. Only God is awesome."

My thesaurus[2] equates "awe" with "reverence" and "reverence" with "respect, love, regard, esteem, devotion, adoration, worship, deference, honor, glorification, exaltation, piety, devoutness, and praise. "

Yep. By that definition, only God is awesome.

The most important thing to remember about our awesome God is that He loves, respects, esteems, adores, and is devoted to us. He wants every being to be drawn to His love, and His wrath is reserved for our actions and attitudes when they keep us from seeking or noticing or listening to Him. In fact, in the Old Testament He wiped out entire groups of people who ignored His wisdom, not because He didn't love them, but because the cultures they created left no room for His soothing, healing presence. Left to our own devices, we would eventually destroy one another. Without God's presence we have no real peace, comfort, purpose, joy, or life. We cling to and claw for whatever we can get, and it is never enough. Why? Because we are made for God.

As Christians, we worship a God of freedom. His love for us is not based on what's in us; it is based on what is in Him. The more we know our Father, the more we love and respect Him. And that, in turn, inspires us to notice Him and desire the things He desires. Faith, hope and love are all important to be sure, "but the greatest of these is love" (1 Cor. 13:13). Abundant love.

God the Father, Christ, and the Holy Spirit are a supernatural being, co-creators of everything, both visible and invisible. (See Genesis 1:26.) Yes, I've mixed my singulars and plurals to indicate the truth — they are God. A.W. Tozer reminds us in *The Knowledge of the Holy* that the Holy Trinity operated together at creation, the incarnation, Christ's baptism, and the resurrection. All are present in the processes of salvation, atonement, and the indwelling of the Christian. They are three distinct persons of one God. We don't have to understand this fully for it to be true. Just as you might present yourself as a parent at home, a worker at the office, and an

---

2 Taken from Webster's New World, Roget's A-Z Thesaurus, Copyright ©1999 by Macmillan USA. 850 Euclid Avenue, Cleveland OH. 44114-3354 All rights reserved.

athlete on the field, you are still one spiritual being. But even that simple explanation does not come close to describing the mysteries of God. This big, awesome God can already see your tomorrows. He wants to equip you today with the character you will need for your life in the future. Do you notice? Are you growing?

This God, our God, is awesome enough to contain His being in human form. He asked us to call this person Jesus Christ. During 33 years on Earth in human form, He experienced the emotional trials and temptations we face. Why would He do such a thing? Because He wanted us to see, hear, and touch Him and believe Him when said, "I'm real, and I understand." He used a human brain and human features to express His will and to sustain our walk here. Christ only taught formally for His last three years on Earth, yet He changed the world forever.

During His time on earth, He revealed He is joyful, patient, and faithful. He knows how it feels to be abandoned, to be so physically sick and mentally exhausted that you just want to surrender. He understands us completely. No one else can make that claim. The day you call on the name of the Lord, He will set you free. Call on Him.

And what about the Holy Spirit? I am shocked that this soothing and wise person of God remains unknown to most of the Christian community. If you are not attracted to this aspect of God, please look again with fresh vision. Christ returned to Heaven so that the Holy Spirit could come to live in us and be our Helper (John 16:7). The Spirit is our teacher, guide, and supporter. When life seems unbearable, the Holy Spirit prays for us in groanings too deep for words (Rom. 8:26). He knows. He is present. He is wise and He is powerful. The Holy Spirit is God's wisdom personified. He, the Spirit, has told us:

- Nothing that is good will be withheld from you. — Luke 11:11
- I will bless you and make you a blessing. — Genesis 12:2

- I will teach you and instruct you; I will guide you. — Psalm 32:8
- I will always be kind to you. — Psalm 100:5
- I know you and I'm familiar with all your ways. — Psalm 139:13-14
- My thoughts toward you are precious; they outnumber the grains of sand. — Psalm 139:18
- I will not forget you. — Isaiah 49:15
- I will love you with an everlasting love. — Jeremiah 31:3
- I am for you; who can be against you? — Romans 8:31
- Trust me. You please me by having faith in me. — Psalm 147:11
- Your times are in my hands. — Psalm 31:15
- I meet your needs. I am your provider. — Philippians 4:19
- I strengthen and uphold you. — Isaiah 41:10
- I rejoice over you with joyful songs. — Zephaniah 3:17

These are promises and blessings.[3] We can count on them even when everything appears to be otherwise. These become etched into us as we come to know Christ and follow His loving teachings. Over time, these truths result in that peace that surpasses all understanding.

---

3 These are all paraphrases of these verses taken from a card given to me many years ago with no author or creator noted. It is important to remember things like, "Nothing that is good will be withheld from us" when it seems God is withholding something good. He, of course, knows what is best for us in the long run.

PONDER

The God of the Old Testament

What if I told you that the God of the Old Testament, who is often misinterpreted because He was willing for entire nations of people to be eradicated, was actually being immensely loving? The cultures He forfeited had become so confused that they had acquired "abominable" ways of living that allowed them to pursue pleasure and avoid pain with no real awareness of God or His ways. Generation after generation, these humans overrode and annihilated their God-given instincts that draw us to Him. Instead, they created sick, pathetic substitutes that included rampant rape and human sacrifice. He lovingly removed these deplorable mentalities from the earth by wiping out the cultures that promoted these sick and faulty teachings so the human race could once again attempt to hear Him and learn from Him. That is not the act of a cruel God. That is the act of a loving God. It is the culture, the mentality, God wiped out. Sadly, mindsets are handed down from generation to generation, so entire cultures were sacrificed for the greater good of mankind. If you were the victim of rape and human sacrifice, you would be relieved to see its advocates removed. If you had to leave this world in order for future generations to live in better, more loving ways, wouldn't you do it? I thank God for His willingness to set us back on the right path and for every human who helps Him.

ANSWER THE FOLLOWING QUESTIONS:

What did you believe about God when you were a young child?
As an older child? As a young adult?

What do you believe about God today?

Where do you get your beliefs about Him?

CHAPTER 7

SEEING THROUGH MORE ACCURATE LENSES

"Anything is possible if a person believes."

—MARK 9:23 (NLT)

I F YOU GET NOTHING ELSE from this book get this: We humans are incessantly loved by God. All of us. It's His nature. It's known as common grace. He wants us to accept His love and pass it on. In order to do that, we've got to let Him take the lead.

The **exchange of your life** is a one-time event. You become aware of your failings and your need for Christ's ransom. You say sincerely from the heart, "I'm so sorry for the way I live. I want You to live in me forever, and I want Your will, not mine, to be done." You mean it. It's done. A change occurs in your spirit. This one-time event is called *salvation*. Some people call this being "reborn" because God has taken up residence in us spiritually, and our old selves die with Christ. We become "new creations" (2 Cor. 5:17) capable of hearing and seeing and acting more like Him because Christ has filled us with His grace and the Holy Spirit indwells us. Some of us have asked for salvation repeatedly and not even known it occurred. Why? Being saved doesn't turn us into robots. It just gives us the option of living in accordance with God's Word. We still have to retrain our minds and bodies. We are told that this exchange (God's grace for our failings) gives us a spiritual set of ears and eyes that helps us to see things from a fresh vantage point. But we can choose to use them or not. Without our spiritual ears and eyes, the Bible and much of its contents "sound like foolishness" (1 Cor. 2:14). Even with them, aspects of God's Word remain complex and beyond our full understanding. (see 1 Cor. 13:12)

The **exchange of your lifestyle** is a daily event. Once you are indwelt, you will realize it only if you begin to live in accordance with Christ's teaching. We are told that we will find God if we seek Him "with all of our heart and soul" (Deut. 4:29, Jer. 29:13). So if you believe you have asked God to reside in your heart, your choices will change only if you make Him the treasure of your heart and begin to interact with Him. The soul is a place of relationship. And when you realize how priceless He is, you begin to live in accordance with Christ's teachings. When His enlightening presence is a mainstay of your lifestyle, you will realize that you are transformed. This lifelong process of making God, not yourself, the treasure is called *sanctification*.

It requires willful choices to learn Christ's ways by studying His Word. For a while, it requires even more energy to live Christ's ways through the endless, loving prompting of the Holy Spirit in us and through the energizing love of other people. Most of us are not accustomed to it. However, behaving as though you have given your life to Christ really does become easier the more you practice it. There is not a moment when God is not encouraging and supporting you to grow, but you must make the choice to notice and respond. Hardheartedness is the consequence of ignoring Him repeatedly, and it can leave you calloused and ineffective even though you're saved.

If you exchange your lifestyle along with your life by giving all of yourself to God—spirit, soul and body—you will notice the change. God's got your back when you anchor your life in His truths, and the best way to do this is through studying His Word.

You have to cling to scriptural anchors in order to mature spiritually. As I studied the Word, there were some verses that convicted me that the ways I was approaching life were wrong. For example:

- "Love is patient and kind. Love is not jealous or boastful or proud or rude. It does not demand its own way. It is not irritable, and it keeps no record of being wronged. It does not rejoice about injustice but rejoices whenever the truth wins out. Love never gives up, never loses faith, is always hopeful, and endures through every circumstance. ." —1 Corinthians 13:4-7 (NLT)
- "Let everything you say be good and helpful so that your words will be an encouragement to those who hear them." —Ephesians 4:29-32 (NLT)
- "In everything you do, stay away from complaining and arguing so that no one can speak a word of blame against you." —Philippians 2:14-15 (NLT)
- "It is better to trust the Lord than to trust in people." —Psalm 118:8 (NLT)
- "In your anger do not sin: Do not let the sun go down while you are still angry." —Ephesians 4:26
- "Do not judge or you too will be judged." —Matthew 7:1
- "Do not make your children angry by the way you treat them. Rather, bring them up with the discipline and instruction that comes from the Lord." —Ephesians 6:4 (NLT)
- "Do not repay anyone evil for evil…. If it is possible, as far as it depends on you, live in peace with everyone." —Romans 12:17-18

These examples are simple and straightforward. When you practice these verses, you realize you are a strong, smart, kind, courageous, and healing being. You feel it. You *experience* it. You will gain the respect of those around you, and exhibit a level of love that turns heads and makes others ask, "How did you learn to do the things you do?" The Bible tells us, "Always be ready to give an answer for the hope that is within you" (1 Peter 3:15). If you live out this Uncommon Sense lifestyle, you will have a lot of success stories.

PONDER

How can I see myself through more accurate lenses?

These are your realities sealed into your being by your Creator, God. Can you let yourself believe them?

- *You are valuable* because you are God's creation.
- *You belong* to a family of people who believe that Jesus Christ and the Holy Spirit are a part of God and are our bridge to Him.
- *You are capable* because when you agreed to let Christ, and not the performing you, be your bridge to God, you were instantly imbued with supernatural power. When you rest in God's Spirit you'll notice this.

These are the best ways to turn your new life into a lifestyle:

- Love abundantly
- Pray
- Fellowship with believers
- Study to transform your thinking
- Read your Bible

Love does not insist on its own way. How, when, and where you feed yourself spiritually is between you and God. Do not compare yourself to anyone else, but *do* let someone know your desires so they can encourage you.

MAKE ROOM FOR GOD: THE ANTITHESIS OF LEGALISM

*"Since God chose you to be the holy people who He loves, you must clothe
yourselves with tenderhearted mercy, kindness, humility, gentleness,
and patience. You must make allowance for each other's faults and forgive the person who offends you. Remember, the Lord forgave you, so you
must forgive others. And the most important piece of clothing you must
wear is love. Love is what binds us all together in perfect harmony. And
let the peace that comes from Christ rule in your hearts. For as members
of one body you are called to live in peace. And always be thankful."*

—COLOSSIANS 3:12-15

I N ORDER TO BE FOLLOWERS of Christ we must keep ourselves and
everything we do clothed in attitudes of love. Christ spent 33 years on
earth to make that point. But legalism forgets this. Legalism is focused
on overt behaviors rather than the stirrings of the heart.

Everyone is to do the same things in the same ways with little regard for
individual differences and preferences. Follow-through can be annihilating

to creativity, a sense of self, and freedom of expression. For the sake of order and respect, love and grace are forfeited or downplayed.

Here's how legalism works:

- Adopt a belief
- Determine what actions and attitudes will support the belief
- Develop a mental or physical checklist
- Assess oneself and others according to how many items are checked off. 100% preferred
- Reward and punish people based on performance and the attitude they apply toward the job

Has it occurred to you that we are all legalists to some extent? When we think of legalism, we think of religious extremists. However, as a mother, wife, and counselor I've noticed something. Many areas of life sponsor legalism. Do you have a mental checklist for the right and wrong ways to manage your home? Your partner's evening activities? Do people get affirmed if they do things on the checklist and reprimanded or mistreated when they don't? Is this what Christ taught?

Legalism can even come from cultural training. A client, Mary, prided herself on her Italian heritage, which taught her to send any guest home with bags of food from her freezer. She loved to cook, and no one ever left her house empty-handed. As she described a party she had attended, she exclaimed, "They had food on tables everywhere but sent nothing home with their guests! Are they too rich to care about anyone but themselves?" I had to explain to her that sending food home with all guests was perhaps not a part of the culture in that part of our city. I pointed out that some guests might have been embarrassed by the hostess suggesting they needed to take food home. Her host's behavior really told her nothing. Mary's checklist of socially appropriate behavior didn't match theirs, so she judged and then condemned them.

When we put on our legalistic hats, we forget that love is essential for success on any front. Christ came to transform our thinking and turn our focus back to soulful, energizing, loving relationships with Him and with one another. Chapter 14 in the New Testament book of Romans is dedicated to helping us understand that our walks are between God and us. Christians are asked not to bicker or argue with one another about disputable matters (Rom. 14:1).

Legalism is a joyless focus on behaviors, attitudes, and activities fueled by fear and rules. Legalism creates feelings of shame and fear in its victims, and, in the legalist, it sponsors an angry disregard for the complexities of human nature and everyday life. Legalism can rob human beings of the richness of who they are by insisting on behaviors that aren't natural to needs, personalities, temperaments, spiritual maturity levels, or talents. Unfortunately, over the years, some Christians have gotten caught up in the details and insisted on behaviors that have little to do with learning to love God and others.

Please do not think I am an anything-goes type. Christ upheld the moral aspects of the laws of God, but He refused to submit to senseless, manmade restrictions. He healed people and allowed his disciples to pick up grain to feed themselves on the Sabbath even though the Ten Commandments required a day of rest. He spent time with unbelievers and drunkards. Why did He do these things? Because the alternatives would have contradicted love.

"SPARE THE ROD, SPOIL THE CHILD"?

Legalism often inspires the use of the well-known phrase, "Spare the rod, spoil the child" to justify harsh forms of discipline. However, that is actually a phrase from a seventeenth century poem, "Hudibras," by Samuel Butler, not an exact quote from the Bible. Christians debate the use of corporal punishment when there are alternatives. Let me give you an example. A man, who I will call John, told me a story about his change from legalism to love. He was a children's Bible teacher at his church and believed that children should respect their elders, sit still with their hands in their laps, open their Bibles, and pay attention. When it was activity time, the children could move around, but during the lesson, they needed to keep their eyes on the front of the room and be still. Okay, so what's wrong with that?

One day, a child came to John's class for the first time. The child wiggled and wouldn't pay attention. John quietly scolded the boy and placed his hands firmly on the boy's shoulders to force him to stay straight in his chair and behave. Just then the director of the children's ministry, Susan, walked into the room and saw the firm grip on the new student. "Is everything okay?" she asked.

"It will be when he learns to pay attention," John replied. Susan looked at John and asked respectfully if she could take the boy into the hall. When they were outside the room Susan whispered to the boy, "What's wrong, sweetie?"

"I'm hungry," he shyly whispered back.

"Would you like a cookie and some water?"

The boy nodded. Once the boy had eaten his snack, Susan returned him to the class and left.

Later, John asked her, "What did you do? He came back to the room and was perfectly behaved."

Susan responded, "He was hungry, and I fed him."

Susan's gentle yet effective intervention was so startling that John was convicted and began to dramatically change his behavior and attitude toward the children. He recognized grace when he experienced the blessings it brought to his classroom. John had been a devout Christian who guided his family with an iron fist and a long list of rules. But he began to loosen up. He decided to allow his daughters to wear fashionable clothes and makeup. John and his wife displayed an energy and affection in their marriage that his friends had never seen before. His wife suddenly seemed kind rather than aloof.

John's story was one of many that inspired me to write this book and to help Christians find better ways of learning to love God and one another and to cope with difficulties. Most humans are chained to fear and rules at times. However, God's perfect love—the love He invites us to share with one another—"casts away fear" (John 4:18).

Not only does God's love cast away fear, but *His* rod also brings comfort. Shepherd's staffs were used to guide and rescue sheep and wound wolves and other enemies. Psalm 23 says, "Your rod and your staff comfort me." Clearly God knows something about the use of the rod that humans do not. Proverbs 13:24 challenges parents to accept their authority and discipline their children, yet we are also called to treat others as we would like to be treated.

When my daughters were very young, our family had a morning ritual for bringing God into our day. We would wake up to candlelight and sit on the sofa together with the children tucked lovingly between Jim and me. They'd cover up with their blankets, and we would stroke their hair as Jim read a little Bible story from a children's book. We would sing songs, stretch, pray, put on our spiritual armor, blow out the candles, and go to the kitchen for breakfast. The entire ritual took only fifteen minutes. Each day one of us would be the person to say a prayer for the family and the world. On Bentley's and Lainey's days, we would have rich, surprisingly mature prayers that coincided with their personalities. When it was Caty's day to say the prayer, she would say, "I love you, God. Amen." Sometimes angrily. Although this was a nuisance, Jim and I chose not to scold her for the shortness of her prayer or for her tone. Thankfully, we realized that it was not Caty's intention to be disrespectful to God. She loved and believed in Him. Had we turned legalistic and demanded that she speak long, loud, and lovingly, we would have ruined the atmosphere. She quickly outgrew this phase. And today, she is often a leader among her Christian peers. So are her sisters. All of the girls give their testimonies in front of large groups and describe the ways God has enlightened, loved, and protected them. All three have friends who know and love God.

I'm not you, and you're not me. We can have some general standards without looking like clones. What we do should be informed by our relationships, not by details. For instance, God says, "Put Me—your Creator—first.

I really do have all of the answers and will support you in every aspect of your life. Don't bring Me down to your level by using My name in connection with that which is base. Don't set goals without considering Me, or put your confidence in anything other than Me...."

You and I see life from different perspectives, but there is much common ground. For instance, none of us wants to be lied to, stolen from, or have the lives of our loved ones taken in fits of anger. That's why God has commanded us to refrain from doing such things. These shared values are designed to safeguard relationships. (See Ex. 20:1-26.)

Legalism is one person's *preferences* running roughshod over everyone else's. It's a tendency to focus on details with a general disregard for relationships. Yes, God is a God of order, beauty, and relational rituals. But those things are in the eye of the beholder. One person's notion of order or beauty is not necessarily another's.

Every team needs a common set of values. But the particulars of how to live into those values need to be informed by the personalities and capabilities of the members. Great leaders model and remind the team of the goals and respect the dignity of the individuals as they work together to create ways of living their shared values. A Christian's primary leader is meant to be Christ. In addition to that, the Bible tells us that God has put our leaders in place and that we are to obey the laws of the government that rules over us. (See Rom.13:1-7.) If you don't like the laws, get involved. Don't simply complain or break them. Finally, we are to live into the agreed upon standards and authority of our homes. (See Eph. 6:1.)

To "make room for God" means you weave Him into everyday life in such a consistent way that His ways become your ways. Strive to make your coping strategies and interactions so wise, kind, and mindful of Him that people are surprised by them. Your loving ways will cause people to ask, "Where did you learn that?" You can answer, "It came from my faith."

PONDER

What's the difference between teaching values and insisting on preferences?

List one of your values. Now make a list of preferences related to that value.

For example, "Take care of what God has given you" may be a value of yours. In some homes, this would lead to a parent's preference that the dishes be cleaned and put away right after each meal. But that is just a preference. It is not a sin to let them sit if you need to spend the time in relationships. Some people are choosing dishes over a relationship, and they wonder why their kids can't wait to get out of the house. I didn't say don't do the dishes. Just consider asking the people under your roof how they would like to approach the task. It's hard to change, but in the long run, it may take less energy than staying the same.

How can you respect and teach values without getting stuck on the details that arise from your own preferences? Collaborate. Keep trying new ways of life until you land on something that works for both you and the people you love. If you are mean or pushy, people won't feel safe to tell you the truth about their thoughts and feelings when they differ from yours. What have you learned from this chapter about insisting on your own way?

Think about asking people you trust to tell you what their preferences are relating to your value. How do other people teach it to their families?

PART 2

An Uncommon Understanding

MAKE ROOM FOR HUMAN NATURE

MAKE ROOM FOR
HUMAN NATURE

"Do not judge, and you will not be judged; do not condemn, and you will not be condemned...for the measure you give will be the measure you get back."

—LUKE 6:37

W HAT DOES "MAKE ROOM FOR human nature" mean? It means to respect the complex ways we are made. It means to realize that to do justice I must understand that the picture I have of anyone at any given time is just a snapshot. And you know those can be pretty unflattering at times; it doesn't show a person from all angles and cannot capture a personality or other intangible traits. Although God sees us from every angle and over time, we see one another dimly while we're here on earth.

I was moved by something I heard Oprah Winfrey say years ago: "We all are created equal. We're just different shapes and colors for the purpose of identification." Our shapes and colors only speak to what is on the outside of us. What makes each of us worth knowing is what's inside; each of us is a beautiful, wonderful, precious child of God. "Make room for human nature" means to consider that we all are doing the best we can with the equipment, training, and support we have. We can do better with a little additional effort and information. "Make room" has everything to do with humility, determination, and wisdom.

As I sat waiting for my daughter in the dentist office one week, I read a magazine article about what makes humans both "good" and "evil." Many sources quoted in the article agreed that we will eventually find the areas of the brain that control destructive tendencies, and then we will be able to create treatments. We are learning how the brain can be adapted with surgery, stimulation, thought patterns, and medicines so a person can behave differently. This truth comes to life in treatment centers of all kinds. Because we're human, we are controlled in large part by our thinking and by the chemical and electrical activity of our brains. What seemed to be missing from the article, however, was a discussion of anything spiritual. It was focused primarily on a discussion of the brain, but what about the heart?

God created us and gave us freedom of choice. Therefore, we have the capacity for both good and evil. The book of Matthew chapter 12 describes this paradox in verses 34-35: "Out of the wellspring of the heart the mouth speaks. The good man brings good things out of the good things stored up in him, and the bad man brings bad things out of the bad things stored up in him." Before you get nervous, remember that God's Word also tells us, "For where your treasure is, there your heart will be also" (Matt. 6:21). That is good news if your treasure is God. These are the words of Jesus!

The Bible teaches us that God created man in His image: pure, good, and deeply in love with Him. In the first chapter of the Bible, Genesis 1, we are told that, "God saw all that He had made, and it was very good" (v. 31). Yet, humans eventually overrode God's will for us. In the Garden of Eden, God provided the *opportunity* for Adam and Eve to know the uglier side of life, but He encouraged them to stay away from it, telling them that if they ever tasted it, it would lead to death: "You must not eat from the tree of the knowledge of good and evil, for when you eat of it you will certainly die" (Gen. 2:17). When Adam and Eve *chose* to go to the source of knowledge of good and evil, they received the education of a lifetime. And it left humankind reeling—filled with damaging thoughts, emotions, and inclinations of the heart.

Have you ever been faced with a truth so disappointing that you never fully return to the person you were before you experienced it? Divorce, the death of a loved one, betrayal by a very important person in your life, or a realization about your own inadequacies strip you of some innocence. It is like the person you were before it happened has died. Once you become aware of evil ways of life, you are destined to try some of them out. After all, you are curious and free.

Now, think about it. Isn't this what every *loving* family deals with? At one point, you have this child who seems so pure and innocent, and you spend your whole life trying to protect him or her from people and places and attitudes that will make their life worse. You wish you could wipe out destructive sex, drugs, hatred, greed, and a plethora of other awful things. You wish your children would never turn to those things because they love, trust and respect you. But that's not the way life works, is it? Human beings are curious. They are destined to go places and do things that do great harm. And if you truly love someone, you have to give the freedom to choose his or her own path—even if that means making mistakes and suffering the consequences that come with them.

Have you ever noticed that we humans use some foolish coping strategies just to be noticed? Some of them are good and some of them are evil. For example, when we don't feel understood, sometimes we raise our voice and scream, or sometimes we just walk away. But neither option is particularly effective. As we work through this world, we seek to know and be known. This is a need inherent in our deepest being and a skill which some of us never acquire. It is not a condition of the brain. It cannot be gained by intelligence, wealth, or position. Indeed, these things can often get in the way of knowing and being known.

For most humans, our own confounding (and sometimes destructive) actions frustrate and disappoint us. Are you too bossy or too submissive for your own taste? Do you tell yourself you will never take a certain risk again only to find yourself taking it? Or, conversely, do you live a relatively boring life and wish you lived more adventurously? Are you ever stingy, impatient, or unkind and wish you weren't?

This section of the book, "Make Room for Human Nature," is designed to help you be more accepting of others and realize that human beings are all works in progress. Approach this section as a guide to help you understand human nature enough to realize that we all live in a constant state of tension and are filled with contradictions. That is an inevitable human state. In an attempt to alleviate our discomfort, we respond in one of three ways: we move toward pleasure, move away from pain, or rest in love—a love that ultimately comes from our relationship with God. When we make the vertical choice and move toward God and His love, we are much more likely to allow God to act out the beauty of His qualities in us. He gives us love, joy, peace, patience, kindness, generosity, faithfulness, gentleness, and self-control.

CHAPTER 9

UNDERSTANDING HUMAN NATURE

*"Your own soul is nourished when you are kind; but
you destroy yourself when you are cruel."*

—PROVERBS 11:17 (NLT)

Just as God is comprised of three entities—Father, Son, and Holy Spirit—He created us to be a combination of three entities. Humans are an indivisible combination of body, soul, and spirit while we are on earth. Even our very makeup is designed to teach us something about our creator God.

G OD TELLS US IN PSALM 139 that He formed our inward parts in our mothers' wombs; we are wonderfully made. He gives each spiritual being life and the opportunity to know and relate to Him with our hearts, souls, minds, and bodies. He has searched us and known us. No one else can make that claim except God, the One whose presence encompasses the Holy Spirit and Christ. Others touch our souls emotionally, but only God has a thorough understanding of us and can satisfy us completely. The more we notice and experience these truths, the more we come to believe them.

The chapters that follow will address the three aspects of our humanity: body, soul, and spirit. If you understand just a few of the qualities of the human makeup (the brain, the mind, and the heart), you will have a better grip on why humans do both ridiculously foolish and incredibly good things. When you understand the influence of the conscience, personality, memory, and spiritual gifts, you can appreciate why we are so confounding. If you take this information seriously and open your heart to it, you will increase your ability to be patient, kind, and nonjudgmental. Those are attitudes prescribed by Christ. And if you acquire them to a high degree, you will know endless moments of peace and pleasure.

DIGGING DEEPER

DO I UNDERSTAND
INSEPARABLE PARTS?

Have you ever considered that the three inseparable parts of us help us understand our triune God? If you could send a part of yourself away for a time in order to help people understand the depth, height, and breadth of God's love and to save the souls of the entire world, would you? Would you endure what Christ went through?

CHAPTER 10

PARTS OF A WHOLE

*"Love the Lord your God with all of your heart, and
all of your soul, and all of your mind."*

— MATTHEW 22:37

ANY STUDY OF HUMAN NATURE can be confounding because no two of us are alike, and many of our qualities are intangible and invisible. But if you know enough about how our bodies, souls, and spirits are put together, you can give yourself and others a break in the hard times, encouragement in the frustrating times, and faith and courage to strive for the very best. You will gain some life-changing, soul-soothing realizations about how you are created, and this will make it easier to love yourself and understand God's love for you.

Remember, God is a combination of three entities: God, Jesus Christ, and the Holy Spirit. Each of us will employ metaphors when discussing our God because there are no words to describe Him perfectly. When I was younger in my walk of faith and in my understanding of God, I thought of the Holy Trinity as a beautiful family. God provides, protects, disciplines fairly and lovingly, and promotes growth, joy, and adventure. The Holy

Spirit nurtures, teaches, and gives us our daily bread. In fact, Jesus called the Holy Spirit our "helper"—the one who explains things to us so we can understand. The Spirit is always with us, supplies wisdom, and supports our efforts. I thought of Jesus Christ as a heavenly, holy brother. In the book of Matthew, He refers to those who believe in Him as His family. He understands us because He is most like us. He walked in human form for a time to demonstrate many things and to show He understands how difficult it can be to be limited by a human body and brain. Yet, He is the perfect brother, because He understands better than any of us how loving God is, how helpful the Holy Spirit is, how capable we can be, and how hopeful life is when we follow the Lord's directions for how best to love and support one another. And, oh yes, I don't want to fail to mention this aspect of Christ: He and the Holy Spirit are always interceding for us. Since Christ understands and has experienced every feeling we will ever have, He not only encourages us to approach life wisely, but He also knows our hearts and gives us credit for wanting what's right; He will approach our Father on our behalf if we ask Him to.

Now considering this family metaphor, I must explain that my faith has matured and that I am fully aware that there is no adequate way to describe God. Whatever words we conjure up can never begin to depict His magnificence and wholeness. He doesn't ask for that. God reminds us simply that He is love. In John 14, when Christ's disciple, Philip, wanted to see God, Jesus said, "Philip, don't you even yet know who I am, even after all the time I have been with you? Anyone who has seen me has seen the Father! Don't you believe that I am in the Father and the Father is in me? The words I say are not my own, but my Father who lives in me does his work through me. Just believe that I am in the Father and the Father is in me. Or at least believe because of what you have seen me do" (vv. 9-11).

The beautiful truth we are taught as Christians is that God is in us and we are in Him. We are triune beings as well. Let's look at three aspects of human nature: the body, the soul, and the spirit. Like the Holy Trinity, these three parts of us are capable of constant communication, they are directly affected by one another, and they are here to stay. So we must allow all three to influence us for the better.

Your Body—Your Physical Experience of Life

The body is the only part of the human being that is visible. It is the tangible part of us—including what's under our skin. It is wonderfully and beautifully made to give us a physical presence and experience on earth. Human bodies enjoy rhythms and balance and moderation. That is why a wise statement contained in Proverbs tells us that too much of one thing and too little of another is not good for us.

The body includes our brains and our five senses. Believe it or not, the brain is a huge part of what makes following the teachings of Christ so difficult for us. Therefore, an understanding of the brain and how it works will help you to stop judging others, help you to have mercy on yourself for your own failings, and encourage you to keep practicing Christ's teachings.

We look at our bodies and think we are seeing ourselves, but we are only seeing one of three important parts of our being. The body is only the physical part of the human being. The Bible describes it as our "flesh" or "tent." This human tent is the form in which we have been placed for a time, and it is influenced by the physical world. Gravity, for example, holds it on earth; light warms it; the sight of an environmental danger causes it instinctively to move closer for inspection or away for safety. Our five senses gather information. Then, nerves in the body send that information to the spinal cord where it is then carried on to the brain and other organs.

Our nervous systems are designed by God to help us take good care of ourselves. They tell the body what is going on outside so the body can adjust inside. When I taught stress management in corporate environments, we discussed how the body reacts to anything we label as dangerous or urgent. Think about how protective the body becomes when we see, hear, smell, taste, or touch something that causes us to feel endangered; the body immediately releases a chemical called adrenaline.

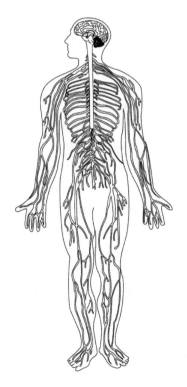

THE HUMAN BODY HAS MANY SEPARATE NERVOUS SYSTEMS THAT COMMUNICATE CONTINUOUSLY TO RESPOND TO OUR DESIRES AND NEEDS.

Have you ever heard of "fight or flight syndrome"? When you face something dangerous, here's how adrenaline helps. Adrenaline makes your pupils dilate so you can see more clearly. You feel your heart pounding because it's working harder than usual to send more blood to your major organs and less to your extremities because, if you are going to run, your lungs and heart will need more strength and energy from the oxygen in your blood. Also, if you are wounded by a wild animal, you don't want to bleed to death, so it's helpful to have less blood in the limbs you might use to protect yourself.

Have you ever had to speak publicly and noticed how cold your hands get? Yep. That means less blood is going to your extremities. You might even feel the urge to go to the bathroom; your body is telling you to let go of the excess weight you'll carry if you have to run from an unfriendly audience. You can't believe how the body cares for itself automatically when it thinks it is in danger. We even want to yell sometimes when we stay and face danger because loud noise can scare living things away.

But notice I said "*when* we label something as dangerous." The brain works in conjunction with the mind (a part of the soul) to decide what needs adrenalin and what doesn't. It's not the sidewalks, trees, or even people who make walking alone at night creepy. It's the thought of being attacked.

The brain, our programmable thought organ, is incredible. It gives us endless ways to express our individuality. And it contains a memory bank, which is pleasurable and helpful. For example, human bodies like rhythms and balance and moderation, so your brain can memorize your habits and spit them out automatically. As you prepare for your morning, think of how many directions your body travels and how many activities it performs without a conscious command from you. Out of bed, body stretches, walk to kitchen, pour juice, drink juice, back to shower, turn on water... Our bodies and brains need sensible amounts of sleep, nutrition, water, rest, exercise, work, and play. When we get enough of these, we feel better, and when we don't, we feel edgy. Children often haven't established good habits, so they forget to tend to their bodies. Give a cranky child a glass of water and a place to run and play (or if he has played or worked for too long, a rest), and his body will literally feel better. If you pause to notice it, you'll experience this change from stressed to relaxed in your body as well when you create the right balance for yourself. Remember that all of life is about relationships. Do you have a nurturing relationship with your body and brain?

Each of our bodies is endowed with talents or abilities that can be used to provide services for others and to give us a sense that the world is a better place because we are in it. Can your vocal cords make a beautiful sound? Can your brain organize life easily? Do you have a good sense of direction? Are you mechanically inclined or creative? Use these skills!

When I taught in a special education facility, I worked with teens who had profound mental disabilities. Several of them could not even dress themselves. They had the physical capacity, but could not understand how to put a button through a hole. But do you know that after a few years of concerted training they not only dressed themselves, but also used simple sign language to express basic needs? They made wreaths at Christmastime and sold them. Why do I tell you this? I believe it's essential to understand that if these students with challenging disabilities could make incredible strides in their lives, we can find the fortitude to change ours, too. The more we exercise our strengths, talents, and abilities, the more they grow. And here's the really nice thing: until our bodies or brains malfunction, we hardly have to give them a thought in order to get through a day. There is only one tough aspect to taking care of our bodies. God asked us not to conform any longer to the pattern of this world, but "to transform our thinking [brains] by the renewing of our minds [soul]" (Rom. 12:1-2). Thinking is a physical activity that takes place in the brain and leads to the release of chemicals that cause the body to carry out certain tasks. Renewal requires that we move from being informed only by our bodies to being informed by our soul and spirit as well.

Your Soul — Your Relational Experience of Life

When you think of the soul, think "relationship" or "interaction." The soul is the combination of your mind, emotions, and will. When we are feeling soulful, we are in touch with our thoughts, feelings, and choices about ourselves, others, the world, creation, and God. Music moves our souls. It touches us emotionally. Did you know that loud music actually stresses the body, but if a song moves our soul, we will crank it up anyway? And what about snow? It is cold and stresses our bodies, but since playing in snow cheers our souls, we are willing to stay out until our fingers and toes are so cold they have stopped hurting. The discomfort doesn't matter because, in that moment, we have moved our attention from our bodies to our souls.

The soul has a mind of its own. It is nonphysical knowing. It is the gut reactions; it is the deeper recognition that, at times appears to be detached from learning. It is the "chemistry" two people have even though they are poorly suited for one another. Sometimes, it informs us in ways that conflict with the brain's limited understanding. There is just "something" about a person or place or activity that brings out the real you and makes you feel connected, even though your brain is telling you otherwise. Have you experienced that? Once when Jim and I were in Ashville we wandered into a little joint for breakfast. The jukebox was playing Natalie Cole's rendition of "Unforgettable." A greasy, poorly groomed big man walked over to us and asked to hold our one year old. He took her and danced with her. My body told me it was foolish to hand my baby to a stranger, but my soul danced as they danced.

The soul can be neglected, and it can also be intruded upon by others. It can be misinformed to the point that it ceases to be helpful for a time. But Christ said, "Do not be afraid of those who kill the body but cannot kill the soul" (Matt. 10:28). God designed the soul to be eternal. And it is clear that the soul yearns to be free. That zest for freedom is instilled in us.

In a soulful moment last week, I asked a group of my friends where they would picture themselves if they could escape the hassles of everyday life and move to a place that would let their soul sing.

> **Jill:** *Italy. The calm beauty, the history. It's just so free I can lose myself in it.*
>
> **Kristin:** *Our smaller home that we left to buy this bigger one. This bigger house with the higher social expectations of the neighborhood is hard on us. That house was enough. We were happier.*
>
> **Sue:** *Any all natural place, the forest or the beach, because that's where I feel and see God.*
>
> **Liz:** *A deserted island with just our little family.*
>
> **Sabrina:** *A city rather than the suburbs. There are museums and activity and a variety of schools.*
>
> **Alison:** *A lake house porch or a log cabin that looks out over the water and trees.*
>
> **Sheila:** *I'm happy right where I am.*

As each woman named a place, her eyes filled with tears. Do you know why? Life is meant to be informed by and poured through our souls. A visit to the soul can be a very moving experience, and our number one soul mate is God. He asked us to have no others before Him. Since God created us, He knew we would have a difficult time relating to someone invisible, so He made Himself visible for a short period through Christ. It's why He said to His disciples, "If you have seen me, you have seen the Father" (John 14:9). And Christ taught us with stories from life on earth — stories of faithfulness and wisdom and of deceit and folly. It's just that from the time we are born, we are surrounded by human beings who forget, or don't know, to tell us to put Him first. So, like Adam and Eve, we look to one another for our cues. In fact, when Adam and Eve agreed to disregard God's wisdom, they traded Him for each other. They went together to the tree and they learned together about evil, even though God had warned them to stay away. Neither of them chose to be loyal to Him. They found comfort in making that choice together. We have been doing that ever since, and it has not been good for us. Ultimately, we know that. We disappoint one another repeatedly. However, if you get to know God well, you will notice that He is never a disappointment. "God will never leave you or fail you." (Heb. 13:5).

We are made in God's image. Remember? Our soul life is what makes belief in God possible. Life is just not soothing without Him. The beauty, order, and wonder around us make our souls want to sing to Him. We know He is there. God created our souls with the capacity to experience a daily dose of His incredible, energizing presence. But human beings can intrude upon that peace. People we barely know can make us believe that God and Christ have no place in our life and that we are only meant to relate to the universe. Don't believe it. Free your soul! It is bursting at the seams. Are you restless? Lonely? Purposeless? Bored? Something worse? These are soulful moments. They can also be turning points.

Do you stop to wonder what God wants for you? Ever curl up in a chair and imagine Him holding and telling you that He loves you immensely? You are everything He needs you to be to serve the people He needs you to serve. Are you willing?

Emotions — Tears are the most obvious physical expression of the soul. They communicate both deep despair and elation. You have a soul designed to be moving in union and in love with God—sensitive, compassionate, determined, and surrendered to Him. You are meant to connect with His creations: the clouds, grass, mountains, water, music, and art. You are meant to celebrate and drink in the wonder of it all. Can you think of times when songs or sights have brought you to tears? If it has been a long time since you've cried, I strongly encourage you to watch shows in which the little guy wins out. It is a very fun and soulful experience. If that doesn't do it for you, what does? As your soul softens, you will also soften your heart, your hugs, your life; your life will become richer.

Will—This is one of the most misunderstood elements of the soul, but it is really quite simple. It is an attitude that inclines us to make a choice based on relationship. To will yourself to do something is to push yourself to make a decision and follow it based on the inclinations of your heart (spirit) in combination with the beliefs you have stored in your brain (body). As I say this, I realize we must take a look at the third aspect of humanity—our spirit—because it is there, at the core of us, where we find the heart.

Your Spirit — Your Spiritual Experience of Life

~83~

The spirit is the hardest part of the human to discuss and to understand. Although it is the core of our being, we aren't accustomed to talking about it. Your spirit is the real you, minus your body. Picture yourself any way you want to, but realize that God made your body the way it needs to be to attract the people He wants in your life and to serve the purposes He has for you here on earth. Beyond this, there are a lot of unknowns. However, that's okay. God also created humans to love mysteries!

Our heavenly Father speaks directly to our spirits when He repeatedly invites us to seek Him. Yet He tells us that in order to find Him, we must seek Him with all of our body, mind, soul, and heart. Therefore, we are spirits who have bodies, minds, souls, and hearts. A relationship makes the connection complete: God actively invites us to know Him, and we actively seek to know Him and feel known by Him. It's why God says outwardly we can be wasting away (we grow physically tired) while "inwardly, we are being renewed day by day" (2 Cor. 4:16).

That "inward" part of you is you, the spiritual being. I remember one day when I was in my forties and was walking home from the children's bus stop. The sky was shades of orange and pink, and the air was springtime crisp. I had just been chatting with a group of women I loved. My body, mind, and soul were bursting with the abundance of it all, and I just began to run full-tilt, like a child. It was a beautiful morning, and I was filled with the joy of God's creation. As I turned the corner and ran across the lawn I wanted to do a cartwheel. I remember thinking, *I don't feel as old as I look.*

Others have agreed with this surprising realization when they look at pictures of their aging bodies. In fact, some of our family friends are people over 70 who still seem young. Is that because our spiritual self and our physical body do not age at the same pace? Is that why a human who looks old can still seem childlike, not only when she is upset, but also when she is happy?

Spiritual Substance

So, your **spirit** is you, the inner you. It moves on into eternity when your body has ceased to function. Your spirit is the part of you that has no physical substance, but houses your invisible qualities such as the conscience, personality, spiritual heart, and spiritual gifts.

1. Your **conscience** is the part of your spiritual being that is comparable to the brain. It comes programmed by God with universal laws that are meant to govern your behavior and soothe your soul.

2. Your **personality** is also knit into your spiritual being. Are you passionate or even-tempered? Vivacious or low-key? Simple or complex? Think about it. You don't clothe a spirit in jeans and tennis shoes. You clothe a spirit in qualities. That's why we each come out looking distinct and precious. When we were told to clothe ourselves with compassion, kindness, humility, gentleness and patience (Col. 3:12), it is because those clothes fit a spiritual being whose loyalty is to God and His kingdom. They are qualities that coincide with the stirrings of our hearts.

3. Your **heart** contains a God-sized, God-shaped cavity that only He can fill. But we choose whether or not to give it to Him. Your heart is a resting place full of both good and awful inclinations, and it is ruled by that which you treasure. That's why God has asked us to treasure Him above everything else.

4. To help us do that, God has added to our spiritual selves a treasure chest of **spiritual gifts** we may claim as we live our lives in the light of His love. (We will discuss these in Chapter 18.)

As we increasingly understand our human nature and why we do what we do, it's easier to stop judging others and ourselves and just learn to love. Love is healing. Human judgment is generally arrogant, often inaccurate, and usually annihilates our best efforts to know and be known. Only God has the ability to comprehend us completely. The more we come to know Him, the more we are able to make the best of what He has given us.

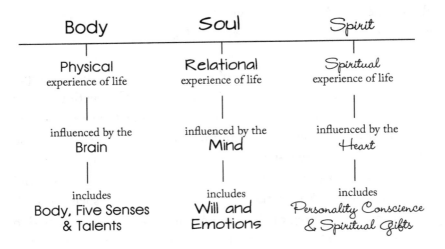

Body	Soul	Spirit
Physical experience of life	Relational experience of life	Spiritual experience of life
influenced by the Brain	influenced by the Mind	influenced by the Heart
includes Body, Five Senses & Talents	includes Will and Emotions	includes Personality Conscience & Spiritual Gifts

DIGGING DEEPER

CAN YOU LOVE THE LORD WITH ALL OF YOUR HEART, SOUL, AND MIND?

The apostle Paul was not the first to recognize that the things we *do* don't always coincide with who we *are*. We are befuddled at times, and we wonder how we end up in some of the circumstances, relationships, and lifestyles we choose. We think of ourselves as good people, but we sometimes do unkind and selfish things. We have an idea or dream and set out to make it a reality, but along the way, we stumble on our own tendencies and/or the inclinations of the people and culture around us. God gave us this freedom: it demonstrates an incredible level of love and respect on His part. Yet He longs for us to listen to and love and respect Him even more than we love one another and ourselves.

- What are some beliefs you were taught by your parents and teachers? Do you still believe them?

    God is...

    People are...

    Your goal in life is...

    You will never succeed if you don't...

- List the people, places, and activities you believe put you in touch with yourself.

- Describe the person you believe you would be if you could change your life circumstances.

- How would life look if you were to cling to and insert the person you long to be into everyday life where you are?

- What do you treasure above all else? Does your life express that? Is that what you want your life to demonstrate?

CHAPTER 11

A THOROUGH EXAMINATION OF THE BODY

*"But, in fact, God has arranged the parts in the body,
every one of them, just as he wanted them to be."*

—1 CORINTHIANS 12:18

T HE BODY IS THE SIMPLEST place to start when it comes to human nature. No one will deny it exists, and since it is tangible, it can be researched and studied. The human form continues to defy our imaginations in its complexity. Brains process thousands of bits of information in a matter of seconds. Bones and tissues reconnect and heal after being damaged. Muscles react automatically to traumatic events.

Your body was designed especially by God to serve His purposes for you on earth—"to give you a hope and a future" (Jer. 29:11). It is the earthen vessel God gave you to attract others and to relate with them. It can also help you to relate to God, to come to know Him and demonstrate His love to others.

Our bodies, however, sometimes instinctively defy our wishes. They are stimulated to action by our most important organ, the brain. There are chemical and physical aspects of our makeup over which we *appear* to have no control. So, unfortunately, we cannot count on our bodies to keep us safe or sane. Sometimes we're rude when we need to be kind, shy when we need to be courageous, or weak when we need to be strong. Why? Because our brains are like computers and have been programmed by our choices and the circumstances and people around us. The habits and thoughts we practice are the ones we are most likely to display under duress.

One day, I received a call from my sister, Jeanne. She was crying and said she needed me to pray with her. She had been taking her dogs for a walk in her neighborhood when suddenly she heard a loud bang. She looked in the direction of the sound. Just then, she heard two frightening screams followed by, "No, Jackson, no! Oh God, no!" My sister bolted in the direction of the sounds. She could see a man's body in the doorway. Another man came from his home and ran to the injured man's side. My sister urgently cried, "Check his pulse!" The man said, "He's dead. Don't come any closer; he's gone." Apparently, he had shot himself in the head.

Later, Jeanne said, "There were all of these workers around me when this happened, and I seemed to be the only one heading in the direction of the disaster. Why didn't anyone do anything? Why did they just stand there when that woman shrieked?" I knew the answer from personal experience: their brains got in the way. In the past, I had been awakened in the middle of the night by emergencies. I understood temporary inactivity.

On one of those occasions, a woman outside my window began screaming for help. People in half a dozen homes awoke to her cries and flipped on their lights. "Help me! Someone help me!" Those were her exact words. Loud. Urgent. Why didn't someone immediately come to help? Why did we all hesitate for even a moment? We needed a second to think. Perhaps, if we opened our doors, someone with a gun would enter; we might endanger our sleeping children. Perhaps we could inadvertently anger her attacker and get the woman killed. How would we approach an attacker? How would we defend her?

We were startled and wanted to do the wise thing. It was only a matter of seconds, but they felt like eternity. Finally, we headed into the dark night, but when we found the woman, she had stopped screaming and became angry. She informed us her husband had fallen into a diabetic seizure and she thought he was dying. But he didn't die. In fact, he was sitting up in his bed seemingly fine, and she commanded us to leave.

Because she had been afraid, her brain overreacted, and she yelled something vague that delayed her rescuers. Had she shouted, "Help, my husband is having a seizure," she would have gotten help sooner because no one's brain would have had to consider the possible dangers.

On another occasion, we awoke to our child's loud, frightened screams. We didn't know which child it was, but there was *not an instant* between her screams and our movement toward the girls' rooms. We moved in to protect, defend, and save whoever was in danger without caring about what it might cost us.

Remember, *the thought you attach to your life circumstances determines your body's responses and eventually your habits.* Human activity stems from input received by our five senses in combination with our minds' interpretation of that input. Then our brains decide what is needed and send the information to our muscle cells so we can act.

Your Senses

What makes one person comfortable in a certain sweater when another says it is too scratchy? Why do some people love vegetables and others avoid them?

Do you love to smell cologne and perfume on other people, or does it give you a headache? Have you ever told someone something was green only to have him or her argue that it is blue?

Genetics are the hardware of the human body. Do you worry a lot? Perhaps you have the worry gene on your DNA strand. You'll have to work harder than some people so you don't fret too much. Are you addicted to nicotine? Same deal. Perhaps your grandfather's receptor sites and urge center were under or overactive like yours. Are you color blind or tone deaf? Don't despair. We all have hardware that isn't what we would like it to be, and we forget that there are benefits to inadequacy and failure. They can keep us humble. All of us get frustrated with our limitations at times, but remember this—What you received from God, your parents, and occasionally medical intervention, is sufficient to allow you to live the life God wants you to live. Each child of God is different, but we are all "beautifully and wonderfully made" (Ps. 139:14; 1 Cor. 12:18).

Take note. I'm going to say something that will save you and your loved ones a few arguments. *Each of us has finely tuned senses, but yours are different from mine.* So if you eat raw oysters, that's fine. But don't tell *me* to eat raw oysters because, to my mouth, well, they feel too slimy. I can't get past the negative effects of the texture to focus on the flavor. You can. Look at this on the bright side—you will never have to share your oysters with me.

My late husband received a bone marrow transplant while battling leukemia. Jim's blood cells had to be completely annihilated so they wouldn't continue to produce the cancer in his body. During the procedure, they were replaced by a donor's cells, and Jim's body reproduced his donor's blood instead of his own. When the transplant was complete, Jim began to like his food without sauces or spice. When he occasionally drank alcohol, he preferred red wine to beer. I asked him why and he said, "My taste buds have changed." Weird, huh? I'd love to meet his donor one day and find out if his tastes matched Jim's new ones.

If someone tells you that a color looks red and you think it looks orange, maybe you are both right. Every color looks slightly different to two different sets of eyes. If someone says, "These socks are uncomfortable," and you say, "They feel fine," maybe you are both right. One day I was golfing with my father. He has the perspective of an electrical engineer and craftsman; he was telling me to line my body up with the hole. I was trying, but I don't think he believed I was trying. I don't have the acute visual perception he has, so I *couldn't* line up my body the way he could. Most of us want people to see, taste, feel, smell, and hear things the way we do, but that is not possible. Let it go. There is plenty in life upon which we can agree.

Today, people understand how the body takes in information and sends it to the brain. It's helpful to know this because you may be expecting too much of the people around you...or they may be expecting too much of you. Instead of assuming someone is just being difficult, realize that *he or she may be trying harder than you are* to get along. Let's take a look at what is happening beneath your skin after your senses collect information.

How the Body Communicates With Itself

Nerves throughout your body collect information about the world and send it on down the line from one cell to the next until it moves up the spinal column and into the brain.

The brain runs on energy and chemicals and is designed to *save* energy. So it receives input from the outside environment (and from our body, soul and spirit to some extent). Then, if a situation looks "familiar," the brain will quickly decide what is needed without going to the trouble of working too hard. It will mix up a chemical recipe for an emotion that has typically been used by its owner under similar circumstances.

For example, if you add a scary thought to a loud noise, your brain will mix up a recipe for fear, and fear chemicals will come together to transmit a message to your muscles. Your muscles then tense in preparation for danger. If you add the thought, "I need to defend myself," your brain may mix up courage and your muscles may spring into action.

On the other hand, if you add the thought, "I'm done for," the ingredients for timidity, might cause you to pull up the covers and pretend nothing is really happening. Recently, I heard a bang in my bedroom in the middle of the night. The same loud noise at a birthday party might have made me laugh. But that night, I had a fearful thought that inspired my brain to release a fearful formula, and I was momentarily tense! I got up and discovered that a large picture hanging across the room from my bed had dropped to the ground when the wire holding it snapped. Was I ever in danger? No.

If you typically become angry when someone lets you down and have learned that it either gets you your way or at least gives you some immediate relief, your brain will offer anger whenever someone lets you down. The problem is this — the more you allow your brain to mix the anger cocktail, the more your brain adjusts to it. Over time, anger becomes an easy emotion to conjure up, and you use it even when you wish you wouldn't. Eventually, your brain may look for angry thoughts so it can mix up some anger. Who is in charge? You or your brain?

Have you ever spent time with someone who seems to go from one negative to another? I hope that isn't you. If you want to experience a healthier emotion, you must stop yourself as soon as your brain begins a distasteful course and tell it — *will it* — to focus on something pleasant.

If a person doesn't like feeling angry, for example, he or she must choose a different emotion (perhaps patience or kindness) repeatedly in order to build a new pathway that becomes easier to travel over time. This will be a deliberate choice until the new neurological trail is well worn. This is where "Seek the Lesson" (discussed in chapter 32) becomes a powerful tool. I'm going to mention this repeatedly because it works.

The brain cannot tell the difference between what is the real and imagined, so negative, skeptical thoughts set the body up to take a beating just as positive kind thoughts prepare the body for healing and repair.

How Cells Communicate with One Another

When I started teaching this subject, few people knew much about cells and serotonin. Today, antidepressants commercials have changed that. Most people know what cells look like and how they process chemicals. So this section is designed to give you a little extra understanding, to help you know why someone may say, "No, I don't *feel* the same way you do about this!"

We have talked about how the *body* communicates. We have *senses* that send information to the brain. The brain processes thoughts and emotions and tells the muscles what to do. Now, I want to take you a level deeper into human variation. By that I mean we are going to look at how humans vary at a microscopic level. We differ in billions of ways molecularly speaking. Your cells and mine are not the same. We're going to look at how impossible it is for me to navigate life the way you do. I want you to understand how complex the body is because it provides the answers for all too common questions like:

- "Why can't they just do it my way?"
- "Why don't you just cooperate?"
- "What's wrong with them?"
- "What's wrong with me?"

Other people can't be you because they don't have your body. They don't have your hands and eyes, and even if they did, their cells could never function exactly like yours because each of their trillions of brain cells has a way of functioning, which differs from person to person. No matter what science discovers, these differences will always exist. We need to be patient with one another.

In elementary school, when we talked about cells, we thought of them as little round things. Actually nerve cells have openings and hallways, so to speak, so messenger chemicals called neuropeptides can move into them and other chemicals can be produced within them as needed.

Let's look at cells and see how they communicate.

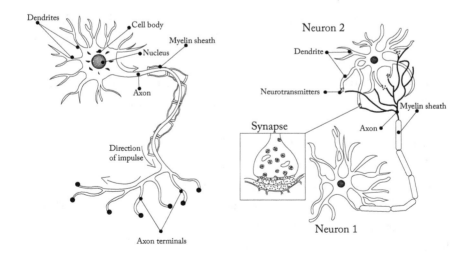

The Manufacturing Plant

One way to understand cell communication is to think of cells as chemical manufacturing plants.

The *dendrites*, like project managers, collect information from other cells to see what is needed for a particular job.

The *cell body* produces chemicals—*neurotransmitters* such as serotonin, dopamine, norepinephren—as needed in order to do the requested job. There are over 100 different chemicals produced in the various cells of the human brain. These chemicals are sent down the cell hallway (*axon*) through electrical impulses. If the hallway has very good insulation (*myelin*) the messengers travel more quickly. If the insulation is thin or broken, it delays the process.

At the end of each hallway is an opening where the chemicals enter an open environment (*synapse*), and the next cell's *dendrites* are waiting in that open environment to "catch" the information from the chemical messengers. This process is repeated over and over from cell to cell until the message is received by the cells that will actually tell and cause the members of your muscular nerves to react. Wow.

A Day on the Job

Stay with me. This isn't easy, but we need to talk about cells and the brain at the same time. I'm going to explain it again using business lingo because almost all of us are familiar with business.

Brain cells create pathways to their destinations to conserve energy. In much the same way that a path created through the woods takes less time and energy than cutting through uncharted territory, a preset neurological pathway through the brain takes less effort. So if two or more things seem similar, the *neurons* (brain cells) will bundle them together and treat similar circumstances alike. You can easily see this at work in young children. If they can climb on one toy, they assume they can climb on another. Petting one dog means they can attempt to pet another. But as adults, we learn to distinguish between similar appearances. Your father's furrowed brow may have been a sign of condemnation, but it may only be a sign of confusion for your boss or spouse.

Why is this important to understand? It illustrates why we must be careful about jumping to conclusions and ask more questions like, "You are furrowing your brow. What are you thinking?" Furthermore, practice taking kind, wise paths no matter what. Use your brain rather than letting your brain use you.

All of human *survival instincts* are located at the lower end of the brain near the spinal cord. So, as the neuron messengers course through the brain, they reach the emotional, instinctive, and the memory departments as well as navigate through other areas before the information arrives at the upper rooms where intelligent decisions can be made. Checking in with all departments may be required, but it doesn't always produce great results.

There are many departments in the brain with different functions. Even in healthy people, any of them can under function or over function. The thalamus projects information to specific areas and controls which information is sent to the thinking part of the brain called the *cerebral cortex*, which has two executive branches—the left and right brains. In the left brain, you hear things like, "Here are the facts and what to do with them." But in the right brain, phrases like, "These are some initial impressions. What are the possibilities? How will we and others feel if we go in that direction?" are more common. A right-brain response to life might be creative, intuitive, even athletic. A predominately left-brained response might key in on facts and logic. Do you think your habit is to lean on your left brain or right brain more frequently? Which one does your spouse seem to call on more frequently? Your best friend?

The best decisions are often made by consulting both halves. In order to do that, the information must pass back and forth. That requires more messengers. When you look at a brain, you might see something that looks like a gap between the left and right hemispheres. That gap, known as the *corpus collosum*, is actually a group of rich folds filled with millions of bundled axons that allow the hemispheres to communicate with one another.

Can you see why it might be easier for one person to make hard, factual decisions while another person seeks symbolic relevance, artistic agreement, and emotional concern? Yet, brainedness is not quite like handedness; it's an inclination, not a must. We can learn how to use both sides more effectively. MRIs have revealed that we all use both sides: we are not left-brained or right-brained.[4] So we must use our whole brain as often as we can.

Although this cell communication business is complex, understanding it helps us realize we are different from one another in billions of ways. We will never see one another completely. Only God has that capacity. This should encourage you to reach for humility. Since you can't see what equipment others are working with, you never really know why other people do what they do.

Holiness, Happiness, Humility

Quarrelling over little things (and sometimes bigger ones) can be resolved if you remember how complex the human body is. We know it is designed to keep itself alive. If humans taste, see, hear, touch, or smell something and it "seems" bad, our bodies tell our brains to avoid it. That comes in handy if you take a swig of gasoline; you're likely to spit it out. Almost all human beings dislike the flavor and smell of liquor the first time we drink it. Why? It can be toxic. How about nicotine? It smells horrid, hurts our lungs, and can even cause us to vomit when we first try it.

We may get to heaven and find out that some of us were given very particular taste buds. I know that some people have a very keen sense of smell. There are actually jobs in the world for professional sniffers. That's how we get the aromatherapists, food critics, world-class chefs, etc. The point? Love does not insist on its own way: love harnesses power. That's humility. With it, you can stop quarreling about unessential things like what foods taste good, what colors look good together, and how long it

---

4 There is rich connectivity in the whole brain, and increasingly neuroscientists are seeing that both sides of the brain are active during analysis and creativity. We can develop our skills by using them. Listening and learning from others is one way of doing that.

takes to complete a task. Simply stop assuming you know what is good for someone else and that his or her brain or body works the way yours does.

The Bible says, "In everything you do, stay away from complaining and arguing so that no one can speak a word of blame against you" (Phil. 2:14-15 NLT). Earlier, we discussed how a caterpillar can only see life from its own perspective, while a butterfly can see a broader spectrum of possibilities. When we Christians behave like caterpillars, we misrepresent our faith. It is God who matters most, and God doesn't care about some of the picky things we value. He sees life from a broader perspective than we can even imagine.

DIGGING DEEPER

WHY DIDN'T ANYONE
ANSWER HER CRIES?

You may still be pondering my sister's question about why the people in her neighborhood failed to move toward the woman's distressed cries. Based on our knowledge of the brain, I suspect they were pondering what the best response would be. There is also evidence that some people's brains react more slowly to the world around them than others. There can be an advantage to that at times. What did you learn about human nature so far that could cause you to pause before jumping to conclusions about others?

CHAPTER 12

OUR INCREDIBLE BRAINS

*"Train a child in the way he should go, and when
he is old he will not turn from it."*

—PROVERBS 22:6

I WAS RIDING A STATIONARY BIKE at the gym one day along with a group
of other health devotees. In front of us was a television with Dr. Phil
talking to a family about their troubling life. Lost in thought about
my own life and those of my clients, I was barely aware of the riders around
me. Suddenly, the woman at my side fell from her bike to the floor. Barely
audible, she mumbled, "I can't breathe." There was panic on her face.

I quickly bent down beside her. As the staff dialed 911, I looked her in
the eyes and explained, "Your body knows how to take care of itself. Relax,
and your brain can tell your body to start breathing again."

The terror left her face. Her muscles relaxed. She began to breathe. I
asked her to rest on the floor for a while and take deep breaths. As she did
that, she explained, "I got caught up in the story on TV, and that it was so
distressing to me, I must have forgotten to breathe."

How did I know? My vocation is helping people overcome anxiety, so the simplest and quickest thing I could do for her was help her relax and let nature take over. What we all witnessed that day was the complex working of a brain focused on the wrong thing for too long.

The brain is the most important organ in the body, because it holds the keys to the body's activity. Signals from the brain tell our muscles when and how to move; they create our perceptions of life; they motivate us to pay attention, recall, and understand.

I confessed earlier in the book that, as a young mother, I was using traditional methods to parent: some good, some not-so-good—lecture, nag, plead, timeout, threaten. None of these appealed to me much. Nor did they lead to the hoped-for results. Why? Because brains do not function as well under duress as they do in a kind and intelligent environment. God has tried to help us understand this.

Our brains are sometimes referred to as triune because they have three critical regions. Simply put, these regions monitor and control our physical, emotional, and intellectual lives. The regions are always working together, but sometimes not in a balanced way. The balance is, to some extent, up to us. Let's examine this.

My favorite model of the brain in on the following page and was created by Daniel J. Siegel, M.D.[5] It will help you visualize the importance of using your whole brain. Put your thumb in your palm, and curl your fingers over it. There's the brain. Your face is in front of your fingers. Your wrist and arm represent the spinal cord, the pathway of continual communication between the body and brain. Your palm represents your brain stem—physical comfort and survival. Your thumb, the limbic system—emotional safety and survival. Your fingers, the cortex—intellectual life, reason and understanding.

---

5 Dr. Dan Siegel's Hand Model of the Brain. © 2012 Mind Your Brain, Inc., Siegel.D.J. (2012). *The Developing Mind: How Relationships and the Brain Shape Who We Are* (2nd Ed.). New York, NY: The Guildford Press. Used with permission. All rights reserved.

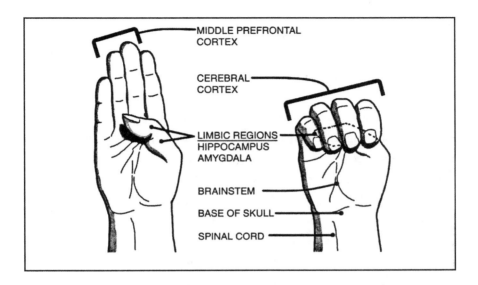

When you lift your fingers, you can visualize what happens when we "flip our lids." We expose our emotions and do not stay connected to the part of us that helps us make intelligent choices. If we want to understand life and be sensible rather than just reacting, we have to integrate all three parts of the brain. And here is the great news: we can live a vibrant life or a sickly life based on today's choices.

Let's compare the brain's structure to a home with a basement, main floor, and upstairs. In the basement (brain stem) is basic equipment that keeps our bodies functioning instinctively. It takes in information from the body and sends signals back. Breathing, heart rate, digestion, hunger, sexual desire, wakefulness, and many more processes are determined here. When we blink away dust, scratch an itch, or stretch to relieve muscular tension, we have our brain stem to thank for these automatic physical comforts being done with little effort on our part.

On the main floor (limbic system) memories and emotions are key players. Here we are enabled to *perceive* life not only inside the body, but also from the environment. From the time we are born, we are receiving input from our bodies. From this we decide that resting in calm arms feels good but talking in front of a lot of people makes our stomachs hurt. We can determine from relationships that when a person smiles, we feel safe and happy, but that same person crying confuses us and makes us afraid. Perhaps you had a beloved dog. If so, your emotions and memories for dogs are likely positive. These signals from early life (positive or negative) become hard-wired over time and are subconscious. Early impressions about authority figures, work, love, people, cultures, and ourselves—some of which occurred before we had language—continue to influence or even control our daily actions, unless we use the energy to go upstairs to the cortex and think things through. When we are tired or angry, hungry or lonely, it's easier to give in to these unconscious cues.

Upstairs (the prefrontal cortex) is where we make many of our conscious decisions and do most of our reasoning and understanding. This is where our memories and emotions are given meaning. It is the interaction of the brain stem and limbic region with the cortex that makes us the intelligent beings we are. Here is where our senses find life to its fullest. Although the brain appears to be divided into a left and right side, these halves are connected and are meant to be used together. We can analyze and understand the complex details of life (left brain) but also learn to empathize with others and create original solutions (right brain). Most of us favor one side or the other. We are blessed to have friends and family members who reason differently than we do and can help us to stay in balance.

God knit you together in the womb, and then He made adjustments based on your circumstances to keep your life challenging, but doable. (Doable means not more than you can handle with His help.) The brain is like a home that is under construction from the time we are conceived until the time we die. We can change its architecture by the way we live and think.

Why do some people handle stress better than others? It may be that they have trained their brains to handle stress, or their brains may have an abundance of a chemical called serotonin, which makes it easier for them to feel calm, happy, and content. We can now manipulate this chemical, but no one can finely tune it for your exact chemistry like God can, so drugs may or may not work for your body. Some people feel worse on medications, some better.

Why do some people seem "lazy" even when they may not be? Their brains may not be designed to rev up easily. Also, they may not have good biological filters for what needs attention and what doesn't, so staying focused may take more effort and make them more tired than others over the course of a day. Oftentimes, they are not designed to be as "high energy" as others, and nothing they do can generate the focused energy they are asked to produce. There are many possibilities.

Why do people react in ways that are immature and inappropriate? It may be that their brains overreact to adrenaline. As a result, they are more responsive in the emotional center. Too many circuits (oftentimes ones that were created when they were children) go off at once, hijacking the person's ability to stay calm and access the cortex where more intelligent choices can be made.

Under what four conditions will you know that you are stressed and less likely to make effective decisions? All of us become more sensitive to pressure when we are hungry, angry, lonely, and tired. (HALT) A wise person told me, "If you are experiencing any of these things, halt before you act."

Why might you repeat a behavior even after you have decided you don't want to do it anymore? The brain has a natural tendency to bundle things together and create chemical pathways to save time and energy. A trigger is a circumstance or condition that leads to a conscious or subconscious thought. This thought, in turn, is like an energy surge that lights up one of your pathways and causes your body to react. One too many people cut you off in traffic; your children are screaming at the top of their lungs; the lawnmower you have to use is not working and you are running out of time for the job—all of these are triggers. You react in a way that you promised yourself you weren't going to react anymore. It seems to happen before you have time to think. We can yell, stomp, or shut down automatically in response to familiar triggers. To change habits, we must think and live intentionally, and we must do so repeatedly. We have to slow down and practice when we are not stressed, because some of the best learning takes place when the brain is running at slower speeds.

The Physical Brain

You now know that your brain is the physical organ that processes the information that comes to you through your body's five senses. Input from the environment travels to the spinal cord and then to the base of the brain called the brain stem. Once the information reaches the brain, the cells there communicate with one another. Then the neurons (nerve cells) in the brain send the information to the appropriate areas to be processed. Where the messages go and how they are processed depends, to some extent, on what they are told by your mind and heart; it comes down to your attitudes, preferences, values, and habits.

Did you know that your brain uses a lot more energy when you are making willful decisions? It has no energy reserves of its own. That's why it is important to eat well and drink water throughout the day. Did you know that the brain is like a tub and can only handle a certain amount of stress before it overflows, so to speak, and chemically malfunctions? Each of us has a different sized tub. Did you know that it requires proper sleep, diet, exercise and rest? Those are healing balms for the physical parts of us.

Even within the population of "normal" functional human beings, brain chemical production and use differs. Some brains produce high levels of dopamine, serotonin, norepinephrine, and other chemicals that provide feelings of peace, energy, motivation, and contentment. Some brains, by comparison, produce low levels of these chemicals. Urge centers differ; some peoples' go off more frequently than others'. Some brains are physically able to filter out unimportant information; others are not. Some brains have properly working dendrites, the electrical receptors that collect information as it travels from nerve to nerve. Some brains do not work as effectively at collecting information and sending it to the proper location to inform the person of what to do. Some brains have nerve cells that are missing myelin, the protective covering that they need to help them work properly.

Did you know that stress has a negative effect on the hippocampus, a small part of the brain that is vital to the storage of memories? Imagine if you live in a dangerous home or environment. You may develop some brain patterns that someone who grows up in a safe neighborhood won't develop, because they don't need them. There are actual physical variations in the brain that influence how we think, feel, and respond to stress.

DEVELOPMENT

Here are just a few things scientists have discovered about our marvelous brains:

- In the womb, trophic (nutritional) factors tell axons where and how to connect.
- Between the ages of 2 and 16, massive pruning occurs (discarding almost half of brain cell connections). In fact, pruning occurs throughout life, especially during our formative years. Only the strong cells survive. So, if you want your children to be articulate when they grow up, make sure you not only talk to them, but also listen so they can talk. You can think of pruning of the brain as similar to the way God prunes earth's forests. Every so often, the forests become cluttered with underbrush and too many trees. From time to time, lightning hits a forest and creates a fire that ultimately cleans out the brush and seedlings. This is how nature freshens itself up and strong roots can grow where overcrowding formerly existed. That is what the brain does. It prunes away paths that no longer appear to be of primary importance so that the stronger, more frequently used connections can develop even further. Humans can promote the growth of brain connections by using their brains effectively.

- Social and emotional learning is vital and is best learned in context. For a child, this means "play with and learn from humans."

Drivers, Start Your Engines — Brain Speed and Intensity

I want to share another important feature of the brain that explains why our perceptions and responses to life vary. We really don't know if a person is lazy or just tired because his or her body uses more energy than ours to do the same jobs. Or maybe there is less electrical activity in certain parts of his or her brain. Did you know that some brains run at low speeds at times when their owners wish they'd run at high speeds? Attention deficit disorder is a condition of the brain in which certain areas of the person's brain appear to slip into a low gear and stay there even when the environment calls for something else. The individual can't do what is "typical" because they don't have a "typical" brain. Let me explain just one of their challenges to help you realize why we can't just assume a behavior stems from an "attitude."

Let's ponder brain speeds and intensities for a moment. Look at the chart below.

Beta: 14-30 Hz
Alert state, focused concentration, analysis

Alpha: 8-14 Hz
Relaxed state, reflecting, creative, problem-solving

Theta: 4-8 Hz
Meditative, drowsy, subconscious, also problem-solving

Delta: .01-4 Hz
Sleep state

Compare the speed of the brain (how alert it is, how much activity it is producing) with the speed of a car. A car shifts gears automatically in accordance with demands. During each day our brain releases chemicals and responds to electrical impulses. It does this at a variety of speeds and intensities.

Now you might be thinking that faster is better. But it actually is not. It is just one of several options we might use during a day. Scientists are beginning to recognize that while we analyze in beta, we problem solve and find many solutions in alpha. Our brains are experiencing a variety of waves simultaneously. Beta is fully engaged, conscious, and analytical. But imagination and creativity occur in alpha, theta, and delta states. Some people are not designed to stay in high alertness for great lengths of time, but others function quite well there. Which state do you think you move into when ideas flow freely, when you are finding solutions to problems, during moments of insight? Which is activated when you do repetitive activities like freeway driving, running, showering, or any other automatic task? Which takes over when completing a monotonous task like brushing your teeth?

The answer to all of these questions is alpha and theta states — lower speeds. And all human beings need to go there throughout the day. We need to intermittently enjoy simple moments. Can you say "water cooler" or "bathroom break"? In fact, lots of us drift into theta states after a big meal if the entertainment or subject is not sufficient to keep us in a higher gear. You know the feeling. One minute you are awake and thinking about possibilities in life, and the next, your eyes begin to droop. You are in a movie or meeting and your brain has chosen to downshift — even though it may be embarrassing!

Now, let's just imagine that Harry has a car that performs normally, but your car is stuck in second or third gear. No matter what you do to fix it, your car can't get much above 40. In fact, you have to crank up the music, rev up the engine, and jam the pedal to the metal just to keep it at a moderate speed. You're working just as hard as Harry is to get through a day, but because of your engine (brain speed), you can't accomplish as much. Your car may look fine, but under the hood you have a liability. Now imagine that every day, someone called you lazy and annoying no matter how hard you work. Most people are breezing through life while you are working hard to no avail. They are admired. You are judged.

If you are the person who must work hard to do what others do effortlessly, you may feel cheated and mistreated. This is the fate of most people who have attention deficit disorder or other brain issues. Their brain speeds may be quirky, their neurotransmitters may not be at typical production levels, and communication from area to area may be lacking, but because they look "normal," they take a lot of condemnation and judgment from people around them.

If you're one of these people, don't despair. Doctors are discovering new, relatively safe chemicals and interventions every day that can help the areas of your brain do the jobs they need to do. In fact, new forms of therapy are being developed that help you use your thinking to change your brain. I know of a lot of success stories. Talk to your doctor. While you're waiting for things to improve, use the abuse you take to help you become a kind, respectful person. We all need education, love, and the right work and home environments to help us flourish.

One thing I have come to believe is that all levels of brain waves are meant to be enjoyed in a given day. And all levels are critical. We analyze life and our brain is fully engaged in beta. But creativity and problem solving are often realized in alpha and theta states. A balance is what we need — even though your balance and someone else's will look a bit different. It is the reason why many of us say, "I want to sit down and do nothing for an hour or two before I have to get up tomorrow and get going again. I don't want to stay engaged all day and all night and then go to bed." Make home a place of safety and refuge for yourself, your spouse, and your children.

It is only for God to judge why we act the way we do at any given moment. He knows what is under each of our "hoods" and why it is there. We don't know if another person is grumpy and has an attitude or if his cells just produce less than average amounts of serotonin and dopamine. Modern science is discovering, at a rapid rate, that there is much more to life than meets the eye. Whether you knew some or none of this, here is the most important thing to take away from this chapter: Be kind. Don't judge. (See Prov. 12:25; 14:21; 19:17; Matt. 7:1; Rom. 14:13; 1 Cor.13 ; Eph.4:32; James 4:1.)

You may keep telling yourself, "I don't want to _____ anymore." But you should always remember it takes time to change. Moreover, there are some things you cannot be trained to do. You are limited by the working of your brain. That is meant to keep you humble. You can be successful by doing your personal best and relying on God because only He really knows your capacity and your purpose. Remember, God gave you the perfect brain to do the things He wants you to do with His help. (See 2 Cor.12:9.)

You can change the workings of the brain and your responses to life to some degree with medicines. What a lot of us need to change, however, is not our brain chemistry, but rather the way we think. Chapter 13 will explain how the mind can help.

SYSTEM OVERLOAD

Everything that comes to us through our spinal cords and minds is processed by our brains. Many of these bits of information are never consciously noticed because a tiny part near the base of the brain called the reticular activating system (RAS) acts like a door. This door is meant to shut out information that is not important to our well-being and let in information that is. For example, while a teacher is lecturing, I need the RAS to shut out the fact that a fly just landed on the windowsill beside me, and I need the RAS to let in the teacher's words. But some people have doors that work differently, so everything gets let in.

That person's brain exhausts him by trying to process unimportant information, and the body responds to too many cues. This makes the owner of the brain seem foolish, overactive, and even annoying. At times, the individual becomes so tired from all of this that he just has to lie down and rest. Then he is labeled "lazy." Knowing what I know about the brain, I have come to strongly dislike the label "lazy."[6] "Lazy" is an attitude. Only God knows our attitudes and where they come from.

---

6 Children who actually are bright and bored are at times misdiagnosed with attention deficit because they do not stay focused on a teacher and sit still in a culture that demands those behaviors. When those same students are given environments that are more creative, challenging and allow for more physical stimulation, they may function at much higher levels. Also individuals who actually do have attention deficit may function better when they are allowed to put music, gum, doodling, even texting and other stimulating activities into their setting to keep their brain in more alert modes. It has been conjectured that some class clowns may be keeping themselves awake by popping jokes throughout the day.

However, when the brain is handling life effectively, and for some of us, when it is medicated effectively, we have a sense that life is manageable. Most times, brain chemicals and electrical activity are being produced at levels that allow us to manage the conditions around us.

Still, brains appear to vary in the amount of stress they can handle and still function effectively. Many factors influence our brain's stress tolerance, but I like this visual description: Some brains appear to have thimble-sized stress cups and others appear to have tubs. Whatever size "vessel" you have, you must respect its size and not take on more stress than you can handle. *A picky, controlling attitude is a stress cocktail—whether it is coming from or toward you.* When your stress cup overflows, you will grab whatever coping skills you have to manage it. Your brain's ability to leave the emotional department and get to the intelligence in the frontal lobe will have diminished. Your natural inclination will be to say and do anything necessary to annihilate the stressor based on your emotional state. Why? Because the electrical activity in the amygdala (emotional department) is going off like fireworks and stealing the energy that your higher brain needs to make an intelligent decision. Counselors sometimes label this over-activity in the lower regions of the brain as emotional seizures. You can tell when someone is experiencing one of these. The person will say and do things that are exaggerated or out of keeping with their typical attitudes and actions because their brain is temporarily out of balance.

A trigger is a circumstance that sets off an emotional seizure. This is where the acronym HALT (Hungry, Angry, Lonely, Tired), which I mentioned earlier, comes in handy. If these stressful conditions exist in our lives, our cups are somewhat full to start with. Add a few triggers like a whiny friend, deadlines, or a sarcastic remark, and *violà*—you have a seizure, which could involve pouting, yelling, shunning, verbal and physical abuse, public reprimands, or negative thoughts and emotions that wreak havoc throughout our bodies. But we don't have to seizure even if we are tired and hungry and our loved ones are rude. We are creatures of choice.

So no matter what memories, attitudes, emotional baggage, and stress cocktails you have stored in your brain during your life, here's the good news: your mind is designed to help. Your mind is a free agent, so to speak, because it is not a part of your body. It is a part of your soul. In the next chapter, we will pause in our examination of the body and look at the ways the mind can help.

DIGGING DEEPER

THE BRAIN

*"In two generations we have moved from a right-brained society
to a left-brained society. There are now more people in prison than
there are farmers. It may be that there's not an epidemic of learning
disabilities. It may be that there's an unwillingness of our culture to
appreciate right-brainedness and an illusion that we're all the same."*

—ANONYMOUS

We can know all of this about the brain and more, and we still
know almost nothing compared to our Creator. So what is the use
of this information?

Quiz Yourself: See if you can recall the explanations for these
questions. (Cover the hint. You may have a better response.)

1. Why do some people handle stress better than others?
    Hint: Do you know what your natural chemical makeup is?
    Is your stress cup thimble size or bathtub size? Can you back
    off when your cup is full?

2. Why do some people seem "lazy" even when they may not be?
    Hint: What's your cruising speed? Does your lifestyle let you
    live there?

3. Why do people react in ways that are immature and inappropriate?

   Hint: Emotional "seizures" result from extreme levels of electrical activity in the emotional and memory centers of the brain. Sometimes we respond like the child we were when a similar condition first happened. Our response depends on the strength of our cognitive maps. Have you created newer, adult maps for yourself?

4. Why might we repeat a behavior even after we have decided we don't want to do it any longer?

   Hint: Our brains have created habitual pathways and we will have to take conscious new paths repeatedly to overcome the old ones. We do this by clinging to new thoughts and creating new cognitive maps.

5. How can you help someone short-circuit an emotional seizure/tantrum?

   Hint: Give them a positive condition that conflicts with the negative one they are having. How do you know when you have found it? Toxic conditions tend to fuel the fire. Loving responses tend to put out the flames. Ask the people you love what they believe will seem loving to them when they lose their cool.

6. Under what four conditions will we know that we are stressed and less likely to make effective decisions?

   Hint: H A L T.

If these hints seemed more like answers, they were. Was that stressful or helpful to you? Perhaps you are able to add to them. Knowing these six small things can simplify and refresh our interactions with one another. We can forgive ourselves and others when we aren't everything we want to be. It takes time to change. How do you see this knowledge helping you in the future?

CHAPTER 13

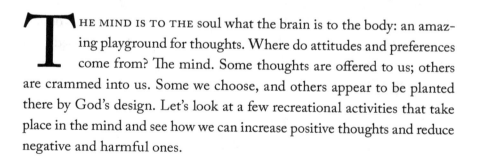

THE MIND: THE SOUL'S PLAYGROUND

"I [God] will put my law in their minds and write it on their hearts. I will be their God, and they will be my people."

—JEREMIAH 31:33

THE MIND IS TO THE soul what the brain is to the body: an amazing playground for thoughts. Where do attitudes and preferences come from? The mind. Some thoughts are offered to us; others are crammed into us. Some we choose, and others appear to be planted there by God's design. Let's look at a few recreational activities that take place in the mind and see how we can increase positive thoughts and reduce negative and harmful ones.

TUG OF WAR

Tug of War is the game positive and negative thoughts play in your mind. You will make many wise, compassionate, kind, gentle, patient, courageous choices if you understand who you can be and why you are here. Alternately, if you accept negatives, you will make fearful, arrogant, hurtful choices and lose track of your main purposes on earth—to love and be loved by God and to care for others.

When I introduced the concept of the soul, I said that it is the part of us that navigates the relationships of our lives. Mental Tug of War is being played every day as negative and positive thoughts vie for victory. To strengthen a team of thoughts based on wisdom, you need to add thoughts to the mix that strengthen your relationship with God. But how can we know what "God thoughts" are? That's simple, really. God wants us to become a people of character and balance. He instructs us to "Love others as you love yourself."

If we live life at breakneck pace with too many competing priorities, it is likely to leave us devoid of peace and tranquility. Likewise, endless self-indulgence does not foster courage, patience, endurance, humility, perspective, poise, or kindness. But neither does endlessly indulging others. Finding a middle ground is the key. In two parts of this book, "Make Room for Miracles" and "Change," we'll get specific about how to do this.

For Jesus Christ, balance included time alone, celebrations and gatherings with everyday people in their homes, teaching and healing amidst throngs of needy people, and fellowship with a close group of friends. People were "amazed" at His brilliant insights about God and God's desires for us (Luke 4:32). In spite of human inadequacies, Christ developed rich, affectionate relationships with people and encouraged us to do the same.

The most difficult decisions in life are not between right and wrong, but between two rights or two wrongs. One example of this is blended families. The inherent desire a parent feels to attend to the needs of biological children tugs against the longing to care for a new spouse. In all families I have watched couples struggle when it comes to loyalties. They wrestle with thorny questions like, "Do we visit his parents for the holidays or mine?" or "Do I leave work early to have dinner with the family or protect my job by working overtime?" The respectful lifestyle discussed in this book will hopefully be a healing balm for those who face these hard questions.

RED ROVER

Our wise Creator designed us in such a way that we will flourish when we live according to His desires for us. When we go against His teachings, we will make ourselves unhappy and sick. It is our choice. Emotions are chemical messengers produced throughout the body, especially the brain. We can now "see" thoughts as they create bits of electricity. A neuropeptide is a chemical that carries emotions. The anger neuropeptide looks different from the resentment neuropeptide, and it in turn looks different from the contentment neuropeptide. I know it sounds odd, but think about it this way—each of your thoughts has an accompanying emotion. For example, what feeling rises up in you when you think of the President of the United States? It is Pride? Distaste? Hope? Curiosity? When a song comes on the radio, it produces an emotion in you. Thoughts and emotions work together.

As you have thoughts, neuropeptides (emotional messengers) are released in your brain. They leave the cell factory and go attach themselves to cells throughout your body and begin to form a path.

If your friend walks by without acknowledging you, you have a choice about how you feel. If you think, *She's so inconsiderate!* you might as well be calling out, "Red Rover, Red Rover, send resentment right over." Alternately, you could think, *She must not be feeling well. That's why she didn't notice me.* Now, the message is, "Red Rover, Red Rover, send compassion right over."

Picture your body as having lines of billions of cells playing the game Red Rover, and there are different teams of cells lined up, waiting for our attitudes to call on them. If you have a difficult time with someone, it is common to rehearse over and over what you are going to do about it, and recall how you were treated. Picture the Red Rover lines. Which emotional team (pathway) are you likely to be building if you feel mistreated? You might call over self-pity or even resentment. Resentment is a friend to entitlement, arrogance, bitterness, and a string of other negative teammates. Over time, those emotions can create a monster called depression. And over time, that team becomes an army. Now, here is the amazing thing: the body functions in such a way that the more it gets of an emotion, the more it wants. Eventually, there is a role reversal, and your emotions will actually begin to inspire thoughts that will make your factory produce and release more of the same kind of emotional messengers. I hope you can see how destructive that trend will be for your health if your emotions are negative. When the team is big, they seem unstoppable. You want to stop thinking about that injustice, but you feel like you can't. But the truth is, yes, you can. With God's help.

You can counter negative thoughts by willfully choosing positive ones. You may have to force them at first by reading them, listening to them, singing them. Whatever it takes. As you do, you will cause the negative emotions to detach from the cells throughout your body and brain, and you will begin to build long, wide, and positive pathways. The bigger your positive team becomes, the more it will influence your thinking and behavior.

Good old science taught me these things about thoughts and emotions. It showed me the workings of the neuropeptides as they attach to cells. What is exciting and encouraging is watching the neuropeptides detach when a contradictory emotion comes around. So you can be right in the middle of a thought that brings about negative emotions, catch yourself, and interrupt the negative thought with a positive one. When you do, negative emotions will detach from your brain cells and weaken. Positives interrupt negatives and reduce their strength.

God created your heart, mind, and brain to all work together. Then He gave you the respect and freedom to design your own destiny. Does He have a purpose and a plan for your life? Yes. Like any parent, He has hopes and insights to what will make your life meaningful and rich. He designed you to have a thought that leads to an emotion, and the combination of those two brings about an action. Every path will eventually communicate with muscular cells, and the body does what the strongest teams tell it to do.

The New Testament is chock full of encouragement for us. It reminds us to keep our minds on whatever is good, noble, right, admirable. It tells us to resist negative thoughts and they will leave. It challenges us to love our enemies, but to avoid spending too much time with people who are confused to the point of destruction. It invites us to encourage one another and spend time among people who are practicing God's loving ways.[7] Now you can see why. Our automatic thoughts will design our minds and our days, so we want our thoughts to be intelligent, courageous, and altruistic.

The wonderful thing about the mind is that it can be changed in an instant by a choice. We don't have to stay stuck in old, hurtful ways of looking at our life's traumas. We can instead make new decisions about old emotional experiences, and we can heal from them.

SITTING UNDER THE SHADE TREE

A playground is a place where we take time just to be with one another. The older we get, the more we use it for this purpose. Perhaps we sit in the swings and gently push ourselves as we chat with a friend or stroll along a path alone and ponder life. If we seldom use our mind for this purpose (introspection), we may spend much of our time experiencing life only at a surface level. We may never discover *why* people make the choices they make unless we take this downtime together. Here's an example.

During a long weekend as a participant in a healing seminar, we participants spent a day reading letters about the highs and lows of our lives. There were twenty of us. The leader had us sit in a circle, close our eyes, and listen to the stories, one after another. I was a counselor and knew I needed to heal from my own old wounds so I could continue to be a positive influence on my husband and children as well as my clients.

Prior to this weekend, I knew that there was one type of client I would not counsel: someone who had committed incest. I had worked with incest survivors, but not their perpetrators. The thought of it was so offensive to me that I couldn't be sure I would treat the perpetrator with the positive regard everyone needs in order to feel safe, be honest, and heal. A counselor's job is to listen, reflect, and help people look at their choices and the consequences. Most people then want to consider choices that will improve life and receive support while they attempt to create new, healthier habits.

---

7 Mark1:35; Luke 4:42; Mark 1:25; John2:1-2;Matt. 9:35; Luke 4:40;Luke10:38-39;Phil 4:8

So, guess what God did during my healing weekend? Our loving God put a man, John, and his daughter in our therapy group to teach me a lesson. The man was short, overweight and cordial-looking with thick blonde hair and a polite beard. He had come in from the West Coast to meet with his grown daughter. He was the perpetrator and his daughter the victim *of incest*.

As each of us read the highs and lows of our lives to a room full of closed eyes and bowed heads, we could hear sniffling around the room. Some stories were typical but many stories included hurtful, even traumatic, events. But as John began to read his story, people began to wail. Yes, wail. It told of a childhood during which he was regularly beaten to the point of his abusers' exhaustion. He was put in a closet under the stairs, in the dark, soiling the floor of his space because no one would unlock the closet door to feed him or allow him common decencies. His relatives, several of them, used him sexually throughout his childhood as an outlet for their frustrations. When he told us these things, he began to sob loudly. As an adult, he had tried and longed to be a good father and to do the right things, but he had failed. He told us, "I'm so sorry. I hate myself. I'm so sorry." Why? Because he had on several occasions abused his daughter sexually as an outlet for his frustrations. She was sitting beside him at the seminar. She was a woman in her twenties who now had children and was determined to break the sick cycle. She read her story. She ended it with, "I forgive you, Daddy."

To this day, this remains one of the most powerful moments of my life. I felt compassion and love for people—including the father of the incest survivor—who had not only been hurt, but had also hurt others. When the highs and lows had all been read, we stood up, our faces red and eyes swollen. Perhaps you are the tough type and can't imagine this display of emotion. I couldn't have either, but I've experienced it firsthand. Many of the lows of all our lives were consequences of our own sorry choices and their results. Either we had not known or didn't have the stamina to use healthy coping skills. We hurt ourselves and have been hurt because of it. Many people met their "enemies" that day, and finally understood them.

That understanding gave the relationship new life. John and his daughter received hugs from everyone. We felt blessed to know them and to feel love for them.

TRANSFORM YOUR THINKING

Disappointments are events. Discouragement is a natural reaction, but it is an emotion that invites jealousy, envy, bitterness, and a host of other things you don't want to have cloud your thoughts. If you internalize these emotions, you start to see yourself as a failure. Instead, take every thought captive. You can distinguish which ones are from God. Your contentment and joy, the richness of your existence on earth depends, to a large extent, on what you choose to do with this aspect of your human nature. Junk in—junk out. Wisdom in—wisdom out. Your brain's choices and your body's choices are largely dependent on the habits of your mind and the meditations of your heart.

I recall hearing a story about a man who was a firefighter and a trained EMT. One sunny afternoon, he was riding in his truck to go home to his wife and five children. Consider his thoughts on that drive. Imagine the relative calm of his brain and body. Perhaps he had his windows down and the sun warmed his skin, the breeze blowing through his hair. Perhaps he was taking in the beauty of a sunset.

Then, he came upon a wreck. His brain waves probably changed from relaxed alpha waves to alert beta waves. He may not have gone into high alert because he was experienced with emergencies. However, when he parked his truck, he saw the bodies of several children strewn across a field beside the highway. A four-wheeler carrying five children had been hit by a car at an intersection. Can you imagine how his thoughts intensified and his brain responded? He may have had a rush of adrenalin, making his vision, hearing, and sense of touch keen. Now, as the man ran to check each body, he discovered that they all were dead—and some of them were his children.

He would later learn that the children had gotten together for a ride. As they approached an intersection of the quiet country road, some tall crops kept blocked the approach of a car that was headed toward them. When the car failed to pause at a stop sign, well, you know what happened. This man, their father, was among the first on the scene.

At this point, it is certain his brain had an emotional seizure: highly emotional thoughts triggering so many brain circuits at one time that the brain went into overload behavior. Yet this man's mind had been trained to work and function in extreme conditions. He had chosen repeatedly to care for the living in the midst of tragedy. And that is what he did. He cared for the living. The driver of the car had lived through it, and the father/EMT/firefighter offered the injured driver medical support while waiting for emergency services to back him up. Amazing.

What does your behavior look like when you suffer from an emotional seizure? Do you cry, yell, condemn, or shun? What thoughts run through your mind when life doesn't go your way? Would you believe that some people seizure/tantrum almost every day? You've seen them on the highway and in stores. Some of you live with a person like this under your roof. This is a common problem because most of us haven't trained our minds. We don't know how. We haven't read the Creator's calming, soothing truths. Our thought life is filled with worry, feelings of entitlement, and justifications that keep us from living the healthy, productive lives God wants for us.

USING YOUR MIND FOR A CHANGE

Your mind is yours to fill with the riches of the kingdom of God. The more of those riches you learn, rehearse, and act on, the wiser you become. "As God's chosen people, holy and dearly loved, clothe yourselves with compassion, kindness, humility, gentleness and patience" (Col. 3:12). Keep choosing good, loving thoughts and appropriate boundaries to respond to the conditions that surround you. Refuse to support negative thinking. Interrupt negative emotions.

On a personal note, I will confess that *Uncommon Sense* came about because I spent the first ten years of motherhood having thoughts like, *They have to respect me... I have to show them who is boss... if I don't teach them how* *to ____ they will grow up to be ____.* I enslaved myself with these dictates and fears, all of which are common, errant attitudes about parenting. If the kids messed up or forgot their manners in front of other people, I took it as a personal affront. I learned quickly that you can make most people do what you want them to do by yelling, belittling, and enforcing a time out. You can. It works. But it only manipulates the outward behaviors of the person. It may break the spirit, but it doesn't infiltrate his or her heart. And enslaving strategies for keeping behavior in line only work as long as you are willing to make yourself a slave to those strategies as well.

My angry, condemning, shunning emotions grew stronger and became more frequent until I couldn't find the playful, compassionate woman I had been when I married my husband. I missed her, and I despised the cruel, fearful, and egocentric taskmaster who ruled the roost. My girls must have been confounded by a mother who was kind and playful one moment and condemning and scary the next. At the time, I couldn't understand how I had become the wretch I was. Now, with my understanding of the brain, the mind, neuropeptides and addiction, I understand it perfectly: the more negative we are, the more wretched we make our lives. The more we expect perfection from humans, the more we will be disappointed. Our Creator will not be mocked. He designed us to flourish if we choose the states of mind he recommends for us. To give in to less than the best is to become less. I'm so thankful for His wisdom.

Be Still

We know that Jesus went away from the crowds and His friends to spend time alone in meditation with the Father. We know that before He started His teaching and healing works at age 30, He spent 40 days alone in the wilderness to meditate and pray. Yet, most Christian churches do not teach the art of meditation. No Sunday school class I ever attended taught me the art of meditating.

When you think prayer, try this: ACTS.

- **Adoration :** Tell God you adore Him and why, or tell Him you want to.
- **Confession:** Talk to God about the wrongs you have done. If you don't know of any, be still. He will bring them to mind.
- **Thankfulness:** Talk to God about the things that are going right or things that aren't going wrong.
- **Supplication:** Talk to God about your needs, the needs of others, and the needs of the world.

Then, just be quiet for a moment. If you practice this art of prayer, over time, you will experience a peace that surpasses all understanding.

DIGGING DEEPER

TRANSFORMING YOUR MIND

*"You will keep in perfect peace the man whose mind
is kept on you because he trusts in you."*

—ISAIAH 26:3 (NLV)

Assumption: If my child just tried harder, s/he would see things my way and life would be better.

Truth: Your child can never see things entirely your way because your child does not have your brain or mind.

Assumption: If my spouse would just grow up, s/he wouldn't feel bad or get angry when I'm only trying to help.

Truth: Your spouse's brain is filled with bundles of nerve impulses created by his or her life before and since you met. Many responses are automatic. Your spouse's mind is filled with dictates and preferences that were handed down and crammed into it or that he or she chose because they seemed the most appropriate at the time. You cannot just get rid of them, but you can create better, stronger, positive pathways in the presence of love, safety, and truth. Be patient with yourself and with others. Move toward love.

We know that theta waves (those which occur during a quick nap) refresh the chemistry of the brain and allow for better, more effective executive function. It would be to your benefit to take a power nap or rest for a few minutes in silence every day. As you rest, train your mind by tucking in a soothing truth you have learned so far about yourself or your God. Repeat it over and over.

To change your mind is often a willful decision. It is worth the effort. Habits of your mind become patterns in your brain. Uncommon Sense is a lifestyle designed to teach you this art of changing your thinking and actions. In the meantime, keep yourself honest about some thoughts you have on a regular basis that make life worse instead of better.

Pause now, and make a list of thoughts and actions you want to change so you can look back at them later and be thankful that you aren't a victim of them anymore. They will go away if you detach from them and substitute healthier ones.

CHAPTER 14

THE HEART: THE DEEPEST PART OF YOU

"Above all else, guard your heart, for it is the wellspring of life."

—PROVERBS 4:23

I N EVERYDAY LANGUAGE, WHAT DOES it mean to give your heart to someone? To whom have you given yours? Pause and consider that for a moment. Those two questions probably bring an old or new love to mind. We may love our children, friends, and parents, but to "give your heart" is a phrase generally reserved for a special someone with whom you share romance, fidelity, and a future. It means you have reserved your deep thoughts, longings, hopes and dreams for that person alone. It means a special part of you is his or hers and cannot be had by another.

Thoughts, longings, hopes, dreams, fidelity, and a special chamber reserved for one great Lover. These are all components of the heart.

Heart Thoughts

What did Christ have to say about the heart? We see, hear, and understand through our hearts. He told his disciples, "the hearts of these people are hardened; they hardly hear with their ears and they have closed their eyes... their hearts cannot understand, and they cannot turn to me and let me heal them" (Matt. 13:11-16 NLT). Christ is explaining that we see and hear intuitively—based on the condition of our hearts. A lack of love for someone can keep us from seeing how important something is to him. It can keep us from hearing the message he is trying to convey. The presence of love in the heart can lead to healing, but the absence of love can lead to pain.

God designed the heart to guide and fulfill us as well as to give us peace and health and inner beauty. He programmed our hearts with principles. The heart is a place where ideas and feelings blend together, and they eventually birth desire.

Anthropologists have noticed that all prevalent world religions espouse some form of the Ten Commandments and a number of other principles that would allow us to live in relative safety and comfort with one another, if we obeyed them. Generally, we call these tenets our "conscience." The first man and woman, at one time, lived well with only these heart thoughts and their love relationship with God and one another. We call this time and place Paradise.

Yet God did not give us just these principles and Himself. He also gave each heart the ability to long, hope, dream, wonder, and wander. The Word says, "Delight yourself in the Lord and He will give you the desires of your heart" (Ps. 37:4). You could interpret this as, "He will give you everything *you* treasure" or "He will give you desires *He* knows will fit your heart perfectly and make your heart sing." Which interpretation do you prefer?

Longings

It is natural for the heart to have longings. As we have said before, we long to be free, to know and be known, to belong, and to have purpose. We are so curious about life and one another that we sometimes risk our lives and relationships to find out things we have no business learning.

All human beings seem to come into the world with an innate belief that we should be cared for and loved. Our hearts are quickly educated when our tired or absent parents tell us through their words or actions that at times they *don't* always care.

An innocent heart believes that life should be fair, people should be honest, and that you do what you promise. The educated heart has learned that oftentimes people aren't fair, aren't honest, and don't keep their word. And the most disappointing thing the educated heart learns is that sometimes the one not being honest and fair is oneself.

Money. Sexuality. Exhilarating states of mind. These can all be gratifying when they are exercised within God's loving boundaries. Yet, the human heart was not designed to be satisfied with these paltry things. We are designed for much more. Each human heart can find its perfect mix, and only God and the individual know what that is. So how is facing all of these facts about human nature and the heart going to help you? Well, if you are willing to learn about and face the facts, you may be able to heal.

God tucked our hearts away so deeply within us that only He can really see them. Nowhere in the Bible are we given permission to be another man's judge. We are told that "the good man brings good things out of the good stored up in his heart, and the evil man brings evil things out of the evil stored up in his heart. For out of the overflow of his heart his mouth speaks" (Luke 6:45).

God knows that it isn't good for humans to be alone (Gen. 2:18). You have a heart deep enough to contain the love that God wants to pour into you. He has saints all over the world ready to fill you with love. You only need to open your eyes and ears to them. When you do, your heart will truly be fulfilled, and you will want to receive more and pour it out freely to others.

Your heart is your spiritual think tank — the deepest part of your being, the wellspring of life. It has all of the essential ingredients to give you a "future and a hope" (Jer. 29:11). Your job is to clean it out enough to let God's light shine in. Look at yourself honestly and be sorrowful for the ways you choose to be unthinking and unkind. Ask God for understanding. Seek it. Accept it.

The heart is covered with trapdoors that lead to old, unhealed damage, damage that was put there by a confused world full of broken people and a host of evil opponents. When someone accidentally (or purposefully) leans against one of those doors, they come flying open, and out of your heart comes all kinds of pent up junk: feelings of resentment and entitlement, of strife and slander, worry, and a host of unseemly things (Matt. 15:19; Mark 7:21-22). But you were not put on earth for this! You are put here for better things. The heart becomes calloused as you defend yourself in ugly ways. Stop. Believe what Christ has told us so that you can watch the trapdoor fly open and use the opening to let the toxic thoughts out and some better thoughts in. Here are some better thoughts (all verses are from the NLT, and the emphasis is mine):

- "I am leaving you with a gift—*peace of mind and heart*. And the peace I give is *a gift the world cannot give*. So don't be troubled or afraid"—**John 14:27**
- "And this hope will not lead to disappointment. For we know how dearly God loves us, because He has given us the Holy Spirit to *fill our hearts with his love*. "—**Romans 5:5**
- *"Don't let your hearts be troubled.* Trust in God, and trust also in Me."—**John 14:1**
- "I pray that *your hearts will be flooded with light* so that you can understand the confident hope he has given to those he called…"—**Ephesians 1:18**
- *"For it is by believing in your heart* that you are made right with God…"—**Romans 10:10**
- *"Christ will make His home in your hearts as you trust in Him."*—**Ephesians 3:16-18**

- "Don't worry about anything; instead, pray about everything. *Tell God what you need and thank him for all he has done.* If you do this you will experience God's peace, which is far more wonderful than the human mind can understand. *His peace will guard your hearts* and minds as you live in Christ Jesus" — **Philippians 4:6-7**

When your junk room door is open, don't brush what comes out under the rug. Move toward love. While you are angry or hurting, turn to someone who you know loves well and let him or her clean up your thinking, hug you, or just sit with you until you are feeling better. If people who care about you pour God's love into you, it will actually be healing.

God doesn't make mistakes. He has designed us to look to Him for the bottom lines of life. He cares. He keeps His Word. He will guide your steps so your life will be filled with enough excitement and adventure and awareness for even the most curious and passionate hearts.

Be an example. Fill your heart daily with God's words. Study Him. Meditate and listen to Him for a deeper understanding of His words and ways. He will enhance the programming of the heart he gave you at birth. Don't waste your time judging other's hearts because people become infuriated and disgusted when they are misjudged. Give the people around you love, and count on God to heal their hearts.

A friend once told me, "It's very soothing to get out of the way when faced with someone who is complaining or being hateful. I've learned," she said, "that when someone acts like a jerk, I can just step aside spiritually and let God, who's inside me, love them. That person's anger is just a mask for sadness. So, when I step aside and let God's love come from me, it really is healing for both of us. It sets me free, and I don't have to come up with responses or explanations like I used to."

There are many ways to do this, such as:

1. **Listen and occasionally say "uh-huh."** That means, "I hear you." It doesn't mean, "I agree with you."

2. **Reflect.** Listen and repeat the person's exact words, without an emotional tone. Without judging. If the other person's words are exaggerated, he will typically correct them himself.

3. **Seek the lesson.** As you are doing it, ask God what character quality would best soothe a hurting or angry heart. Exercise the quality that God whispers in your ear. (Remember, the fruit of *God's* Spirit is love, joy, peace, patience, kindness, generosity, faithfulness, gentleness, and self-control.) God's choice will sometimes surprise you, and once exercised, it will quickly soothe *you* as well as the other person. God instantly knows what is needed because He can see all the way to the heart.

DIGGING DEEPER

What would you do today with $86,400?

I heard a sermon in which the pastor asked us to ponder what we would do if each of us was given $86,400 every day. It would be deposited in a bank account, and you had to choose how to spend it because whatever you didn't spend would be lost. It cannot be saved. The next day, you would again be given $86,400. And again, at the end of the day, whatever you didn't spend would be gone. This would occur every day for the rest of your life. To what or to whom would you give your money?

List what comes come to you mind:

-
-
-

God gives each of us 86,400 seconds a day, irretrievable and more precious than gold. You are a cracked vessel, running around trying to get a sip of living water from other cracked vessels. We don't have enough to go around unless we drink from the enormous fountain of God's love and let it flow from each of us into one another. The next time you spend your seconds smiling at or hugging someone, think, "You hug them through me, God."

CHAPTER 15

HUMAN MEMORY: THE FALLIBLE COMMODITY

*"I praise you for remembering me in everything and for hold-
ing to the teachings just as I passed them on to you."*

—1 CORINTHIANS 11:2

MEMORY IS AN IMPORTANT CONCEPT to discuss because many arguments occur as a result of disagreements about the past. In fact, some people hate to go home for holidays because of the way they remember their families treated them. This heart wrenching damage could be nipped in the bud if we all could learn to say and accept two simple sentences: "We remember this differently. Where can we go from here?"

Memory is simply a combination of perceptions, opinions, emotional needs, and reality. It involves the brain, the mind, and the heart. Remember that the brain is an incredible, interactive network of chemicals and electricity. The "reality" that is processed by the brain is tinted by our perceptions, needs, hopes, and fears—material from the body, mind, and heart. When it comes to recollection, sometimes reality has been changed before we have a chance to discuss it.

Years ago, I went to a one-day seminar on memory. The speaker was telling us about various memory research studies. One point he made is that counselors must proceed with some caution when clients share childhood (as well as present-day) memories. To drive his point home, the speaker shared the results of a brilliant memory study conducted by Ulrich Neisser, a psychology professor at Emory University, after the Space Shuttle Challenger explosion in 1986. You may still recall this historic moment because it was extraordinary. An everyday person had been chosen to travel into outer space. It was the stuff of childhood dreams. Her name was Christa McAuliffe, a science teacher from Concord, New Hampshire. As a nation, we were all excited for her. The world was watching, and then something went horribly wrong. Within 73 seconds of takeoff, the Challenger exploded. The seven crew members were killed.

I remember where I was. Do you? Do you recall who was with you? Well, those are the questions this professor asked his Psych 101 students to answer the day after the explosion. He had them write down their recollections of the moment when they heard about the explosion. Who was with them? Where were they? What were they doing? He collected their written responses. Three years later, they were asked to rewrite their answers to these questions, and their recollections were mostly inaccurate. For example, one girl first said that she was at lunch with a group of friends, and when she heard the news she wished she could get up and run to express her distress. Three years later, she stated that when she heard the news of the explosion, she ran down her dorm hall in distress. Her desire had become a part of her recollected reality. Other students' recollections were equally "corrected" because of emotional reactions that could not be lived out at the time but later became a part of the "memory." It is clear that emotion both adds to and deepens memory unless it is so repugnant that it escapes our memory or is suppressed and largely unavailable.

What's the point?

Human memory is not perfect. It is littered with emotions, fears, hopes, intellectual regroupings, and defense mechanisms that encourage us to lie, to save face, and so much more. It doesn't take an explosion to plant or change memories. It happens every day in both significant and insignificant moments.

When I first told this story to my friends, their faces beamed with insight. Jill was the first to speak. She said, "This makes some of the events of this week make so much sense. The other day, Jake was protesting that he had put his shoes away, but they clearly were not where they were supposed to be. He knows where they belong, and he probably thought of putting them away. He wanted them to be there, so he remembers having done it. He's not making something up. He really has a memory of putting his shoes away—it's just that his memory may not be accurate."

Decide not to waste time on earth arguing about memories. Realize that you can move forward without arguing the past. Scripture tells us, "Don't have anything to do with stupid and foolish arguments, because you know they produce quarrels" (2 Tim.2:23), and "If it's possible, as far as it depends on you, be at peace with everyone" (Rom. 12:18). Only God has an unencumbered awareness of what actually happens in the past, the present, and the future. If you can embrace that truth, you can begin to understand humility.

So from now on, when you and another person are trying to make decisions based on recollections and you reach an impasse, do something different: Keep it simple. Just say, matter-of-factly and with a kind tone, "We remember that differently. Where can we go from here?" Then, my friend, move on.

If the other person persists with recollections, as some will, then just listen rather than argue and keep the mantra going. Ask God for insight as you do it: "Since we remember it differently, what positive direction can we go from here?"

DIGGING DEEPER

MEMORY

Memories: They are trap doors to your heart. Jot some notes below about times you remember when you:

- Were betrayed
- Had no status
- Were misjudged
- Were excluded
- Were ignored
- Overreacted

- Failed to defend yourself or someone else
- Needed to react, but were afraid
- Were bullied

Something good came from each of these hardships. What? Sometimes it is just that you developed compassion for someone else who will experience the same trial. That person will be thankful you are alive because you are there to help him or her through it. Hopefully, you also developed resilience, endurance, and fortitude—all things that will benefit you as you go through life.

CHAPTER 16

THE CONSCIENCE

"I will put my laws into their hearts and I will write them on their minds."

—HEBREWS 10:16

THE CONSCIENCE IS A GIFT given to every human heart by God. It is designed to protect us. [8] At its core, is a set of God-given principles with basic information I refer to as our "core conscience." In its purest form, it inspires us to consider one another and ourselves and, in so doing, to "spur one another on towards love and good deeds" (Heb. 10:24). All over the world, human beings have created cultures with values that correspond to this core conscience such as share, be honest, respect your authority figures, don't steal, and don't kill. All of these are relational principles. If you're interested in learning more about this subject so that you can notice what you have in common with people of other faiths, I

---

8 Did you know that in a Yale baby lab, babies as young as 3 months old watched rude guy and nice guy puppets act out scenes. Then the puppets were offered to them. The babies consistently preferred and accepted the nice puppets. Are we born knowing right from wrong? Researchers at the Infant Cognition Lab at Yale have been studying babies for years and believe we are. http://www.cnn.com/2014/02/12/us/baby-lab-morals-ac360/

suggest *Oneness* by Jeffrey Moses. In it, he names 64 principles that the major religions appear to share.

The conscience is also a programmable part of every human heart. We can add to and override the basic principles we instinctively know are best for us. So, in the same way that your computer comes preloaded with basic programs to make it immediately useful and functional, all human hearts begin with some basic thoughts and feelings that help us operate. Then we begin to make adjustments to them. This is why Christ told us little children are better equipped than adults to inherit the kingdom of God. They haven't yet been trained to override their core conscience and adopt one that is complex and faulty.

Are you taking care of your conscience by surrounding it with affirming truths from God's Word? Are you spending time with people who share your faith and are loving, kind, and caring? Oddly enough, your conscience can be blurred or overridden by attitudes and actions that contradict it. God leaves you with the choice to ignore His standards and adopt your own. I've done that before, have you?

Dr. Charles Stanley has preached many wonderful sermons about the human conscience, and I want to share my notes here to help you understand why you do what you do and help you guard against basic falsehoods.

Remember, to make good decisions, we often have to leave the emotional department in the brain and consult upper levels where thinking and reasoning take place. The conscience is to the heart what the executive branch is to the brain: a guide. As you read about each type, jot some notes about your own conscience. It's important to recognize the good, bad, and ugly about yourself. Awareness is the first step to change.

A **good conscience** is one that helps you live in accordance with your basic programming. It is active. In Acts 23: 1, Paul says, "I have always lived before God in all good conscience." In 1 Timothy 1: 12-13, he admits, "Even though I was once a blasphemer a persecutor and a violent man, I was shown mercy because I acted in ignorance and unbelief." In other words, Paul's intentions were good, but over time, he approached life in a way that was not in agreement with God's way. Since God looks at the heart rather than our behavior, we may experience mercy based on our intentions.

A good conscience, one that is active, is not good enough. A person is truly successful on earth when his conscience is not only good, but also clear and blameless. It is informed by God, and the individual is striving with all of his heart to rely on Him, not on others. You may live in good conscience, but you will live with the consequences of how you allow yourself and others to enhance or detract from your core.

A **clear conscience** is quiet and clean and has not been overridden by intentional actions that contradict it (2 Tim. 1:1-3). It is true to the Word of God and doesn't compromise on convictions. For example, I know that theft is wrong. I have not taken something that is not mine, so I have a clear conscience in that area.

A **blameless conscience** is one that is quiet, approving of us as we work to live a healthy life (Acts 24:14-16). We do our best to walk in the will and way of God. We're living in accordance with what we know. The apostle Paul is an example of someone whose life began with a good conscience. He was well trained when it came to Jewish law and cultural practices, but was cruel to those whose beliefs contradicted his. After He encountered Christ on the road to Damascus, he awoke to a new way of seeing life. He adopted and became learned in the Christian way of living. In fact, next to Jesus, Paul is the most learned teacher of the Christian faith.

A **weak conscience** is one that has not been exercised (1 Cor. 8:4-6, 9-12). If I have never been placed in settings where I have been tempted to ignore or override my conscience, it hasn't been strengthened. For example, if I'm wealthy, I may never have been tempted to steal to survive. If I haven't been asked to give, perhaps I've not been tempted to be selfish. If I'm single, but no one ever asks me out, it could be that I haven't been tempted with promiscuity. If I'm not a parent and don't spend time with children, perhaps I've not been tempted to mistreat them. Some people keep their lives so isolated that they seldom face temptation. Unfortunately, some of these well-protected and well-meaning people will be unequipped when they are challenged.

The Scripture tells us to be "in the world, but not of it" (1 John 2:15-16). I'm not suggesting you throw yourself in the midst of chaos to build your conscience. However, some of the best counselors are people who have followed a poorly-trained conscience or ignored a well-trained one. Either way, they did some irresponsible things with their lives, realized their mistakes, and turned around. Because of this, they have compassion on those who make the same mistakes. It's also likely that they don't give in to their faulty programming anymore. They have strengthened their conscience by not giving in to urges, and they are better able to help others do the same.

Remember that the conscience is a gift given to you by God. A weak conscience allows you to do or accept destructive and dangerous attitudes and behaviors. You probably don't even realize you're hurting yourselves and others. Gossip, for example, is a behavior that can occur when a weak conscience allows a person to talk negatively about another person without feeling uncomfortable. Gossip simply means you have said something that demeans someone else. The information you are sharing may be true, but God calls us to build one another up, not damage one another. A strong conscience will nip this in the bud.

The **defiled conscience** is one that is comfortable with things that contradict God's loving truths (Titus 1:15). Having a defiled conscience is like looking through a filthy window. If your conscience is defiled, God's truths have grown dull and incomprehensible because they have been repeatedly overridden. Over time, damaging and destructive attitudes and actions fog the window to our core conscience so we can't see the light. In certain areas, we begin to live in darkness (Prov. 2:12-13).

A **seared conscience** is the result of willful, conscious acts against the core conscience (1 Tim. 4:1). A person who has seared his or her conscience this way is sometimes called "hard-hearted." A conscience can be active in one area and seared in another. For example, I've seen otherwise loving parents yell at and condemn their children so often that it becomes a way of life. One woman said to me, "I don't know when I got into the habit of yelling at my kids. I'm sure that when I first started doing it, it seemed wrong. I certainly don't like to see other people do it. I feel guilty if I don't give them time, teach them manners, and hire responsible baby sitters. But I've gotten really good at rationalizing my willingness to rip them apart verbally when they fail. My husband even does it in public thinking others are impressed. Why have I adopted this pattern of behavior when I really love my kids?" She had a seared conscience in that area.

A **false conscience** is misinformed. It develops when we believe incorrect teachings about what is good and necessary in life. One Easter, I sat beside a woman who was dressed in very old, dirty clothes. Her hands were icy cold as I held them during the greeting, and she kept her head down and spoke quietly. She apologized for her clothes and appearance. It's been over 20 years, and I have not forgotten how beautiful she was. Why did she apologize? Had someone taught her to be ashamed if her clothes were not pressed and clean? God is not a strict, picky parent. Her guilt was not from God and ours was a casual church.

"The Lord has already told you what is good, and this is what he requires: to do what is right, to love mercy, and to walk humbly with your God" (Micah 6:8 NLT). These requirements all pertain to treating others well, which is what our conscience is designed to keep us doing. A false conscience is a place in the heart where we store important people's prescriptions for life — *ones not prescribed by God but by people.* Christ came to release us from unnecessary rules and restrictions.

ENHANCING OR DETRACTING FROM OUR CORE CONSCIENCE

This is pretty simple. How do we add unhealthy aspects to our healthy God-given core? Some philosophies we adopt so that we can live peaceably with our own selfish or confused desires (James 1:14). Some we inherit inadvertently. The people around us are living them out, and they make sense at the time. Some we were pulled into. If we want to clean things up, we can ask the Holy Spirit to guide us back to God's truth—"Come near to God and He will come near to you" (James 4:8). Christ has told you this repeatedly. (See Matt. 7:8-9; Matt. 21:22; Luke 11:9; John 14:14.) God's Word tells us, "If anyone wants wisdom let him ask God who gives generously to all without finding fault, and it will be given to him" (James 1:5). "You do not have because you do not ask God" (James 4:2-3).

How can a faulty conscience keep my life off course?

Write your own recollections of a time when you experienced each type of conscience.

- I had a good conscience when… (Think of a time when your actions lined up with your beliefs.)

- I had a blameless conscience when… (Think of a time when you did what you believed was right and didn't blame others for the ways you cope.)

- I had a clear conscience when… (Think of a time when God's loving dictates were being lived out in your life.)

- I had a weak conscience when… (Think of a time when you had it too easy and were not yet tempted in a certain area of your life.)

- I had a defiled conscience when… (Think of a time when you did something you brag about with one person but you would be horrified for another to learn.)

- I had an evil conscience when… (Think of a time when you did something you don't want anyone to know about.)

- I had a seared conscience when… (Think of a time when you knew it was wrong yet did it repeatedly until you became comfortable with it.)

- I had a false conscience when… (Think of a time when you felt guilty when you knew you probably shouldn't have.)

Remember the question you were asked early in this study:

Acquiring	→	Establishing	→	Reaping
1. No holy beliefs	→	No holy actions	→	???
2. Holy beliefs	→	No holy actions	→	Discomfort or despair
3. Holy beliefs	→	Holy actions	→	Life, peace, thankfulness

Did a faulty conscience affect the life course you were on?

Remember to take good care of your conscience by surrounding it with affirming truths from God's Word.

CHAPTER 17

PERSONALITY

"For you created my inmost being; you knit me together in my mother's womb. I praise you because I am fearfully and wonderfully made; your works are wonderful, I know that full well."

—PSALM 139: 13-14

P ERSONALITY[9] IS HOW YOU APPROACH life. It is the myriad ways you respond to the world around you and includes your disposition, nature, and temperament. It is colored by what you are taught. Generally, that's good. But sometimes your personality can control you rather than you being able to control it. Let's look at personality from those different angles.

A GOD-GIVEN APPROACH TO LIFE

Doesn't it really make life more interesting if we all don't have the same approach to life? Humans love variety. Life would get a little dull if we

---

9 The terms personality and temperament have both been used by the psychological world for many years. There is still some debate as to when either should be used. Both describe a group of qualities that affect attitudes and behaviors in the individual. Both, when extreme, can be destructive, but temperament tends to be a milder descriptor.

all got up, ate, worked, rested and slept at the same time and for the same reasons. Your heavenly Father doesn't want your life to be dull. Instead, He wants it filled with possibility.

I have already told you that I don't believe we come into the world as blank slates. In Jeremiah 4:11, we are told that God knew us before He formed us in the womb. Our DNA is in place, and so is our conscience and a basic personality. Oddly enough, after years of study and practice with a variety of psychological assessments, one of the most useful models I've found for describing personality to people is a simple and memorable assessment developed by two well-known Christian counselors, Gary Smalley and John Trent. There are a number of aspects when it comes to personality, but it's helpful to start with some basics.

THE SMALLEY-TRENT PERSONALITY TEST

Are you a lion, beaver, otter, or golden retriever? These are the names given to four personality types because the animals exemplify them.[10]

Lions are natural leaders. They enjoy challenges, are confident, bold, self-reliant, purposeful, and determined. They can be cold and unaware of the toll their "follow me now" attitude takes on others.

Beavers enjoy instructions. They are practical, detailed, predictable, analytical, deliberate, inquisitive, persistent and sensitive. They can be perfectionists and overly critical expecting others to live up to their high standards.

Otters are fun-loving, enthusiastic, creative, group-oriented, and inspiring. They take risks, motivate others, and enjoy change. They can be messy and distracted, leaving details to others while they try to find fun ways to work things out.

Golden retrievers are loyal, sensitive, calm, non-demanding and tolerant; they enjoy routine, avoid confrontation, and are dependable. They can also be stubborn and passive doing their best to keep things from changing.

---

10 The Two Sides of Love Gary Smalley and John Trent, website which offers the assessment for the 4 personality types http://smalley.cc/images/Personality-Test.pdf

Did you see yourself in one or more of these types? Perhaps you're a lion with golden retriever tendencies. Interesting. A real life example can help you understand what to do with this knowledge.

THE VALUE OF UNDERSTANDING PERSONALITY TYPES

Mary and Janie were supposed to hang out at Mary's house one Friday night. But on Friday afternoon, Janie got invited to a party. Janie called Mary and invited her to go, but Mary declined, so Janie went without her. Later, Janie's mom called Mary's mom to tell her, "I'm sorry. I'm embarrassed and upset that my daughter changed her plans and let Mary down." Mary's mom cheerfully explained, "That's okay. Mary knows that Janie is an otter. Since Mary's a golden retriever she doesn't let things like that interrupt their friendship. Mary loves to stay home with the family. Sometimes their plans will work out, and sometimes they won't. My youngest daughter is an otter, too, so she might have done the same thing."

I know this doesn't sound real. However, it is. This woman teaches in the church and likes to educate others about these personality types. She's one of the least judgmental people I know, and when I'm tempted to criticize someone, I go to her for counsel because she keeps me honest and humble. What I love about this story is how Mary's mom kept a positive regard for Janie, even though she knew she'd let her daughter down. She didn't become disparaging.

You may be reading this story thinking things like, "It's wrong not to keep your word. You always should keep it, even when it's hard work!" Or you may be someone who would like to come right over to Janie's house and tell the whole family how to do what needs to be done. Or do you think everyone should just loosen up and live big?

The point of this illustration is to show you that each human is a complex mix of personality types, so if we want to love and understand others, we cannot ignore each other's innate tendencies. The healthiest families live by a common set of standards that are based on values, not preferences. The healthiest people are adaptable and set up boundaries and consequences to keep bad habits from becoming damaging and destructive.

In the Bible, Joshua—one of the great leaders of the Jewish nation—made this statement: "As for me and my house, we shall serve the Lord" (Josh. 24:15). He meant that they would live a lifestyle that had God at its center and gave Him the respect He deserved. As believers, we can all agree that this is a good way to approach life, but otters, lions, beavers, and goldens will put this into practice in different ways. Research demonstrates that each personality type is valuable and that the most effective teams are composed of a combination of all of these types.

Colored by Life Experience

As a counselor I have had the privilege of getting to know individuals at a deep level. People who seem to others to be aloof are actually shy. Anger turns out to be sadness. Quirks of personality are actually the remains of old wounds because life has dealt someone an awful blow and he or she has learned to cope with it by putting on an air of confidence, arrogance, silliness, or some other quality that hides the discomfort and pain underneath.

My friend, Sheila, told me that she had an easier time getting along with family members after she studied the work of Milan and Kay Yerkovich, authors of *How We Love*. At a seminar she had attended, the Yerkoviches asked a poignant question: "Thinking of your first eighteen years of life, do you have specific memories of being comforted by a parent after a time of emotional distress?"

I'd like *you* to answer that question. Perhaps you were touched by a trauma such as death, divorce, or abuse. Or maybe you felt rejection when you didn't make the team, a friend moved away, or a trusted individual wounded you. Did your parents notice, ask questions to find out more about your feelings, or offer some kind of caring, physical touch? Did you walk away feeling relief from your pain?

Your answer to these questions, either the consolation you experienced or the absence of it, could reveal more about your current relationships than any other insight you might uncover. Giving and receiving comfort—which usually encompasses appropriate, caring touch, listening, and relief—creates an emotional bond that's key to a fulfilling relationship.

Sheila was taught to use this information to remind herself why some people will avoid, control, play the victim, vacillate, or people-please.[11] That's how they learned to adjust to relational difficulties (wounds) when they were young. They may do those things in extreme ways! She can decide not to take those coping strategies personally. She realizes that the other people aren't playing the victim or avoiding because of her; it's just a style they *added* to their personalities earlier in life because they believed it would make life better. She can decide not to give in to unhealthy coping styles. Now she can love them without judging or acting in a demeaning way.

What about quirks of personality on a cultural level? In his book *To Thine Own Self Be True*, Lewis M. Andrews sites an anthropological finding concerning the personality propensities of two neighboring tribes. He writes:

> The Eskimo tribes of the Northeast, for example, are well known as a warm, communal people, friendly and self-assured, while the tribe just a few miles away are a sullen and hyper-sensitive lot with suspicions that border on the pathological. There are no geographic factors to explain this incredible differ-ence—both tribes have to cope with the same severe climatic and food shortages—yet the child-rearing practices are telling. From their earliest years the friendly, self-assured tribes are taught to be forthright and openly emotional, not ashamed to ask each other for help or to admit weakness. The sullen tribes, on the other hand, are taught to be secretive, mistrustful, and to expect the worst from any forthright behavior—which is exactly what they get.[12]

---

11 Yerkoviches call these connecting styles and describe them in their book, *How We Love*.
12 Andrews, Lewis M. *To Thine Own Self Be True*. New York: Doubleday, 1989. p.94.

So, do you see how soul-level, relational interactions can take any basic personality and slant it in a positive or negative direction? Our homes and support systems can ultimately make our life seem easier or harder depending on their positive or negative attitudes and approaches to life.

COLORED BY BIOLOGY

The *Harvard Mental Health Newsletter* is a professional publication filled with articles to help counselors keep abreast of new discoveries and research. Many of them are of interest to mental health professionals because they discuss personality disorders. Personality disorders are out of the ordinary, persistent patterns of functioning and thinking that make a healthy social life very difficult for those who struggle with them. The April 2005 issue included an article on children with conduct disorders that said:

> Some impulsively violent children may have low levels of the neurotransmitter serotonin in their blood…caused by head injuries…or reduced activity of the prefrontal cortex, a center of judgment, planning, and decision-making. It's possible that in many cases, conduct disorders arise when a child with a tendency to irritability, impulsiveness, or fearlessness, or some subtle deficiency in the prefrontal cortex, perhaps genetic in origin, is raised by a family in a social environment that is a particularly bad fit for these temperamental characteristics. These children sometimes conceal their symptoms and other problems because they would rather be considered bad than admit to weakness or suggest in any way that they need help.[13]

You could exchange the word "conduct" with any number of types of disorders (eating, attention, obsessive-compulsive, etc.). Each type is related to atypical brain function, and each type can be alleviated, to some extent,

---

13 Harvard Mental Health Newsletter, Vol. 21, No. 10, April 2005, p.5.

with medication. But this is not a perfect science, and the final paragraph of that article is the most telling. It reads:

> Many experts now believe that the most promising approach to preventing and rehabilitating children with conduct disorder is parent management training. Controlled studies have found it to be more effective than psychotherapy. Parents are taught to issue and enforce stable rules, negotiate compromises with older children, and substitute sensible discipline for inconsistent harshness.[14]

Mental health professionals have not changed their attitudes about this since then. We believe that the most effective way to help children change is to teach their authority figures, monitor brain health, and offer emotional and intellectual support.

OUT OF CONTROL

As a young counseling intern, I remember one of my professors defined mental health in this way, "A *mood* disorder is like onion breath: you know you have it, and the other person knows you have it." Examples of this kind of problem include short-term depression or anxiety related to an event or circumstance. A person who has it is atypically sad, anxious, and just different than she used to be. The mood won't last for long and will usually leave when the circumstances improve or the person gets better at coping with them.

According to my professor, "A *personality* disorder is like garlic breath: the other person knows you have it, but you don't know. And it's hard to get rid of." You may recall movies about schizophrenia, borderline personality, histrionic, manic-depression, or narcissism. You can read about these disorders to learn more, but please don't decide that someone has a

---

14 Harvard Mental Health Newsletter, p. 5.

given disorder. Labels often lead to treatment and inaccurate treatment can make things worse.

On the way home from a day-long course on personality disorders, I realized something very important. The hardest disorders to improve are those that cause the person to be shunned. Without feedback, touch, kindness, and sensible goals, mental health tends to get worse, not better. People with difficult personalities need love just like people with easy personalities do. If your words and actions are loving but the person isn't receiving them, pray and seek healthy support.

DIGGING DEEPER

Uncover Your Personality

Go to http://smalley.cc/images/Personality-Test.pdf and ask your family members to take this short personality test. If they are very young, you may want a copy of The Treasure Tree, a storybook about the lion, otter, beaver, and golden retriever and how they learn to respect one another's different personalities. Your child can decide who he or she is most like.

At a family meeting discuss how different personalities bring a richness and variety of abilities to your family. Don't be surprised if the lions and beavers at your house are the ones who hold people accountable for their responsibilities — it's more their nature. Don't begrudge otters and golden retrievers if they go easy on people. That comes more naturally to them. Remember, balance is what is best. The combination of accountability and grace is actually helpful.

Also, be careful not to label people. If anyone feels their score does not fit them, accept their assessment. It's offensive to be misjudged. For a more thorough description of the meaning of each of these four personality strengths and weaknesses, check out websites and books by John Trent and Gary Smalley and others.

I also encourage you to research the Meyers-Briggs temperament descriptions. They are excellent and often used in business to help colleagues understand one another and work together. The Myers-Briggs information will help you understand why:

- Some people are energized by parties and others are exhausted by them.
- Some people trust their gut and others trust what they can see, hear, smell, taste or touch.
- Some people bank on logic and others bank on feelings.
- Some people love surprises and others hate them.

The point is my way or your way isn't always the *right* way. We need to make room for one another's personalities and preferences, stay humble, and ponder.

CHAPTER 18

SPIRITUAL GIFTS

"God has given gifts to each one of you from his great variety of spiritual gifts. Manage them well so that God's generosity can flow through you."

—1 Peter 4: 10 (NLT)

A SPIRITUAL GIFT IS A GOD-GIVEN ability to do something effortlessly. Sometimes Christians refer to these as *motivational gifts*. You may recall from chapter seven that the word *salvation* refers to the time in a person's life when he makes a decision to let God act on his behalf so He can do good things for humankind, things we cannot do on our own. When you make that decision, the Spirit of God chooses a gift for you. This gift is meant to help others who want to do His loving work on earth in a way that will benefit all of God's children.

Whatever gift God gives to you, you almost cannot keep from doing it. Some examples are the gift of encouragement, teaching, or administration. Other gifts are service, evangelism, giving, faith, and hospitality. The books of Romans and 1 Corinthians mention others. God knows when you are ready to exercise this privilege.

What is the difference between talents and spiritual gifts? All people have natural talents, and they are as beautiful and varied as we are. Some of us are mechanical; others of us are athletic or artistic. All of these are natural talents that are genetically inherited and can also be improved with practice. Some people have a talent for remembering details, and others can find a theme in a mountain of seemingly random details and make sense of it all. I believe these talents are meant to provide us with an altruistic purpose on earth.

We are accustomed to talking about and recognizing one another's talents, yet spiritual gifts are even more extraordinary. To exercise a spiritual gift is to act on God's behalf—to demonstrate His love to the world. I want to introduce you to the concept in case you've never heard of it, because understanding this aspect of human nature can help you respect the variety of ways humans can support and care for one another supernaturally. We are, at our core, supernatural beings.

My favorite illustration of spiritual gifts is one in which several people are sitting around a table eating when one of them spills a glass of milk.

The person with the gift of **serving** stands up, gets a towel, and starts to mop.

The person with the gift of **teaching** analyzes the situation and explains how to avoid it in the future by moving the milk away from the edge of the table.

The person with the gift of **administration** assigns responsibilities to get the mess cleaned up and the glass refilled in an effective and expeditious way.

The person with the gift of **giving** sees a need and tries to fill it by refilling the glass.

The person with the gift of **encouragement** is more concerned about the feelings of the person who spilled the milk and will try to make him feel better by offering positive feedback and emotional support.

The person with the gift of **mercy** will identify with the person and take pity on him in his embarrassment.

The person with the gift of **prophecy** will point out the greater truth, that milk is for drinking not spilling. If wise, this person will not belabor the obvious.

Uncommon Christians believe that God wants to function through us in ways that don't come naturally. For example, once I counseled an adulterer, and God used the gift of encouragement through me. Sam was leaving his wife and children for another woman. Although I was normally repulsed by this behavior, I came up with an endless stream of encouraging words and ideas while I was working with him and his wife. I would point out all the things he was doing well and encourage his wife to shower him with love. I couldn't believe some of the things I said. They came out so effortlessly, it was as if they weren't my own thoughts at all. I always prayed before I met with them and asked God to talk for me. Clearly, He did.

WHEN A GIFT IS NOT A GIFT

If you take your gift and use it without God's help, you will make mistakes. You also may annoy people who don't understand your gift. This is common. All humans act on their own initiative and misjudge others at times. Pray. It will improve your odds of avoiding such mistakes.

More Christians are blessed with the spiritual gift of service than any other, so we will look at it a little more specifically to let you see how spiritual gifts can affect us.[15] People with the spiritual gift of service:

- See and meet practical needs
- Free others to achieve their goals and appointed tasks
- Disregard weariness
- Have difficulty saying "no" (Others say it can't be done, but they show them it can.)
- Are alert to people's likes and dislikes

---

15 These notes were inspired by a sermon from one of my journals during my years at 1st Baptist Church of Atlanta.

- Have a strong desire to be with others, to identify with them and meet their needs
- Need approval and appreciation to confirm that what they are doing is important
- Like short-range projects and will chop long-term ones into short-term chunks to see progress
- Meet needs quickly (Red tape and talking about a task rather than doing it drives them crazy.)
- Have a tendency to feel unqualified, but their need to get things done as well as determination, love, and joy fuel their fire

People with this gift can be misunderstood because:

- Their quickness may seem pushy
- They avoid red tape and just start working (Others may feel excluded from the job.)
- Their eagerness may prompt suspicion of self-advancement
- They have a hard time letting others serve them
- Their interest in practical things may appear to be a lack of interest in spiritual things
- They may look distracted from a job because they are taking care of someone's emotional need

If you have the gift of service, here's how to know when you are on the right track:

Our attitude when God leads	*Our attitude when we ignore God*
alert, hospitable, generous, joyful, flexible, available, persistent	unconscious, loner, stingy, self-pitying, inflexible, self-centered, gives up

If someone you know seems to be misusing their gift, what do they need?
- A) A swift kick in the rear
- B) Withdrawal of privileges
- C) To be judged, nagged, and pushed
- D) Feedback and love

Answer: (D) of course

The truth is, someone who doesn't really have the gift of service may just have learned the habits of service by watching someone else. We don't really know who gets which gift. In fact, as Christians mature in their faith, they acquire new gifts. If this notion of spiritual gifts intrigues you, I strongly recommend that you read or listen to a series on it so that it will not seem a mystery. There are a number of good tests online to help you assess your gift, and I'm willing to bet you'll learn some things about your spiritual self that you never knew before.

DIGGING DEEPER

Spiritual Gifts

Ask: Do the daily activities of your life require a spiritual gift that you do not seem to have? Are you sick of serving, administering, giving, encouraging? Christ teaches us, "whatever you have asked for in prayer, believe that you have received it, and it will be yours" (Mark 11:24). It is God's nature to give lavishly, so don't give up. And don't read a delay as a refusal on God's part. He knows what you need, and you will receive it at the perfect time. Ask, wait patiently, and stay open to receive it. One gift after another will be given to you as you grow into your relationship with Him. You'll see.

Write: What spiritual gift do you know you need? What spiritual gifts do you hope you are given?

Act: Create a "Wisdom Room" in your home—a place where you keep music, books, blankets, pictures, and anything else that makes you feel at home with God. Add things that make you feel happy, protected, comforted, encouraged, and strong. You can create a space with each member of the family in mind so that any of you can retreat there. If you want to realize your gift, enhance your relationship with God.

Act: There are a number of spiritual gift assessments online that can help you begin to familiarize yourself with this supernatural area of life. Consider taking one.

CHAPTER 19

DEFENSE MECHANISMS

"Now you are full of light from the Lord and your behavior should show it!
For this light within you produces only what is good and right and true."

—EPHESIANS 5:8-9

"Jesus said, 'Father, forgive them for they do not know what they are doing.'"

—LUKE 23:34

A DEFENSE MECHANISM IS AN AUTOMATIC, and often subconscious, response to a difficult situation. It is an innate ability to protect our souls from loss and distress. These mechanisms distract us from looking at the ugliness that lies within ourselves and the inherent weaknesses in any human relationship. Some of the names psychotherapists use for these unconscious defense mechanisms are: rationalization, denial, regression, passive aggressiveness, minimizing, maximizing, intellectualization, projection, displacement, fantasy, and acting out.

Since awareness is the first step to change, make a check beside the defense mechanisms that you realize you have a tendency to use. When you do, you are usually *unaware* of it, so remember that others can sometimes see these in you better than you can see them yourself.

- **Rationalization** — Explaining or excusing behaviors that you typically believe are wrong. For example, you might say, "This was a tough situation, so I had to do it."
- **Denial** — Saying something isn't true when it is. For example, you might strongly dislike a man at church who puts down his wife in front of everyone. You find him to be rude and cruel, but when someone mentions him, you want to take the high road. You attempt to convince yourself that you feel differently about him and say, "It's not that I think he's a bad guy...."
- **Regression** — Doing something you are too old to still be doing. For example, after your spouse rants at and nags you, you turn to your adult daughter and subtly stick your fingers in your ears as if to say, "He/She can't make me listen."
- **Repression** — Trying not to notice unpleasant realities. For example, as a teenager, you might have been vaguely aware that the popular group didn't care about you, but you hung on the edge of their circle and tried to ignore their disinterest in you.
- **Passive aggression** — Acting like things are okay while you make others pay for ways they have hurt or offended you. For example, if you don't like that your coworker takes frequent smoke breaks, you'll tell him it's fine but then avoid working with him and "forget" to copy him on important emails.
- **Minimizing** — Protecting yourself from anxiety or worry by making something seem smaller than it is. Imagine a coach engaging in a 15-minute rant, but afterwards, he tells a parent, "I have to raise my voice a little with the players from

time to time." (Addicts have this one down to a fine art: I drink, shop, work, philander, smoke, yell...but just a little.)

- **Maximizing**—Enlarging or intensifying a situation so that no one can deny its importance. A teacher might tell a parent, "Mrs. Smith, Tommy has been pestering the other children all day" when Tommy actually did it only three times in eight hours. The teacher is acting on the assumption that if she makes it sound big enough, the parent will do something about it.

- **Externalization**—Believing that something outside yourself is the reason for your actions. An employee might tell his boss, "Sorry I'm late for the third time this week. The traffic is awful." The truth is, the employee leaves home too late to be sure he will be on time.

- **Intellectualization**—Using lengthy discussion or focusing on details to distract others from the topic you should really be facing. This is a common mechanism used in abusive parenting. Parents intellectualize to explain their inappropriate reactions to children. It would be healthier to address how scary it is for children to see adults out of control and then apologize for the behaviors. That's a tall order.

- **Projection**—Attributing your thoughts and feelings to someone else. For example, a son says, "I'm sorry I'm such a disappointment to you, Dad." The dad is not disappointed in his child at all. The son is disappointed in himself or is fearful of disappointing the father, so he projects that feeling onto his parent.

- **Displacement**—Holding an emotion in when it occurs, and letting it out on your spouse, the dog, the boss, the kids, or any other convenient target. Some people justify their own angry emotional displays at home when they have had a stressful day at the office.

- **Fantasy**—Escaping reality, including daydreaming or tuning out. Our hectic, demanding culture and the advent of electronics has made most of us experts at this. As a result, our face-to-face social-emotional skills are taking a beating.
- **Acting out**—Displaying what you're feeling in exaggerated or intrusive ways such as slamming doors and throwing things. Physically expressing feelings that the person isn't able to express verbally can have a calming effect on the person acting out, but is destructive and scary to those caught in its path.
- **Undoing**—Trying to right a wrong by drawing attention away from it or attempting to undo the damage by doing something unrelated. For instance, you might cook a special dinner for a person after a screaming match. What's wrong with this? Spiritual damage from frequent bad habits cannot be traded out for a nice meal. Regret, an apology, and a determination to change are needed. A loving meal will only be healing if these other conditions are also in place.

One theory that I have about defense mechanisms is that they are universal security blankets for the soul. All humans use them. Remember when you were frightened of the dark when you were a child? Did you pull your covers over your head, thinking the Boogieman couldn't get you if he couldn't see you? That's how these defense mechanisms work. We think if we cover up with them, they'll keep us safe. If we pretend that we're not mean, angry, sad, scared, perturbed, disinterested, disappointed, or feeling rejected, then we'll be protected. But security blankets don't really shield us, they just make us feel more secure while we are using them.

God has a better plan. Instead of using defense mechanisms when life becomes difficult, He wants us to think before we act, be courageous, and bring up difficult conversations at the right time and place so we can have intimate, healthy relationships. He wants us to create safe environments where we can mess up and be weak, fallible, and foolish while still giving and receiving love. Remember the two different tribes that we discussed in chapter 17? Both tribes deal with the same severe shortages, yet the children who were taught to be secretive and mistrustful became sullen and hyper-sensitive adults. Conversely, the children who were allowed to be open, show emotions, and admit weaknesses became warm, self-assured, and friendly adults. Let's decide to loosen our grasp and expose ourselves to a lifestyle that's simpler, safer, and more in line with our Creator's wishes for us.

Understanding How You Cope

Below are some of the most commonly used defense mechanisms. Check the one you most frequently use. If you aren't sure, ask someone who loves you to tell you the truth. Try to catch yourself using it and then make the decision to live without it. Be still and listen for God's voice, and depend on Him to give you an alternative such as courage or wisdom.

- **Rationalization** — Providing "explanations" to excuse inconsistent or irrational behavior without being aware that this is happening.
- **Minimizing** — Protecting yourself from worry or anxiety by viewing significant events or problem behaviors as being less important (smaller) than they actually are.
- **Maximizing** — Viewing significant events or problem behaviors as more important (bigger) than they actually are to protect yourself from potential damage or harm.
- **Externalization** — Believing outside forces or circumstances are the cause of your self-destructive behaviors. This defense mechanism allows you to avoid accepting responsibility for behavior.

- **Intellectualization**—Using lengthy arguments or small details (deflecting behavior) to distract from the task at hand.
- **Projection**—Ascribing your own undesirable traits or thoughts to another person.
- **Displacement**—Redirecting emotions such as anger form the source of frustration and discharging them onto other persons, objects, or ideas.
- **Undoing**—Engaging in behavior designed to symbolically make amends for or negate previously unacceptable thoughts, feelings, or actions. This is not to be confused with actual and direct amends made to persons you may have harmed.
- **Regression**—Returning to a less mature level of behavior.
- **Fantasy**—Escaping from an unpleasant or undesirable situation through daydreaming, "tuning out," or not paying attention.
- **Acting out**—Acting without reflection or apparent regard for negative consequences.
- **Passive aggression**—Indirectly and unassertively expressing aggression toward others.

PART 3

An Uncommon Attitude

MAKE ROOM FOR MIRACLES

Make Room for Miracles

"Do you believe that I can do this?"

—Matthew 9:28

Y ou can change the world. And you won't be doing it alone.
I want to help you see the enormity of the investment you are about to make. When you take on the task of living out God's wisdom, life does not become painless. The rubber meets the road, and the road is rugged at times. You will not stop your bad habits instantly. Neither will the people around you. It's not humanly possible. Yet, God has told His children what will cause them to flourish. We can prove to the world that love, respect, and prayer—through the flow of the Holy Spirit within and among us—is the way to a better life.

If you choose to live a life defined by Uncommon Sense Christianity, something wonderful will happen in your soul. You will become increasingly hopeful, capable, and caring. And then your very being will change; you will realize that no day can pass without the possibility of you breathing God's love in and breathing it out onto the world. Every day, no matter what else you can or can't do, you will have influenced the world for the better.

Across the world, young people have hit the streets and are declaring—and are willing to die for—their desires to promote freedom and respect in a world starving for both. Let's help them make it a reality. Uncommon Sense is such a positive alternative to manipulation, violence, materialism, and escapism. You will realize this if you live it. You won't want to go back to the way you lived before because intimacy through loving friendship is better!

God's love can be the most powerful love of your life, yet it is only as amazing as the bond you share with Him. So, in order to ignite the fire within the relationship, you must notice the daily gifts He brings your way. That is, you must begin to live with Him in mind. How can you do that if you don't try? You can't. He isn't visible, or audible, or intrusive.

The tools you are given in part four are revolutionary because they will help you begin and end your days—and spend every moment in between—remembering who you are and what you are called to do, which is to demonstrate love at all times. But before we get to them, we want to create a home environment that makes the use of them practical, sensible, and efficient. The Bible reminds us to win people over by our loving and constant hearts. There is a curious verse in the Bible that explains that if we love others when they are hateful to us, we heap burning coals on their heads (Prov. 25:21-22). Did you know that people actually used to carry pots of burning coals on their heads to publicly demonstrate when they felt remorse for a bad decision? If someone is hateful to you and you don't retaliate, the perpetrator has an opportunity to notice his own ugly behavior. If you react in anger, the focus shifts from his wrong behavior to yours, and he feels justified to be hateful again. Christ came to take the hot coals of self-condemnation and shame away and replace them with love. Even in the Old Testament God tells us that He gives "beauty for ashes" (Isa. 61:3 NLT). Love convicts humans better than condemnation, and with it, remorse takes on a completely different look.

I once worked with a man who had been unfaithful to his wife. He was a high-powered executive, so his betrayal became public. He was being sued by his former lover, and everyone he knew got wind of it. His home life was a wreck, his wife was reeling from the immensity of the mess their lives had become, and his children were in shock. The public exposure put a spotlight directly on the deeds he'd done in darkness, and he hated himself. He felt ashamed and was disgusted by his past. During one session when he was reviewing his choices and cursing his foolishness, he began to weep. "The person I am the most sad to disappoint is my mother-in-law," he told me. "She is such a sweet person and she believed in me. She doesn't deserve this." It was people's love, not people's condemnation that broke his heart. By the way, the mother-in-law never stopped loving and believing in him.

It may seem ridiculous to be loving and peaceful when someone harms you, but the time to challenge him is later, when he is not feeling contentious. In the moment, you must choose to either give him the floor and try to understand him (a high calling) or distance yourself a bit, gather your wits, and then go back to loving him again. Humans have this capacity. You will see distancing on your child's face the next time your lecture gets too long, or you may see it on your coworker's face if you talk more than she wants to listen. But distancing yourself isn't as important as what you do during that time. It is in these moments that you tune in to God.

In this section, we will look at a lifestyle that promotes the kingdom of God—a lifestyle that favors the loving, authentic, and relational way encouraged by Christ. Doing so will remind you of who you are and how to respond to your circumstances accordingly. You'll learn loving ways of dealing with the behaviors that make you want to scream, cry, or hide. You'll learn how to change hearts rather than manipulate behavior.

DIGGING DEEPER

CAN I REALLY CHANGE THE WORLD?

What feelings and thoughts did you have when you were introduced to the notion of changing the world? Do you realize that you can literally change it physically and spiritually by the healing things you say and do on a daily basis? Write your thoughts here in response to what you have just read.

If your thoughts are pessimistic, disappointing, or downcast, think of a person you know who has a positive take on life. Will you commit to call him or her when you are discouraged and soak in that person's impressions of life?

CHAPTER 20

A NEW ATTITUDE

*"Give all your worries and cares to God, for he
cares about what happens to you."*

—1 PETER 5:7 (NLT)

THERE ARE TWO MAJOR ASPECTS to the Christian lifestyle: attitude
and actions. To set you up to take the necessary actions, you must
have the right attitude.

Many years ago, I was blessed by a movie called *Matthew*. It was shown
at a church I enjoyed attending, and it gave me a freedom and perspective
on Christ I'd never had before. All of my life, I'd heard certain stories and
phrases from the Bible that gave me a confusing sense of who the Son of
God was. I understood, "Jesus loves me this I know" but wondered, *Why is
He so hard on people who misunderstand Him?* Sometimes when I was young,
I saw movies in which the Bible and Christ's words were read with a tone
of disdain, frustration, or distance. It was the way I had been treated by
some of my teachers when I let them down. This led to my inaccurate perception that Jesus was hard on people who misunderstood His teachings.
I also saw pictures of Christ and didn't like most of them. I wondered,

Why does He walk around looking all sad and messy? Doesn't anything make Him happy? Even when He has kids in His lap, He looks blah. These were my honest impressions of Christ.

Yet, *Matthew* portrayed Jesus Christ as healthy and full of life. Jesus had a sense of humor. He seemed strong. He knew how and when to tell hard truths. He even *yelled* at some of the Pharisees because they had alienated others from God through their misunderstanding and hypocrisy. For the first time, I heard Jesus speak Matthew 23 , "Woe to you…" with a new attitude. He wasn't disgusted. Rather, He was determined and imploring! What a difference.

Prior to seeing this movie, I attended a church where a professor from an elite college read the Bible during the Sunday morning services. Some of the people at the church thought she was too animated and cheery. But I told the clergy how much I loved her reading, and they told me, "The Bible should be read without emphasis so that the listener can choose his or her own intonation." Okay. But what if the reader's intonation is out of keeping with God's character? What if it is downcast, disconnected, disappointed, damaging, or even destructive?

Here's all I know. The Christ in the *Matthew* movie had hair that actually moved in the wind. He laughed, hugged, joked, and pleaded. He was healthy looking and had genuine emotions, and for the first time in my life I was able to hear His words with playfulness or pleading rather than disdain.

If you are going to introduce new ways of living into your home, office, or circles of friends, you want the atmosphere to be respectful and warm. You also want to have the maturity and constancy to keep your word when you have collaborated and come to agreements. When you change your mind, you want to inform the people with whom the agreements were made rather than sneaking or carelessly having your own way. When you blow it, you want to apologize and dedicate yourself to getting back on the horse and trying again. You want to repeatedly collaborate and update decisions as needed with them. This atmosphere leads to the development of respect and rich character.

I remember a woman who lived across the road from me. She had five children, and since I was already challenged by my three girls, I used to observe the way she parented because her children appeared to be respectful, well-behaved, and generally happy. One day, we were outside on her driveway—the place where all of the neighborhood children loved to play. She called out to her little three-year-old who was headed toward the street and said, "Jordie, bring your bike over here." Jordie did not come over. He looked at her, turned toward the street, and began to pedal. Again she called, "Jordie… come this way." Jordie looked but didn't come. Then with a tone that was sweet and regretful my friend said, "Oooh, Jordie, now you have to go inside." She lifted him into her arms, held him lovingly, and took him into the house. Yes, he cried. But my take-away was the way she responded to his consequence. Rather than becoming angry, she was compassionate and consistent.

That should be the atmosphere of a loving Christian environment—consistent enough that you can count on it and compassionate enough that you can learn the meaning of the word grace. Grace means I won't always get what I deserve, but when I do get a consequence, I know that it will be accompanied by a level head, compassion, and love.

As you read the following chapters, try to imagine what life would look like if your interactions with the people around you were marked by simplicity, a kind sense of humor, and a large dose of respect and compassion. Even if you are the only one striving for it, your life will improve.

DIGGING DEEPER

Attitude

Can you think of someone you knew when you were a child or a person you know now who exemplifies the qualities discussed in this chapter? What was it that made you remember him or her? Would you like to acquire more of those attitudes you admire?

Do any of these attitudes fit?

- Healthy
  sense of humor
- Determined
- Thoughtful
- Strong
- Affectionate
- Playful
- Respectful

- Reliable
- Willing to apologize
- Interested
- Inclusive
- Adaptable
- Compassionate
- Forgiving
- Generous

Add some of your favorite qualities or attitudes:

CHAPTER 21

ESTABLISHING FAMILY DYNAMICS

"But as for me and my family, we will serve the Lord."

—JOSHUA 24:15 (NLT)

THE WORD *DYNAMIC* IS DEFINED as "energizing, vigorous, active, potent, compelling, magnetic, electric, vibrant, effective, and influential."

Imagine a home defined by dynamic love. Imagine that as you live among the people in this dwelling place, you become more loving yourself. There is a vibrant, compelling force that causes you to notice what people are doing right rather than what they are doing wrong. When people want you to improve, they encourage you by modeling the behavior. Once you have learned, they may mention it to you or remind you of it, but nagging and lecturing are no more. Tough situations are handled one-on-one with predictability and respect. Weekly, the entire group spends loving time together to help everyone become more acquainted with one another and to reassure each member that they belong in this place.

That is the dwelling place you are about to create. I know it is possible. I live there.

THE FAMILY DYNAMICS OF UNCOMMON SENSE

- Listening to God
- Learning to Wait
- Teaching His Ways
- Experiencing Love

LISTENING TO GOD

God isn't a fool. He won't talk to you if you aren't going to listen. So you must begin by telling God that you want to hear His voice in your heart and then be still repeatedly throughout the day so you can listen for healing words. The Bible tells a story of a woman who goes to a judge over and over again until the judge gives in to her and gives her what she wants (Luke 18:1-8). That story, told by Christ, is meant to encourage us to keep sharing our hearts with our God until we feel heard. Christ lovingly and playfully said to a crowd, "You parents, if your children ask for bread do you give them a stone instead? Or if they ask for a fish, do you give them a snake? Of course not! If you sinful people know how to give good gifts to your children, how much more will your Heavenly Father give good gifts to those who ask Him?" (Matt. 7: 9-12).

When we share our hearts with God, He will give us what we need — more than the most loving human father or mother could give. Honestly, it will be so perfect it may make you chuckle sometimes. Are you asking and then listening for His response?

As you interact with loving people who are in love with God, you will begin to understand Him. The easiest way to do this is to tell God you want to listen to Him and then start reading about Him or listening to loving, wise teachers. I have included a list of possibilities in the appendix of this book that have helped my friends and me get to know Him. If you don't have a Bible you read regularly, I recommend you purchase a modern version, one that's easy to read and filled with study notes. As you spend time studying and learning about God, you will understand more about the spiritual realm in which we live.

A question, for example, that is often asked of Christians who love God is, "Why does a loving God let bad things happen to good people?" The answer is really quite simple. "Because there is more good to be had from their circumstance than bad." We may not be able to understand that. We may not want to believe it. But we can because God's nature is loving and good, and He has set us free to make choices. If we all were taught to listen to God from a young age and live in accordance with His loving dictates, the world would not be as messy and cruel as it is.

LEARNING TO WAIT

You are going to learn to wait if you practice Uncommon Sense. You will wait for yourself and others to change old habits, for the right time to voice your preferences and concerns, and for God to fill your heart with His desires for you. The wonderful thing is that as you wait for God and experience the peace and joy of His kingdom, you will find yourself thankful over and over again. You are going to make room for God, for human nature, and for miracles during those wonderful pauses in life. You are going to stop expecting your child to have an adult's mental and emotional capabilities when he or she is still learning and growing. Have any of us arrived? I know I haven't, but we can feel really good about how far we have come.

TEACHING GOD'S WAYS

Even young children can learn God's ways when they are taught to affirm others daily and listen reflectively. Uncommon Sense includes ways to do this such as loving wake-ups, devotionals, meals, and quality tuck-in times. Fun activities become standard fare. Life is made simpler by using coping tools such as baskets, Character Tickets, Loving Payback Time, and habit-changing Potter's Clay. These will be defined in part four. Electronics will be limited. (Did I hear a sigh of relief?) There will be more time spent building relationships, which is also good for building social skills. Add a pinch of collaboration. Energize it all by focusing on positives, and you can create a daily rhythm that lightens everyone's load.

Soul and Soil

I enjoy gardening. One day, a woman I know told me how she took gallon milk jugs, filled them with a blend of nutrients, poked a hole in the bottom, and let the mix slowly seep into the soil around her newly-planted flowers. I followed her advice that year, and I had the kind of plants you see in magazines. They were so big they made us laugh! In the same way that nurturing the soil is critical to the growth of a plant, nurturing our souls is critical to physical and spiritual growth.

Is the soil of your life too hectic? Would you define it as removed? How about numbing? Would you say you're careless because of it? Impatient? Or do your daily habits intentionally draw together the people you love for conversation, laughs, and repair? Does your lifestyle provide for soulful, artistic, or athletic expression for each member of your family? Does it provide for encounters with and awareness of our amazing God?

You can teach God's relational habits by using them thoughtfully and playfully. This allows Christ's nurturance to seep into your soul. Over time, His habits become a part of you. As you acquire increasing amounts of Christ's life-giving ways, timewasters have less space.

Experiencing Love

I have heard many stories of unexpected love from people who have adopted even one aspect of this lifestyle. Not *feelings* of love, but *experiences* of love. What we know in the world of psychology is that the cruelest, most arrogant, judging, and self-centered people in the world are in the most pain. Though they seem to be the ones inflicting hurt, it is only because they have little relief from their own unrelenting insecurities and challenges. Christ has asked us to be people of grace and compassion, to pray for relief for one another's pain. So we pray while refusing to support damaging attitudes and behaviors. We pray while offering undeserved kindness. Then we watch as the most difficult people in our lives begin to meet daily challenges with considerate responses rather than rash reactions. The good things your children do occasionally when they're eight will occur frequently at age eighteen because doing so has become a way of life...because love feels good. The experience of it is compelling.

DIGGING DEEPER

How can I embrace these family dynamics?

Which of the family dynamics speaks to you? Why?

Which dynamic, if any, do you think will be most difficult for you to embrace? Why?

- Listening to God
- Learning to Wait
- Teaching His Ways
- Experiencing Love

As you can see, much of what you will need to create a life filled with love has to do with your own willingness to get rid of habits, memories, and attitudes that are not Christ-like. Many of your old ways will be in direct opposition to your new ones and will keep you from becoming the person you want to be. I commonly remind my students to *replace* ineffective parenting habits with better ones rather than just adding new ones to the mix.

Listening to God and waiting are the hardest parts of living well. People do not change overnight. Dieters don't get tiny waists overnight. Athletes and artists and workers of all kinds develop their talents and skills over many years, not hours. Experts are experts because they have put the time into honing their minds and talents. Nurturing a healthy home life is no different. Traditional parenting doesn't change children or parents overnight. Neither does Uncommon Sense. It just makes the waiting more soothing because you are becoming someone you like and are experiencing God as you do so. Once you get the hang of it, you won't be able to go back to some of the defeatist approaches to life you have learned.

CHAPTER 22

POSITIVE COMMUNICATIONS ALL DAY

*"Let everything you say be good and helpful, so that your words
will be an encouragement to those who hear them."*

—EPHESIANS 4:29 (NLT)

I s it possible to have only positive communication throughout the
day? Yes! How and when do you handle adversity if you don't talk
about life as it comes up? You carve out a few minutes from each day
and come together to discuss life in a very brief, thoughtful manner. You
apologize for hurts and make plans for support. Once a week when everyone
is rested, you tackle the big problems if there are any, and then dream and
celebrate together.

When human beings disagree or are disappointed with one another,
they want to set things straight—usually right here, right now. The problem is that when we give anyone unexpected criticism or challenges, the
victim's face, body, mouth, and heart says, "Ouch." A better way to address

concerns is at the right time and place for both the giver *and* the receiver. (See Prov. 15:23)

In the real world, when one person catches another off guard with a painful perception like, "What you did or who you are was offensive or ridiculous to me," it hurts. It feels a bit like an emotional bee sting that comes out of nowhere. The person who receives a stinging communication reacts: "Ouch! I want to get away from you or do something to you to hurt you back. I want to make sure you don't hurt me again." Bee stings in human families are unexpected moments of criticism and judgment or feedback given in a devaluing tone or attitude that is loud, rude, assumptive, or insistent. Bee-like people are individuals who require immediate gratification for their own perceptions of right and wrong. Some beestings come in the form of words—some come in body language.

If you want to live an energizing, extraordinary life, you're wise to obey God's Word and use your words to encourage others and build them up (Eph. 4:29-32). But if you are in the position I was years ago, you probably can't imagine how people can still be human and avoid negatives throughout the day. But I don't wonder about it anymore. I know it is possible to talk positively all day and save negatives for a small, designated time. I've done it. My children have learned to do it. The tools and strategies in this book came from my desire to address difficult topics and teach people how to communicate important things in very small windows of time without interrupting the flow of love and respect in our homes.

Instead of bringing up negatives during the day, jot notes on a notepad or your phone to remind you of things you want to discuss during an *evening update* (usually 5-10 minutes long), *character time* (between 5-15 minutes), or a weekly *family meeting* (between 30-45 minutes). Your total time to discuss difficult topics is concentrated into a few respectful hours each week, and you maintain the positive and safe atmosphere of your home the rest of the time. You do so by limiting comments throughout the day to these three categories:

- **Positive Affirmations** — "That was kind. You're funny. I like the way you hang up your coat every day when you come in the door."
- **Positive Interests** — "There are only three weeks left of school. Will you miss some things about it?" Any subject is fair game as long as you *both* agree it is pleasing to talk about and doesn't stir up strife. Some people even find political debates positive interests as long as there doesn't have to be a winner.
- **Positive Invitations** — "Want to help me cook? Would you like to run to the store with me? Let's go play basketball!"

Although I said it is possible to have positive communication all day, it's not easy. This is the challenge that drove me to create a nontraditional lifestyle. These categories given to us at Van Horn's seminar brought passion back to my marriage and my life. But I needed new habits, including the meetings and tools found in this book, in order to stick with positive comments all day. They quickly and effectively addressed the needs and concerns that had been addressed with ongoing criticism, nagging, and other conversations that no one wanted to hear.

DIGGING DEEPER

BEE STING RESPONSES

When someone says something you don't want to hear, what does your bee sting response look like? Some people respond to stings by opening their mouths; they start defending their choices or blaming someone else for them. Some people roll their eyes, sigh, poke fun, or purse their lips. Some people walk out. Others just tune out. Few bee sting responses are attractive, and few "bees" feel sorry for the victim after they strike.

How often do you say too much when you need to be still?

How often do you say nothing when you need to speak?

Would you be willing for people you love to say "ouch" quietly when they feel a sting from you? Are you courageous enough to say "ouch" when you get stung? If you are trying to change, keep trying. Let yourself be gently amused by how hard it is to shed the old you rather than constantly get frustrated. Have compassion with the people around you knowing they may be trying to change as well.

Each of us is different. If you want a relationship with a person, you will want to care about what she cares about and stop telling her what should and shouldn't matter to her. If she tells you a certain topic or behavior is an issue or hurts, assume that something in her brain is attached to a chemical recipe for emotional discomfort when you bring up that topic. There may be an old wound there. Remember that we said that the brain is filled with messenger pathways. Roses make Susan happy because her father gave them to her for her 16th birthday. However, they make Jane sad because her father had them on his casket. Their brains have paths attached to roses. And we said that paths become interstates if they are traveled repeatedly. But those pathways can change over time. You and the people you love will create new ones together. But you must travel the roads you have today. If you callously stir up discomfort in another person, your relationship will suffer.

Consider it a good sign if someone you love still tells you when you hurt him or her. It means you care and that there is hope that the two of you can do better. And when you do stir up discomfort, apologize earnestly and apply lots of love. The damage will slowly begin to heal. Old brain pathways will weaken as painful feelings and thoughts are interrupted and replaced with new, pleasurable ones. This lifestyle will help with all of that in an uncommon yet intelligent way, because each tool is designed to respect God's creation, our differences, and His dos and don'ts for our relationships.

CHAPTER 23

ESTABLISHING A NEW LIFE RHYTHM — DAILY ACTIVITIES

*"And what does the Lord require of you? To act justly,
love kindness, and walk humbly with your God."*

—MICAH 6:8

TO EXCHANGE YOUR CURRENT LIFESTYLE for one based on the teachings of Christ means you must alter your way of living as dramatically as you did your identity. The world will notice that you are different and that there is more joy, peace, and love in your life than that in the lives of culture-driven individuals. They will notice because you will have an atypically kind and affirming attitude toward yourself, life, and others.

If you want you and your loved ones to understand and experience Christianity, you have to *live* it. Living life as Christ teaches is radical. Before Christ came, we were confused. We thought God wanted us to control our behaviors and perform religious rituals, but Christ teaches us to open our hearts and learn about love. It's an attitude of surrender that produces endurance and perseverance and character and hope (Rom. 5:3).

When I first set out to make this change to my life, I did it with a lot of support. I was attending "Lifestyle of Love" seminars with my husband. The leader continually reminded us to make decisions based on wisdom, not feelings. Our teacher and the friends I made in those seminars encouraged me to make the flow of God's love in my marriage and my family a priority every day. I had several close friends who knew the good, bad, and ugly about me, and they loved me anyway. If I called on them, they reminded me to live what I'd learned. I call people like that my IHRs (intimate, healthy relationships). You will need at least one IHR to help you make this lifestyle change because it is hard, and someone will need to remind you of the person you want to become.

Over the past decade, I have gathered a set of Christian friends who are IHRs. They have incorporated some aspects of Uncommon Sense living in their homes. On hard days, when I am disappointed, frustrated, or feeling down, I can call one of them and say, "Remind me of what I believe." I can even briefly share my concerns because they care about the people I love and know all humans are worthy of love. These friends will not demean me or the people in my stories. Instead, they will listen, remind me of the positives, and tell me the essential truth I have forgotten. I end the call renewed and refreshed. (Some of their testimonies and tips are in part five.)

Now, before you read the following list of daily actions and feel overwhelmed, remember that you don't have to do it all. As my friends and their families have learned, you add a few at a time in the order that works for you, and your IHRs will support you to make the change.

A DAY OF UNCOMMON SENSE INCLUDES:

- Loving Wake-Up
- Family Devotions
- Meals Together
- Affirmations
- Energizing Positives
- Affection
- Limited Electronics
- Shared Fun
- Tuck-in Time
- Brief Collaborations

Before you or the people you love leave home for the day, you can already have several of these under your belt. I hope the following descriptions of these lifestyle elements will enlighten, encourage, and free you to realize what a precious child of God you are. You're created for intimate, healthy relationships with God and with the important people in your life.

Loving Wake-up

The first and most important thing you'll do each morning is remind others of who they are: lovable spiritual beings. You don't have to go all "deep and weird" with this, but kiss them on the head, give them a hug, and tell them they are beautiful. Then act like it. Rather than frantic mornings filled with cries of, "Hurry up! Where's your book?" the time spent together is calm and kind. Support them in any ways they need, and resist topics that result in bad feelings. If something goes wrong, provide support to make it as right as you can. Later in the day, you can troubleshoot what went wrong and determine how to make it better. If authority figures cannot model intelligence, patience, and poise when things go wrong, then they should not expect it from others.

Morning is a perfect time to breathe Christ in and breathe His love out onto others. Tell your family members you love them as they walk out the door and show them you mean it by being pleasant the entire time.

Family Devotions

There are Christian bookstores filled with wonderful, applicable books to help families learn about their faith and their Father. God's kingdom really is in our midst, but many people don't live like it. In fact, few Christian families read or pray together. Most Christians are embarrassed to pray aloud because they've never done it before, but that can change. A Gallup poll in 2013 indicated that although fewer young adults attend church or claim a religious affiliation than earlier generations did, nine out of ten young adults do believe in God. They are seeking spiritual experiences and new ways of connecting with God without all of the rules.[16] They can be introduced to Him by reading and listening to Christ's wisdoms through great teachers, music, or retreats. There is simply no excuse to live life with old, broken notions about Christ and His desires for us. Look in the appendix of this book for a few ideas.

When the girls were young, our family devotions were a rich, 15-minute period of time spent reading from a children's devotional or Bible, singing, stretching, and praying prior to breakfast. If we didn't do this before breakfast, we would sit on the deck with popsicles and do it after dinner. As the girls grew up and became more mature in their faith, we simply read a childhood or teen devotional each morning while the girls ate breakfast then asked what prayer needs everyone had for the day. Then we would pray as a family for international or national needs, family members, friends, and challenges at work and at school.

I firmly believe that spiritual beings need spiritual food in order to feel strong and live a vibrant life. We wouldn't think of starving ourselves by skipping meals day after day. Christ is the bread of our lives as Christians. And we must have a little every day. We partake of Him when we think, read, or sing about Him. His presence is penetrating, and over time we'll find we want increasing amounts of it and will grow to love His Word and His companionship.

MEALS TOGETHER

This is increasingly difficult because our culture has us active morning, noon, and night. Still, either breakfast or dinner needs to be a time each day when all of you find yourselves in the same room at the same time to break bread. There is something special about eating together. It creates a sense of warmth, bonding, sharing. Whether your family members stand at the kitchen island and just drink juice or sit down for a meal, this blessing must be added to your day. And by the way, you can offer a brief prayer before

---

16 Michelle Boorstein, "Religion is in trouble. The word, that is." *The Washington Post,* online edition, http://www.washingtonpost.com/local/religion-is-in-trouble-the-wor d-that-is/2013/07/11/759c6644-e416-11e2-aef3-339619eab080_story.html , July 11, 2013.

you eat. It reminds us that our food comes from God and we are blessed to have it. Some simple prayers can be found in the appendix.

Affirmations

Avoid the trap of feeling like your spouse or child is getting all this ooey gooey self-esteem fake stuff. How? By giving them real food. Don't say something just to be saying it. Each day, lean on the Holy Spirit and ask Him to affirm your loved ones through you. Listen for what He has to say. Sometimes, you'll be amused by what comes out. You'll know it's the Spirit because you wouldn't have thought to say it. The gift of encouragement is a quality of God's that is strong in some people, but seems largely missing in others. Practice and surrender yourself and you can let God's loving words of affirmation find their way out of your mouth and into another's heart. This is essential "For the kingdom of God is not a matter of what we eat or drink, but of living a life of goodness and peace and joy in the Holy Spirit" (Rom. 14: 17).

In the book *Transforming the Difficult Child,* authors Howard Glasser and Jennifer Easley point out that the best way to strengthen a child on the inside is to catch him or her doing the right thing and comment on that rather than only when he or she does wrong. I prefer that mode of affirmation when others are commenting on my choices, don't you? God tells us the same in His Word: "Fix your thoughts on what is true and honorable and right. Think about things that are pure and lovely and admirable. Think about things that are excellent and worthy or praise." (Phil.4:8 NLT). Build on successes. Water what you want to grow.

Affection

God created us to flourish when we are richly nurtured from birth on. It is His design and desire for us. Children who fail to receive affection can grow up to be anxious adults or lack important social skills.

Affection creates sturdiness, assuredness, warm resolve, and the ability to bond in humans. If you hug with your body at a distance, pat a lot, and generally stiffen up, try a new way. Try to remember the last appropriate loving touch you received and pass it on. The best way to know what a child likes is to gently offer and then notice his or her response. And remember, affection doesn't always involve touch. Can you imagine the difference for the child who comes off the field from a bad inning and looks up at a parent? One parent has affectionate encouragement written on his or her face, the other critical disappointment? Which one would make you want to hold your head up?

Limited Electronics

There is so much in educational and therapeutic literature about this. Turn off the TV for a while every day and do something that does not require the use of an electronic device. Find a time to shut down the computer and cell phones so you can enjoy the people you are with. Under normal circumstances, healthy people spend time with other people and use technology in a balanced way. They aren't limited to electronic friendships except in extraordinary or devastating circumstances. Some parts of our brain are best stimulated when they are reading and interpreting human facial expressions. This can only happen when you are looking at and engaged with the humans around you.

Shared Fun

Long ago, I was told of a study in which college students were given individual tutors for each of two topics: one was academic, and the other was sports-related. Later, they were asked which tutor they would prefer to date. Guess which tutor was most frequently chosen? The one who participated in the fun event, of course. If the only part of you that you show to your family is the taskmaster or even the nurturer, that's all you will be to them. And you will both be cheated. Balance is a crucial quality in life.

Cards. Board games. Electronic *physical* games. Croquet. Ball games. Hopscotch. Crafts. Woodworking activities. From a young age, we need to play and create because it helps us bond with others and builds social skills. That's why it's important to find something to do together even if your family members are at different stages of life. Learn to congratulate good effort and attitudes on the opponent's part with a matter-of-fact, believable tone. That lets them realize that (to you) the win isn't the only important quality in the game. Create an environment where everyone can enjoy activities without performing excellently. Remember they have probably already been called to perform all day. And so have you. It's time to relax.

Brief Collaboration

Evening updates. These will be described in more detail in chapter 25. They let everyone know you care about your lives together and that you are a team. It also helps people think about tomorrow before it gets here so they can be prepared. This collaboration may happen at the dinner table or on the steps before everyone heads upstairs for bed. It's another opportunity to show a display of togetherness and camaraderie by asking things like, "What's going right?" or "How can I support you?" "I want to remind everyone..." Easy. Quick. Powerful.

Tuck-in Time

Growing up, my siblings and I had a nightly ritual of kissing our mother and father and saying goodnight on our way to bed. Our father often read to us and tucked the covers around our little bodies while mom would offer us water and sit on the bed so she could stroke our hair. With our own children we added a simple prayer of thanksgiving to God for good things that happened that day and for the bad things He didn't allow to harm us. We finished with The Lord's Prayer, "Now I lay me down to sleep," and "God bless (the people we loved, and the President), and peace on earth, good will to men."

DIGGING DEEPER

WHO ARE MY IHRS?

Will you need support to adopt and become skilled with new life rhythms and coping strategies?

Who will allow you, even *encourage* you, to simplify your life, energize positives, and nourish your soul with kindness? Here's what to look for.

INTIMATE

To be intimate suggests being known. It's generally easy to tell stories about the positive choices you have made in life. But real intimacy (a feeling of really being loved for *all* of who you are) occurs when another person also knows the not-so-good, bad, and ugly things about you and loves you anyway. Who is the person to whom you've told your most private, intimate stories? What allowed you to reveal yourself to that person?

HEALTHY

To be healthy, a relationship must have a *wise* freedom in its midst. God has created us to have personalities, gifts, talents, and dreams.

- Who gives you permission to be yourself?
- Who respects you enough to give you the freedom to find your own ways of living?
- Who is courageous enough to tell you the truth when you are headed down a destructive path?

If you came up with three different names, you may need all of them on your support team.

Relationships

To relate is to connect, understand, and have common ground. Healthy relationships not only offer camaraderie, but also boundaries and safety.

- Who gives you the courage to be honest, but not careless, with your precious life on earth?
- Who reminds you to sacrifice earthly treasures for heavenly ones?
- Who will walk this exciting but challenging journey with you?

Remember, the Holy Spirit is your number one IHR, but God said it is not good to be alone. He wants another human being to come along side of you—someone who understands your desire for God and who, like you, wants to be loved. The Bible says that three is even better than two, so expand your support system whenever you can.

CHAPTER 24

UNCOMMON CONSENSUS— GETTING STARTED

"Make my joy complete by being like-minded, by having the same love, being one in spirit and purpose. Do nothing out of selfish ambition."

—PHILIPPIANS 2:2-3

I OPENED A BOOK THE OTHER day and a treasure dropped out. It was from one of our many family meetings when the girls were young, but this had been an especially rich one. I had given the family a paper labeled "Coplin Lifestyle of Love." Beneath the title was a list of our lifestyle philosophies, and each of the girls had initialed the items on it. Their initials signified they understood why we chose to live the way we did. We all agreed to:

- Share positive communication throughout the day
- Write and recieve Character Tickets when we felt devalued
- Pray to remind us of whose we are and why we are here

- Honor God's relational hierarchy of Himself, marriage, family, others
- Give nightly apologies and affirmations to keep our relationships healthy

I smiled to myself as I looked at their little-girl signatures. If you met my daughters, you would know that they love the life they lived, but it was a bit different from the norm. I can recall their shy giggling as they explained the tools on our kitchen counter — the ones that served as forms of discipline and reminders of what we believed in — to their friends. The girls were thankful not to live traditionally, but they sometimes gave me good-natured grief for setting up our home with these unconventional tools.

Uncommon Sense creates a system of communication that takes care of details in a succinct, constant, and kind way, so you can make space for God's undeniable and inevitable presence in your life. When you live this way, it is a pleasure to get up in the morning.

I used to teach stress management seminars in which I addressed work, home, and individual stress. I often asked the audience what they thought the leading cause of divorce is. What do you think? Infidelity? Financial distress? Actually, the leading cause is poor communication. We often fail to communicate our needs, hopes, dreams, and values with one another, and we let minutiae litter our time with tedious verbalizations. Life within the kingdom of God is not meant to be handled like this. There is a better way.

Consensus Replaces Confusion

Does your family dynamic look more like a congested city highway or a trip through the countryside? If you live in the developed world, you may have created a "spaghetti junction" in your home. The way to untangle the roads and make life feel a little more sane and soulful is to start holding brief, effective meetings when you want to communicate. Go ahead and groan and then keep reading because these meetings in our family have resulted in a lot of laughs, dreams, respect, compromises, and brilliant solutions! An uncommon consensus exists in the family that adopts this lifestyle because hit-and-run parenting and backtalk are greatly reduced. A rich sense of belonging and respect develops when family communication becomes civil, predictable, and collaborative. Wise decisions replace abrupt reactions. Parents learn to stop lecturing, judging, punishing, and nagging. Children learn the habits of participation and renewal. Predictability and discipline replace fear and threats, and grace and love abound. Those who really participate both in the meetings and the lifestyle interact with the Holy Spirit throughout the day and become very familiar with His voice. The experience of love becomes real. God is made manifest.

GETTING STARTED

The first step is to begin with a habit you will need to adopt: Collaborate with your family. Some people like flowcharts to help them know where they are headed, so here are the first few steps you will take to build this new way of life.

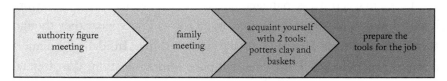

Once you have had two initial buy-in meetings, you can begin to use the daily tools. Both meetings are designed to discuss *your* desire to change the way *you* are living. You ask to hear other authority figures' thoughts, and attempt to gain their approval and support. If they don't want to participate, you can still use many of the tools and philosophies. It will be harder going it alone, but you will grow spiritually and experience personal peace as you make each loving move. The second meeting is to discuss with those under your authority how you are going to interact with them in new ways.

MEETING 1: INITIAL AUTHORITY FIGURE BUY-IN

Until the authority figures under your roof agree that you are a team and that values and responsibilities need to be shared, you may feel more like you are running a hotel than a home. The first meeting you design will include: an explanation that you intend to build the use of positive communication and accountability into your lifestyle; a discussion of five or six values to hand down to the next generation; a list of household responsibilities and privileges that are necessary to get through the week; and a look back at who you were before you began to use complex and desperate measures for managing or manipulating other people.

Let's look at the important details that must be addressed for you to feel on top of life rather than consumed by it. If you want things to change but aren't sure if your spouse will want to participate, ask permission to try some new things and just see if he or she will take part in this initial meeting.

Your first meeting will likely be a doozy, but you may never need to have one like it again. What's more—you'll love the results. You and the Holy Spirit and any other authority figure in your environment are coming together to consider a fresh lifestyle for the people who live under your roof. Go away for the weekend with your spouse if you are married or take a treasured and wise friend if you are single, and take a hard look at your life. (If you don't have a wise friend, go with God.) I have to keep most people honest by pointing out that if a loved one died, they would set aside sports and work and leave town to honor him or her. Well, it may be far past time to honor your family unit by setting aside a weekend to look at why you live the way you do and how you can live more soulfully and richly. If you cannot afford to go away, clear your house of children for one day, and get a good night's sleep. Decide to be honest and polite and patient, and don't feel you have to settle everything in one sitting. Instead, take breathers, go for walks, and decompress periodically.

VALUES

Make a list of five or six key values you and your spouse want to pass on to the next generation. Your stated values will lay the foundation for everything else you hold dear in life. What do you want your children and spouse to know about God? Others? Themselves? Their purpose? Daily life? Trials?

Your values, the ones you live into under your roof, will either become a foundation for wisdom or a foundation for confusion. To say that you value something is to say that you hold it dear and prize it above all else. Christ told us His opinion on the matter when He said that two commandments fulfill the Law: Love God and love others as you love yourself (Matt. 22:37-39).

For example, one potential value you might teach is **life is about love**. Isn't that what we just read? God incessantly loves us. One of our purposes here is to share the love of God from person to person all day and acknowledging Him for the part He played in it. Our job is to teach our families about a 1 Corinthians 13 kind of love. When we miss the mark, we apologize, accept loving consequences, forgive one another, and try again. If this is one of our family's core values, then our daily, weekly, monthly, summer plans reflect our efforts to make love a part of our lives.

Don't we have to teach our children the importance of money, hard work, and giving back to the community? Yes. All important aspects of life are taught. But they must be approached from a loving angle. Recently, our daughter who is a photographer took a trip to another country. She was stepping out on a rooftop to take a picture when the roof caved in. She called me later that day and told me she'd miss much of the trip because she was bedridden by her injuries. She wrote on her blog that the experience made her more sensitive to the losses she had seen during some of her travels as she watched crippled men and women make their way through the streets. She also wrote emails to me explaining her desire to teach art to children in disadvantaged environments and to learn from them. She wanted to share not only her art supplies, but also her love. Her writings were rich and wise beyond her years. By the end of that same week she called again. She said, "Mom, I feel really bad. You paid all of this money for me to see these places, and I ruined it." I replied, "Caty, I sent you on the trip for you to grow in character and heart. I more than got my money's worth."

When your values are about love and giving from your spiritual gifts, you can't miss. You don't have to have money to give love. Your children don't have to work twelve-hour days. They don't have to get rich quick. They don't have to be straight-A students. We never have to worry that our integrity, patience, endurance, and joy will be unwanted. The time you take now to look at your values, what you believe about God and what you want your children to believe about Him, is critical for them to feel grounded. If your children understand that God is good and wise, they will know they are ultimately safe and at home in His kingdom. It is critical for them to realize the magnitude of their activity here and that what they do with their lives matters. It will affect the friends they choose. And they, not you, will be told by the Holy Spirit what their purpose is. So your job is to open the doors and let them discover who they are spiritually. Let's not break their spirits. Let's walk solidly, but inquisitively with our children and leave room for love and self-discovery.

Another potential family value is to **make decisions based on wisdom, not feelings**. For example, the Bible says, "In your anger do not sin" (Ps. 4:4). Negative feelings chisel away character; wisdom builds it. Negative feelings also can leave depression and anxiety in their wake unless you use them to make positive changes in yourself. Wise coping skills (such as Character Tickets, Potters Clay, Seek the Lesson, baskets, reflection, meetings, and lists—all of which will be detailed later) interrupt feelings so you can live by God's power rather than your own. Healthy coping skills do one of two things: give feedback to try and improve a relationship or delay gratification of an emotion by waiting until the emotion subsides. Remember that an emotion is a chemical that can make us feel out of balance. Once we're steadied, we may decide the thought we had wasn't a big deal.

Family first is a critical value. Simply put, it means your family members come before friends and other activities. Uncommon Sense makes investing in family relationships simple and quick, so when the people under your care hurt one another, they can quickly reinvest in the relationship to prove their importance to each other. We live under the same roof. We're either related by blood or we took a vow to care for one another for a lifetime. God doesn't make mistakes. We may make mistakes in our choices of friends and where we invest our time outside the family, but we can be sure we are meant to make the flow of love a priority within our own home. So it comes first.

I will add a word of precaution here. I certainly understand that there are exceptions when family members are not safe to be around. I'm also making the point that it's family first, not family only. We cannot focus on relatives to the point we no longer understand the creativity and healthy diversity that exists in the society at large. We are designed to be curious and called to be respectful, and rich relationships outside the home are essential to learning to love people who are different from us.

Thankfulness rather than entitlement is a quality that every missionary mentions when they share their experiences from the field. People surrounded by poverty have nothing, but they are happy simply to have each other. This value can be taught in so many ways in a family. In part 5, I offer a suggestion for helping children learn how to handle money, but this value is about helping a family focus on thanking God often for what they do and don't have. In America, children are taught that taxes pay for police, military, firemen, streets, bridges, and people who take on the responsibility of governing us. Rather than complain about these people, our children would profit from hearing us give thanks that some people are willing to spend their lives working to ensure that we can live as freely as we do. Thankfulness lines up with the scriptures about focusing on that which is good. If I have eaten, am relatively healthy, have a warm, safe bed, and had someone speak kindly to me, I am so blessed.

RESPONSIBILITIES

Once you have made a list of the core values you want to live out, it is time to look at the hard facts of everyday life on earth. Make a list of all of the things that have to be done to get through a day such as carpools, chores, errands, and afterschool activities. Then, make a list of those things that require your attention on a weekly and monthly basis. That shouldn't take more than half an hour. Sit down with your partner/soul mate and assign responsibilities. You may want to let your children choose a few at a later family meeting, or you may decide that their full-time job, school, and their part-time extracurricular activities (sports, arts, homework, learning to socialize) are enough responsibility for weekdays.

Each person can put in an hour of house cleaning or lawn care on the weekend, and they will learn responsibility and a good work ethic. And the best thing of all? Once you finish this list, there will be no need to discuss "who does what and when" any more. All you will need is the list and integrity. Most people are not accustomed to doing what they say they will do. Over time, your new lifestyle will change that.

Put this list in the front of a pocketed notebook and ask each family member to sign their initials beside their responsibilities. By signing, they confirm that they know their own jobs and are willing to be held accountable for doing them. All of those conversations about, "I thought you said *you* were going to do it" will not need to happen. You can talk about pleasantries instead. You can find an example of a responsibility list in the appendix, and in part 5 we'll talk about responsibilities and jobs.

Later, you and the family will want to make a list of privileges because sometimes having privileges is contingent on having first met responsibilities. Privileges are activities or objects that bring pleasure. Electronic devices such as phones, for example, are typically given to a child when he or she is old enough to afford and care for one. Sleepovers, parties, and eating out are typically seen as privileges earned by children who behave responsibly outside the home. In most cases, it is a good idea to state the privileges as time-limited and based on performance. "You can play basketball this season, if you maintain a C average." "You can have a phone if …" That way, maintaining the privilege is up to them, not you. By the way, if you micromanage, it will not be a privilege. It will become another chore.

Free time is not a privilege; it is a necessity. Free time is an individual's window to take time for him or herself on a daily basis to do whatever he or she wants. It can be high energy, low energy, secluded, social, laid back, or intense. You may discuss which games or shows they choose, for example, but they are allowed a time for them. It is a time slot when they get a dose of whatever their soul needs. It is a necessity. It allows for self-expression.

Toxic Coping Skills

List some behaviors that your family has adopted for dealing with difficulties. Toxic coping strategies are ways of handling things that do damage to the user or to others or both. Fake crying, tattling, tantrums, yelling, shunning, screaming, lying, drugs, overuse of alcohol, complaining, gossiping, backtalk, lecturing, whining, arguing, bickering, nagging, interrupting, hitting, running away, acting out—these are ineffective and immature coping strategies. We call them ineffective because the person who uses them stays stuck in a level of immaturity. Healthier, more mature people prefer to converse about problems, try to hear one another's perspectives, and then either move toward compromise or agree to treat one another lovingly despite their differences.

Some people convince themselves that giving someone a cold shoulder is an effective way of coping. They shun routinely and explain it away by saying, "She's unpleasant, and I can't have that around me," "I'm just not going to be around him when he's like that," or a number of other things that justify a lack of love in the face of pain.

A trigger is something or someone that causes you to experience bad feelings. Moving away from a trigger for a few moments until you can clear your head and recall the good things about a person is wise, but if it takes you hours or days to get over your bad feelings about someone, the problem may be more about you than him or her. If this describes you, seek counsel with a loving person and have them help you find a better way to cope. People heal in the presence of love, not in the absence of it. Running from your problems won't make them go away.

Remembrance of Better Times

I was at a church concert last summer. The band played music from the 70s, 80s, 90s, and today. Many of our friends were there. Couples were dancing as if they were still in college. We talked later about what a free time that had been and how different we had been before we started families and took on so many responsibilities. People looked wistful as they recalled gentler, more easygoing versions of themselves.

Always remember to encourage one another. Before you leave this day of hard work, chat about a time when you can recall really liking who you were. What qualities did you most enjoy about yourself? Think of a person you liked being around. What did he or she bring out in you? Think back to when you first felt important to someone else. What made you feel special? A marriage without soul talk lacks luster. Talk to one another about a time when you were a person who responded to life more positively more often. Choose the word you prefer: responsibly, kindheartedly, respectfully, thoughtfully, patiently, generously, joyously, honestly, adventurously, whimsically. Write a celebratory statement that your life can be approached from that simpler, more playful, positive angle and you are going to get started now.

Meeting 2: Initial Family Buy-In

At family meetings, the tone should *always* be kind, respectful, and upbeat. If you hog the stage or speak sternly, others will keep their mouths shut and will loathe participating in them. Bring a notebook that has your family name written on the front, values and responsibilities listed inside, and lots of blank pages for contributions, updates, and meeting notes.

Share Values List

During this initial meeting, share your list of values with your family and let them add to it if they want. Ask them what they think of the list you have made together. If your children offer values that you disagree with, offer to think about them for a while rather than arguing about them in the moment. Sometimes, children have a simple wisdom that defies our own. Explain that this list of values is like having a map that keeps you on track and focused on what is really important as you decide how to live together as a family.

Prepare the Family for a Lifestyle Change

At this meeting, you will tell your family you are going to adopt a new lifestyle with them and that you need their help. Tell them that instead of the typical disciplinary methods that most families use to help their children learn, you are going to use some simple coping skills and fun tools. Give them some modeling clay,[17] tell them to turn it into anything they want, and have them put it on a little plate. (This clay will be used to help change habits and will be discussed in chapter 31.) Keep them in suspense about what they will do with it. Just explain that it is one of the new tools and that you'll be using it a lot.

Explain Toxic Coping Skills

Most of us have heard of toxic waste. *Toxic* means "damaging or harmful," and toxic coping strategies are ways of handling things that do damage to the user or to others or both. They are ways that cause us to either vent our emotions or stuff our emotions without considering the cost. Raging, stuffing, and numbing are never satisfying. Communication and intimacy are what we want. It takes courage to admit to your children that some of the ways you have been parenting are wrong. Yet it is foolish to pretend that they will not adopt your strategies and to assume they do not recognize when you are out of control, mean, or insensitive.

Explain that the lifestyle you are about to introduce is designed to make you a more loving partner to your spouse and a more loving and likable parent. Tell the children it is based on the teachings of Christ and that, with their help, you are going to give up some of your bad habits. Better yet, ask them to tell *you* what you do that they don't like, and see what

---

17 Modeling clay can often be found at dollar stores or other inexpensive places in the craft or children's section. If you use playdough or a substance that hardens quickly, you'll need to let them make some toothpick holes in it before it dries up.

they say. Try to make this fun. If no one will talk (because they don't want to hurt you or they fear retribution) you can get the ball rolling this way:

"What if I give up my habit of talking rudely when you do something I don't like? How about my yelling/complaining/grounding/spanking based on mood rather than wisdom/confronting you in front of others/interrupting you to demand my own way? Do I ever do those things? Do you wish I'd give those habits up?"

This level of authenticity and intimacy is intoxicatingly freeing. It makes people laugh, cry, or wonder. It seldom shuts them down. Rather, they are likely to feel free to confess their own failings and desires. The precondition, of course, is to offer your truth out of honesty and love, not manipulation.

EXPLAIN HEALTHY COPING SKILLS AND ANCHOR SCRIPTURES

Explain that you've discovered that in order to get to know God better and to inherit the life He wants for you, you have to let His ways be yours. Then, before they have time to groan and think you're about to buckle down, reassure them that they are going to learn how God brings freedom, not slavery, and read them some of the Scriptures this lifestyle is going to teach you to use. As you read them, ask if others agree that these Biblical ways of life would be nice. Look at the two examples below:

> **Read:** "Let everything you say be good and helpful, so that your words will be an encouragement to those who hear them" (Eph. 4:29-32 NLT).

> **Share:** "That means I'm going to try to focus on what you're doing right rather than what you're doing wrong!"

> **Ask the buy-in question:** "Would you like that?"

Read: "Do justice, love kindness, and walk humbly with your God" (Micah 6:8 OAB).

Share: "That means that if you've had a good day and then do a few wrong things, I'm not going to act like the whole day was bad. Doing justice means looking at the whole person or situation, not just a snapshot. Being kind means realizing that we all fail and we all stumble. I'm going to try to be as nice after you fail as before. Walking humbly with God means letting humans be human and not trying to control everything they do. I will try to remember to offer a wise response rather than rudeness and vengeance when things don't go my way."

Ask the buy-in question: "Do you agree with these philosophies?"

An anchor is designed to keep a ship in place. Scriptures are designed to keep our lives in place. Uncommon Sense "anchor scriptures" are verses that keep you from drifting back to old parenting styles and old rationalizations. It's hard to keep telling yourself that you have to yell and be mean, if you remember that God has told us that "man's anger does not produce the righteous life that God desires" (James 1:20).

I found that when I anchored my life with some simple, loving scriptures I began to like myself and my family more. If you have a spiritually mature family, you may want to bring this book and read some of this lifestyle's anchor scriptures (listed in the appendix), or some of your own that have convicted you to transform your everyday habits. Ask your family for some of their favorite passages if they have some and talk about what each anchor scripture means in everyday terms. Put your favorites in your family book.

Introduce One or Two New Tools

Explain that you have some fun new tools to help everyone handle little challenges in everyday life. Before this meeting, familiarize yourself with one of the tools and introduce it to the family. For example, the basket tool may be an easy one for the family to adopt because it is very helpful and user friendly. Or you may want to teach them to put up their little finger this week (or say "ouch") if you bring up a topic they don't want to talk about.

A fist with a raised pinky finger is an "i" in sign language. At our house, it stands for "issue." That means, "What may be a positive interest for you, Mom, is an issue for me. I'd rather not talk about it." Remind everyone to keep a pleasant demeanor when they lift their pinkies. No words. No scowls or stiff, angry gestures. Just lift a pinky, and the speaker will respectfully change the topic. Truthfully, this usually makes people laugh, but sometimes it hurts their feelings. In time, it becomes an effective way to get to know what topics are pleasant and unpleasant to someone else. Remember that an issue is something we set aside for an agreed upon time, not something we ignore and never discuss.

It's critical for this first meeting to go well and leave everyone feeling good, so keep it simple and cheery. The new family standard is "uncommon consensus." It is important to know where everyone stands. So if they don't talk, ask. Everyone gets heard and no one has a "stupid idea."

End the meeting by letting the family know that at least once a week you'll be having a meeting (shorter than this one) to discuss important family topics, and the rest of the week you're going to try to talk about positives. Also, tell them that by next week's meeting, you'll teach them more about the clay and some other tools you'll all be using for your "out with the old, in with the new" way of life. Finish the meeting by telling each person one thing you like about him/her and share a hug.

DIGGING DEEPER

(AND ACTING ON WHAT YOU LEARN!)

Go to the store before your family meeting. Get a big notebook with pocket dividers. In the first section, write the key points you want to make at this first meeting. Remember, one of the keys to this lifestyle is simplicity. A notebook with a family picture on it is a simple place to store and recall ideas and decisions for the family as a whole and for each member. If you attempt to store these details in your minds, you will have to deal with clashes in memory and information overload.

During the meeting, use the first section of the notebook to chronicle the values, as well as bad habits and things your family members want to see changed. They will know their thoughts are important to you because you are writing them down. This is a demonstration of collaboration.

Take notes about family values, toxic coping skills, and any topics or concerns that come up. You may or may not be able to discuss everything. Be sensitive to your audience's age and ability to sit. Make it fun with refreshments if appropriate and remember that timing is everything. The meeting should be announced well ahead of time, so no one has made other plans. You want a friendly crowd.

CHAPTER 25

UNCOMMON CONSENSUS — MAINTAINING THE FLOW

"Again I tell you that if two of you on Earth agree about anything you ask for, it will be done for you by my Father in Heaven. For where two or three come together in my name, there am I with them."

—MATTHEW 18:19-20

U NCOMMON CONSENSUS IS A TERM my oldest daughter, Bentley, came up with one day when she was driving to Nashville pondering my chapter on meetings. Meetings are designed to get everyone in the know, and *in agreement* as much as possible. One extraordinary quality of the Uncommon Sense lifestyle is that the forms of discipline are practiced by *all* family members — parents included. In other words, not only do parents give children feedback, but children are also taught to give their parents feedback in respectable, predictable ways *so the children are learning subconsciously, by the parent's example, how to* receive *feedback with poise and appreciation.* Parents, as well as children, are held accountable for the ways they behave. At meetings, all family members are encouraged to offer ideas for ways to improve life at home, assign responsibilities, determine needs, schedule vacations and family projects, and troubleshoot problems. Of course, parents have the lead and the final say, but all members are aware that their opinions make a difference in the final outcome.

Weekly collaborative meetings are the only way to minimize, but not avoid, tough topics, agree on how challenges will be handled, and acknowledge the importance of freedom and accountability. Since we are trying to keep love flowing as much as possible, these meetings are a welcome relief from all those annoying and mediocre interventions. Over time, I found that almost all issues of daily life could be handled with four simple types of collaborative meetings:

- **Family meetings:** Held once a week to keep us on track as a family and help us understand, love, and support one another
- **Evening updates:** Held daily to manage spaghetti junction under the roof and affirm what we are doing right
- **Heart-to-hearts:** One-on-one meetings held as needed to discover if we are still in agreement of what is important in life
- **Character time:** Held as needed to do damage control for struggling relationships

WEEKLY FAMILY MEETINGS

Once a week, you should round up the family and sit together to talk about what is going right and what needs improvement as well as dreams, hopes, preferences, and family standards. This is a great time to reread your family values and ask everyone if they think they are living into them. These are lengthy (30 minutes to 1 hour) depending on the members' abilities to stay involved. All family members *collaborate*. You want to come to a consensus. Why? Because now that you have read about human nature you understand that there are a variety of brains and personalities and gifts that your family standards need to fit.

Family meetings are meant to be upbeat and led by an authority figure. Ideally, the parents come to the meeting with a short list of topics they think need to be discussed. This is "buy in" time. In other words, this is the time you strike agreements so that during the week, when life is difficult and hectic, you can live what you believe, not just what feels good or what has been typical for you. Family meetings are a great opportunity to teach people to talk one person at a time, stay on topic, and enjoy one another. Having said that, if you don't allow a certain amount of fun, encouragement, and honesty, people will dread coming to these. This is not a time for public condemnation. If two of you have a beef, save it for after the meeting. And there should be no verbal pile-ons. (A pile-on is when more than one person jumps on another.) If you are leading the meeting, you have the job of keeping it safe and sane.

Topics for Weekly Family Meetings

- ALWAYS compliment the family on the positive, healing choices that have been made during the week.
- Remind the family of standards that were agreed upon and make sure everyone still agrees on them (this is called "buy in"). The important standards to cover are the ones that are being ignored. But make note of the ones that are going well to encourage them. Everyone's opinion counts. Sometimes the reason standards are being ignored is that they are too strict, unnecessary or just need to be tweaked. This allows for brainstorming and for everyone to feel respected and heard.
- Decide on a family project for the month. Put it on the calendar and make it a priority. (Examples of these projects include: cleaning the garage, painting a room, washing windows, giving away things you no longer need, or helping an elderly or sick neighbor.)
- Change daily or weekly responsibilities, if necessary, so that each person is doing what they do best.
- Converse about hopes and dreams as well as vacations, holidays, friendships, and faith.

- Use a family notebook to take notes. Let people initial the meeting notes page to make the point, "I was here to hear this information. You can hold me accountable for it." My daughter, Caty, was often our note taker because she was the most restless during these meetings. I still have one of the papers that says, "meeting #3486." Trust me, there haven't been that many! It's fun to go back to the book when someone says, "You never told me that." Once they see that you did, and that they initialed it, you will both get a laugh out of it instead of a scowl.

Evening Updates

These are my personal favorite. They are frequent, quick meetings (5 to 10 minutes) always led by a parent with a pleasant, upbeat attitude. I come manned with my calendar, a notepad, and a list of issues that came to mind during the day but were not mentioned at the time because they would not have been received as positives. If I have five things on that issues list, I'm going to choose and mention only the most important to my peace of mind. Too much content overpowers the participants and can be forgotten more easily.

Evening Updates have four parts:

- **Affirmations:** Mention what we are doing right. *Always begin the meeting with affirmations.*
- **Needs:** Ask who needs support. What materials or encouragements are needed for work or school? Christ poured himself out as a fragrant offering. This is my chance to demonstrate what that looks like.
- **Calendar:** Ask and let everyone know what is happening this week. Write it down.
- **Reminders:** Issues. Quickly note what needs improvement. Remind family members of basic commitments that may be forgotten. These should not sound like a lecture. They're not meant to be rude or preachy; just a few upbeat sentences to keep things on track will do. (For example, you might say,

"Remember to empty your baskets, and put your dishes in the sink. Thanks, everyone.")

Note: If only one person needs a reminder on a certain topic, hold him/her at the end of the meeting and mention it to them in private. And do so quickly and kindly. This is not the time for a heart-to-heart because the people attending are coming for what you promised would be a quick meeting. Heart-to-hearts need to happen when both people have agreed to give an extra measure of time to one another. Remember, if these update meetings become lengthy, people will *dread* them.

With older children, these updates can be done standing up: call the family into the room, have them stand around you, and make it happen. If your family life is uncomplicated, you may not need them every night, but they really eliminate those late-night trips to the office supply store for poster boards you didn't know your kids were going to need. Also, every time you bring the family together as a whole and create a positive moment, you are telling them subconsciously that they belong to something good.

Heart-to-Hearts

These are one-on-one meetings. (Occasionally they include more than one parent, but always only one child.) The next chapter includes a description of them since they are one of the key ways you will teach your child to navigate life when modeling, mentioning, and reminding doesn't work.

Character Time/ Issue Time

Some families like to call these Character time and others call them Issue time because they deal with more than just tickets. These are meetings that are designed to bring an authority figure and two children together to review Character Tickets, experience conviction, offer forgiveness, and assure that loving time is being poured back into relationships after damage has been done. They are explained in detail in chapter 30.

DIGGING DEEPER

MEETINGS

Which of the meetings will be most difficult for you? Why?

For example, let's say one of your children is a morning wreck waiting to happen. Your mornings are difficult because he forgets his homework, can't find his shoes, and isn't making it to breakfast with the family, so tucking in a quick family devotion and prayer isn't happening for him. He's struggling and starving, and it is affecting all of you. He needs love and support. During a heart to heart you might say, "It seems like you are not getting everything you need for school ready the night before."

You want to say, "It's driving us all crazy!", but that probably isn't true. The other children in the family are probably busy running their own lives, unless you make a spectacle of him in front of them. Perhaps your children don't like *your* anger when he fails, so they blame him for your angry behavior. (Lots of projection going on.) When someone triggers you, you may be triggering others with your toxic responses. This book is going to help you correct this. That was the way you used to think, and you have to do something new to build a new interstate to morning kindness and a day that doesn't start out with issues. So, instead of saying, "It's driving us crazy," you say, "I don't want your mornings to be stressful. Can I help you put your things together and sit them by the door before you go to bed?" Whether he is two or 22, he may not have a brain that organizes things easily.

Recently, I was conversing with a mother whose adult son is living with her. She said, "He is very messy and disorganized." I recommended to her that she come beside him and model how to clean and organize his room. She teared up and responded, "I can't. *I don't know how.* No one will want to marry him. And I'm divorced, so I'm no example." Can you hear how her response to his messiness is based on her fear that he will end up like her if he is messy like her? Yet millions of messy people are married, successful, and have friends. She just needs to do her best to help him do his best and then pray and have hope, faith, and love, but the greatest of these is love (1 Cor.13:13).

Now, I'll ask the question again. Which of the meetings will be the most difficult for you? Why? Remember, awareness is the first step toward change.

- **Family meetings (30 minutes to 1 hour):** Focused on values, coping strategies, dreams, responsibilities, and belonging
- **Evening updates (5–10 minutes)**
- **Heart-to-hearts (Time Varies):** Focused on values. Do we still agree about what is important?
- **Character time (Time Varies):** Focused on accountability and repair for damaged relationships

CHAPTER 26

INTERVENTION STRATEGIES

*"Let your speech always be gracious, as though seasoned with salt,
so that you will know how you ought to answer everyone."*

—COLOSSIANS 4:6 (OAB)

What is an intervention? It is an attempt by a group of loved ones to help someone admit and overcome a damaging habit. It is an intrusion into someone else's affairs.

What is a strategy? A strategy is an effective plan of action. It's an artful means to an end.

It takes time to change. I have a delightful friend, Sandy, who quoted a verse of the Bible one day while we were discussing how children grow, rebel, and think they are wiser than their parents. Children think parents just don't get it. The verse Sandy quoted was, "Train up a child in the way he should go, and when he is old he will not depart from it" (Prov. 22:6). I heard that verse often as a child. But Sandy's emphasis was on the word "old." "When they are *old*," she repeated. "Never forget, it takes time. It all takes time."

We have talked about the importance of keeping the atmosphere of a home positive and uplifting. While you are waiting for yourself and others to become more responsible, wise, and capable, you can practice nagging and lecturing—which you already know doesn't work and makes you feel like you want to crawl out of your skin—or you could map out a new plan of action to help yourself and the people you love. Here's the positive plan.

Begin with the least intrusive intervention and move to increasingly intrusive support as it is needed. When someone lets you down by forgetting or ignoring his agreements with you, *model* the behavior you want. If that doesn't work, *mention* it. If that doesn't do the trick, *remind* him of the commitment. The next step is to have a *heart-to-heart* with him. And if that isn't fruitful, establish relationship-building *consequences*. This order—model, mention, remind, heart-to-heart, consequence—moves from least intrusive support to the most. These forms of support can be given in the right place at the right time, and they will work. This system is designed to integrate kind communication and show respect for the individual at every level. It avoids nagging and insistence, something Christ asks Christians to give up.

MODEL

You told your spouse you would love for him to mute the TV when you talk to him, kiss you when he walks in the door, and take the dog for a walk after dinner. He agreed. But it will take a while for him to make a habit of doing these things. So while he is transitioning, model the behaviors you want: mute the TV when he talks to you, kiss him when he walks in the door, and offer to walk the dog with him.

Do you want people to sit up straight at the table? Without a word, straighten your own posture while they are watching you. If you actually had an agreement that someone would sit "properly" at the table, your example will be more effective than verbal correction. Want someone to lower his or her voice? Lower yours. It can be catching.

MENTION

If modeling the behavior is going straight over a loved one's head, *mention* the agreement with a word: Kiss. Dog. These verbalizations—delivered at the appropriate time in a pleasant tone of voice—are more powerful than giving a history of failure, asking why it isn't happening, or pleading for it to be done "sometime tonight."

Remind

If you have mentioned the hoped for behavior and nothing changed, you can move to a bolder strategy: *remind*. But it is best to set up this strategy ahead of time. Let's say your husband decides at a family meeting that it is a nice idea for family members to greet one another affectionately when they get home rather than ignoring one another by continuing to talk to someone else on their cell. You can say to him, "I want to support this change. Do you want me to remind you when you forget?" If he says, "Yes, remind me," then he probably does want to incorporate this change into your lives, and he has given you permission to help. If he says "No," he may have faith in his ability to handle it without you. Or he may not like the way you support him. Also, you may have just discovered that an affectionate greeting isn't a behavior he really believes in, and it is unlikely that he will change his old ways. In any case, move on. There is a scripture that says these four words: "Mind your own business" (1 Thess. 4:11). As hard as that can be, there is an intelligence to it. When your child sees you're disappointed in your spouse, it does not make life more pleasant. Don't be the family policeman.

Remind means one short sentence: "You want to greet others affectionately when you walk in the door." That's it. If they do it, fine. If they don't do it, fine. If greetings are important to you, then *you* do it and move on. Remember that the adults in the house set the example, including how they treat one another when they fail. Children receive great value from their parents' simple, intelligent actions. When they are old, they will remember being blessed by your ways.

Heart-to-Heart

We just mentioned this under the section detailing meetings, but it is worth mentioning again. You know what a heart-to-heart is. It's a conversation two people have when they share their truths, remember what they believe in, and uncover the deepest parts of themselves. A heart-to-heart is done away from spectators. It's special because your agenda is to hear and understand one another. When you do this, some of your agreements will change, because you will understand one another on a different level than you did before the conversation took place (2 Thess. 3:5).

If I had a nickel for all of the times I have corrected my children in front of one another, I could take the family on vacation. I *don't* believe in it. Public reprimands are foolish. When humans are corrected publicly, they are so busy trying to save face in front of the crowd that they don't hear half of what is said. Furthermore, they don't want the insensitive chastiser to profit from hurtful, ill-timed words. Have you ever felt embarrassed when you saw someone else be corrected in public?

Did you ever play a game called "Pile-On"? One person is lying innocently on the floor, and someone yells, "Pile on!" One by one, people rush over and pile on top of him or her until there is a mound of humans. I don't recommend it. The person on the bottom can be hurt or smothered. I don't know what the purpose was except to make the person on the bottom miserable and everyone else laugh. "Pile-on communication" is when one person has a criticism of a person in the room, and someone else adds *to* it. Sometimes, several people will agree with the criticism, and the victim feels ganged up on or humiliated, or smothered. Nothing good comes from this. Too much salt covers up the flavor that the food was intended to have. People tend to assume an arrogant attitude when there is a preponderance of agreement on a subject. It sounds like this: "We're right. You're wrong. You need to change." Well, that may be true, but because the pile-on and arrogance were distasteful, the victim is less likely to want to please anyone by changing.

Undoubtedly, heart-to-hearts are preferable to public correction, but too many of them will lessen their effectiveness. These intimate conversations need to be well timed. You need to be in a kind mood; both of you need to be ready. Ideally, you will ask the other person if there is a good time to mention a concern of yours (in private). Remember the family dynamic of being willing to wait. A well-timed meeting will often produce a good result. A poorly-timed meeting may produce more strife. If you want others to be okay with these heart-to-hearts, make them short and be a great listener. Be willing to work their impressions into your future standards whenever possible. Model the value of these intimate conversations by being willing to stop what you are doing when they ask for time alone with you. When you and another person have said you are in agreement about family, the home, character, beliefs, and standards but then ignore your commitments to one another, you both need to figure out what is going on. (See Matt. 18:15; Gal. 6:1.)

CONSEQUENCES

Make it count. If others don't follow through on their responsibilities, what are they willing to give or sacrifice to show that their word matters? Remember to discuss consequences ahead of time. If possible, let them decide, and don't make consequences too severe. Frequent, unexpected or harsh consequences can change people, but they can also lead to wounds that last a lifetime and can often ruin a relationship. Why? Your loved ones will learn that they can only count on you to be unpredictable and harsh.

I am often asked what is different about this book, what makes it special. I believe it is the loving windows of time this lifestyle produces. I recommend that small increments of time be given when we fail one another repeatedly and unapologetically. (See chapters 29 and 30 for more on this.) These minutes spent together build good memories and enhance the love within the relationship. Privileges may occasionally be pulled, but more loving activity is being added. Furthermore, the person who needs to change gets a say in how and when the loving time is spent. Ideally, the activity reflects the personality, gifts, and interests of both the person who is trying to change and the person who is hoping for the change. A list of loving consequences can be agreed upon before they are needed. (You can find some ideas in part 5.)

DIGGING DEEPER

AND ACT

Get a Post-it Note or a 3x5 card, and write down these five intervention strategies. Begin to intervene with these forms of support from least intrusive to more intrusive. Over time, you will see improvement in your relationships with others, and you will be more pleasant to live with, too.

- **Model** — Set an example by doing it yourself
- **Mention** — Say a word or two
- **Remind** — Reach an agreement on how to remind someone of a commitment
- **Heart-to-heart** — Seek to understand whether they are still in agreement
- **Consequences** — Make it count (If possible, let them decide what will help them follow through on their commitment. Look for a positive.)

If you are trying to instill a behavior and these strategies aren't helping, look at chapter 40.

CHAPTER 27

WEEKLY/MONTHLY ACTIVITIES — ESTABLISHING A NEW LIFE RHYTHM

"But the Lord said to her, 'My dear Martha, you are upset over all these details! There is really only one thing worth being concerned about. Mary has discovered it — and I won't take it away from her.'"

— LUKE 10:41 (NLT)

NONE OF THE ACTIVITIES I am about to define were a part of my routine growing up. When I was a child, backtalk wasn't applauded on TV. My nights weren't littered with endless homework or sports. I didn't drive four hours to play a one-hour game. A greater percentage of fathers lived with their birth children and first wives, and they were home for dinner at night. By and large, that's not the way it is anymore.

So after trying to parent traditionally for eight years, I realized we needed new ways to make home life predictable, safe, and soothing. We needed a way to do chores quickly and infrequently, and we needed everyone to contribute to the maintenance of the home. I was unwilling to constantly interrupt everyone's relaxation and joy to get domestic needs met. I had done it for years and had had enough. I wanted to make time to have dates with my husband, enjoy my children, and teach values rather than preferences.

Here are the areas which needed regular, but not necessarily daily, attention.

- Church
- One hour of chores per person (Weekly)
- Couple's date (Weekly)
- Family meetings (Weekly)
- One-on-one child/parent date (Monthly)
- Family work day (Monthly)
- Couple's getaway (Monthly or Bimonthly)
- Pay off debts (Varies in accordance with children's ages and needs)

CHURCH

The richest days of our family's lives were when we were attending a church where the people were fun, "normal," friendly, and enjoyed eating and spending time together. There were literally Sundays when we would arrive at church at 9 AM and return home twelve hours later after having spent the whole day with fellow believers and then finishing the day at a pizza joint together after the evening service. Our children attended Wednesday night Bible studies, and we ate dinner at the church, which I loved because I didn't have to cook or clean that night.

The funny thing is that the year before our family began this activity, I couldn't imagine how the family down the street worked it into their busy lives. Susie and Jim had five children, and we only had three. Their children were popular and active in school. They all had good grades, excelled in their extracurricular activities, and were always impeccably dressed. Both Jim and Susie were active professionally and taught at church. Know what I learned? God has a clock of His own. Jim and Susie invited our family to a musical at their church. It was so fun! Then we attended a service. It was moving. Then, Wednesday nights became a refreshing ritual, and we still got home in time for an ice cream cone and a little TV time.

Church doesn't take hours that you don't have. God makes the time up to you. Honestly, He does. You will find that out if you start giving time to Him. Over the years, the hours we spent at church have varied according to the changing rhythm of our life as a family. What does God want for you? Listen to your conscience. There can be no doubt that He wants you in His house with uncommon, loving, joyful believers. You might be the person they have all been waiting for.

One Hour of Chores

Every home requires maintenance. All the parents I know want their children to learn the value of hard work and taking care of what they have been given. This can be learned in one hour a week by expecting your child to chip in on the weekend. Home maintenance is something that must be done in order for us to keep life in order. Don't pay your kids for this time. Don't yell or nag. Have a day of the week when you expect each family member to chip in and tell them all matter-of-factly what needs to be done. Tell them that if they do it with a good attitude and happen to finish before the hour is up to come and show you; that's it. Be sure to notice what they did right, and be cautious about perfectionism.

Our culture has our children working at night as well as during the day. Homework seems to increase every year. Sports are not played freely — they are overseen by adults who tell your children what to do. To be healthy, people need down time, so consider easing up on household responsibilities during the week and compile chores for one serious window of time. This approach eliminates nagging tired family members who just need a balance of relaxation to refresh themselves for their work tomorrow. On a weekday, by the time you could nag for help, you could have done the job yourself and been less tired than if you fussed at someone. Not everyone does the dishes at night, makes their beds daily, keeps their clothes picked up or washed, or dusts and vacuums weekly. Some of those people who don't are your neighbors. Did you know that?

Couple's Date

I don't know if there is a better way to help a family feel stable than to have both parents (biological or not) under the roof and in love. If you are married, have a date every week. (A list of ideas can be found in part 5.) The idea is to spend a couple of hours of uninterrupted companionship doing something you both enjoy. If the children are young and you are a little short on funds, just go into the bedroom and do something outside of the routine while the children sleep or watch TV. The purpose is to recapture time alone combined with romance, play, or some other positive and freeing emotion that reminds you of why you are journeying through this challenging life together as friends and lovers.

One-on-One Child/Parent Date

Once a month, give each child time alone with you for two or three *uninterrupted* hours. Go to the park. Buy an ice cream cone, and sit, chat, and laugh. There is no better way to tell a child that you love him or her than a monthly dose of love. A child psychologist once told me that she considers this monthly date the most important thing a parent can do for a child because it provides him or her with undivided attention, relaxation, and fun. Jim used to spend money on his dates with the girls. My dates were mostly free. Hiking, skipping rocks, baking mud pies, and window shopping were popular. We visited lots of parks and libraries, collected leaves, and made collages.

Family Workday

Once a month, demonstrate the value of community service. During these times, the members of a family work together toward a goal. Participate in a project that benefits the whole family, the community, the church, or the world. Clean out a room or closet and take some of it to a charity. Clean up the yard or plant flowers for a neighbor. Paint a dingy room to show the family how inexpensive and simple it is to modify and beautify your home. This is a wonderful time to teach your children the domestic skills they will need when they have their own homes and vehicles. Work on a Habitat for Humanity house. Run a relay for a special cause. At Thanksgiving break, we each take a bag and give away the things we don't use or need and give it to others as a way of saying "Thank You" to God for all we have. If your house is in good shape, you could go to a nursing home and read or work in an elderly neighbor's yard. You can even take your children to the Red Cross and let them watch as you donate blood.

Spend at least three hours *or* the amount of time it takes to get the job done. Explain ahead of time that attitudes have to stay positive or else the clock will stop and more service will be required from the grumbler to compensate for time and energy lost. No worksite can afford workers who grumble and complain; it is exhausting to everyone involved. (Do keep in mind that not all workers are beavers. Don't punish your otters for occasional playful pauses. Short breaks will refresh everyone if you allow them. Assign jobs and appreciate contributions with personalities and talents in mind.)

COUPLE'S GETAWAY

Once every month or two, get away with your partner overnight. Chat. Rest. Read to each other. Take walks. Watch romantic movies. Make love. Select a topic that's important to both of you and spend a few hours on one of your days away discussing it to help you get and stay on the same page.

PAY OFF DEBTS

With this lifestyle, loving time spent with others is the primary form of discipline. At some point in the week, each family member will be required to pay time to the relationships they devalued. It may sound like a consequence that doesn't hurt and won't change people, but it does hurt in the sense that it is a major imposition. No one wants to be required to give up free time, yet that is what the lifestyle requires, and it does inspire people to think before they act.

There are two major ways that we can make loving deposits back into relationships that have been robbed.

- **"I'm sorry. Will you forgive me?"** Nothing can be substituted for these six simple words. Period. No buts, no explanations, no excuses.
- **Positive Action.** Our words matter, but our willingness to exchange a hurtful attitude or behavior for a more loving behavior is also key.

At least once a week, draw a line in the sand, so parents and children are required to put family first and set friends and electronics aside. Perhaps that will be a Sunday because it is set aside by many Christians as a day of relaxation and restoration, but any day will do. Perhaps your family will be good at paying debts as soon as they are incurred rather than waiting for a specific day of the week. When children are young, a parent needs to be available to monitor time together and be sure the time stays loving. Whatever day you choose, free time doesn't begin until debts are paid. Once each person has paid their debts, they are free.

Audacious behavior

This includes actions that are extremely hurtful and make the home feel unsafe.

Time cost — Big

Jim and I each identified toxic coping strategies we used when we were angry, strategies that made the girls afraid of us. If we used one of them to cope with our frustrations, we owed the recipient three hours of loving time. What do you do when you throw a temper tantrum? Stay away from someone for hours or days? Yell at the top of your lungs? Get physical in your anger? Intimidate? If you don't know what makes people afraid of you, ask them. Let's not kid ourselves, these behaviors are damaging.

All five of us also agreed on three or four audacious behaviors for the children. We are talking about behaviors that need to stop immediately. Those will depend on the age of your children and what you think is way over the top in terms of damage. A couple of examples might be:

- Blocking the path to freedom during a physical fight with a sibling.
- Out of control anger that leads to cursing at a parent. (If this occurred because the parent's behavior was exasperating, you may owe them a date anyway. See Eph. 6:4 and Col. 3:21.)
- Direct disobedience (I said you could not go to Joe's house after school. You went. It was a lengthy discussion that just took place. There's *no* possibility that you "forgot.")

For audacious behaviors, the child pays time to a loving parent — even if it was a sibling who inspired the behavior. Why? The child needs love. Two children are unlikely to be able to sustain loving behavior for hours at a time. It is not the sibling's love that the child really wants anyway. So the parent will decide on an activity that needs to be done for the family or home, and the child will participate. The activity is simply designed to give you something constructive to do while you are spending loving time together. If you know how to do things around the house, this is the perfect time to teach them to your child — lovingly. (But remember the experiment with the college students. All time spent together cannot be work-oriented.)

Instead of overreacting, the parent can simply write a note that the audacious behavior occurred, date it, hand it to the child, and ask him or her to put it in a gift box labeled "IOU." By the end of the week, request payment. The child may help you clean a closet, paint a room, cook a meal, exercise, play a game or two, or just get in the car and tag around with you while you do your usual errands. Whatever the task, it will be done with an authority figure who is treating him or her well. You are demonstrating a life well lived. If you are bossy and perfectionistic, avoid activities that require work. The idea is to expose a child to your world while you fill him or her with love. That's it.

Words of caution:

- This is hard to remember, but you must give the ticket, not a lecture. The lecture was the old way. Keep treating them well and move on with life. Your composure and kindness will shock them as Christ's composure must have stunned the prostitute who received no condemnation from Him (John 8:1-11).

- Decide how much audacious tickets cost ahead of time. Charge the same amount no matter what the behaviors are. An audacious behavior costs X in your home. After all, God does not have a list of sins with value points beside them.

- If you tell your children that they are going to owe time but never require them to pay it, they probably won't change.

- If they have no life because they owe too much time, ease back on your expectations. A little of this goes a long way, and too much will break their spirits rather than build character.

- If you are a lonely parent, find a friend. Sadly, some parents find excuses to punish their children and keep them around. It is not your child's job to befriend you. They need time with friends their own age in order to grow intellectually and emotionally.

- If you integrate these weekly and monthly rituals into your family life, you will teach more about work, marriage, and family than anything you try to enforce on a daily basis. Because they are infrequent and predictable, they will become natural, and you will have enriched and simplified your life by doing them.

DIGGING DEEPER

ACTIVITIES

Was there a weekly or monthly activity that you can't imagine adding to your life? What's the hang-up?

- One hour of chores
- Couple's date
- One-on-one child/ parent date

- Family workday
- Couple's getaway
- Pay off debts

Is there a daily ritual that you can't imagine deleting from your life? Perhaps this is a good time to pray and ask God to help you find a way to unshackle yourself from the need to have things accomplished every day. Ask Him to teach you and your loved ones that less is more. Ask God to help you relinquish any of your daily patterns that are unimportant in His eyes.

CHAPTER 28

AN OPEN HEART

"The message God has planted in your heart is strong enough to save your soul."

—JAMES 1:21 (NLT)

THE SUBTITLE OF THE BOOK was going to be *Revolutionary Strategies for Experiencing God and Living Life in His Kingdom*. Pretty bold notion. And yet, the Bible tells us that the kingdom of God is in our midst (Luke 17:20-21). If God is near and longs for a relationship with us, let's reciprocate. Let's live according to the most espoused philosophies of the New Testament. Let's realize that the tone of Christ's teachings is one of consistency, wisdom, and even humor that we all find palatable. We are invited to live in the land of miracles, but too often we choose the path to ruin. Some people don't want to go home at night to a sobering, if not hellish, environment that they, themselves support because they have chosen human tradition over loving truth.

This section of the book—Make Room for Miracles—was designed to help you open your eyes and heart to new possibilities. You have been invited to rearrange your attitude, family dynamics, life rhythms, strategies, and communication styles. Why? Because an open, positive environment is an easier place for the breath of heaven to circulate. Ask God to blast into your life with this prayer:

Search me, O God, and know my heart;
test me and know my anxious thoughts.
See if there is any offensive way in me,
and lead me in the way everlasting.
　　　　　　　—PSALM 139:23-24

Pray it every day and watch what He reveals to you. Some of us have taken a long, wild ride as a result, but it's worth it in the end.

Make room for God. Remember your identity. You are overcoming the habits of the body by lining up your thinking with God's truth.

I remember a story of three middle school girls who decided one night to see what it was like to drink alcohol. They had someone buy them a bottle of vodka. They poured it into some water bottles. Later they walked over to a park to swing and drink. Within a matter of hours, one girl's parents, who were away leading a Christian parenting retreat, received a phone call:

"Meg has been brought to the house. She passed out from drinking too much alcohol, and we are afraid for her life! We don't want to get her into trouble, but poison control recommended emergency help."

What did the parents do? They were authentic. The retreat they were leading was designed to be intimate, and that was what the audience observed when they decided to explain the situation to the audience, pack up, and head home. Calm. Concerned but hopeful. Not angry. Unafraid to tell the truth to the audience about their child.

They met Meg and her caregiver at a children's hospital and spent the night. The next day, she was told she had ingested a near-lethal level of alcohol and was blessed to be alive. The girl felt physically better because she had received fluids throughout the night but was distraught because she had disappointed her parents. They kissed and reassured her. All of the parents confiscated the girls' phones and explained that there would be no interaction with one another or the outside world until their stories lined up. Only when they all told the truth about who gave them the liquor and why they decided to drink it would they be given access to one another. Other than that, the parents maintained a loving and concerned attitude and continued to treat their daughters with the same affection they had received before the incident occurred. Within hours, the stories lined up.

Later that year at a Christian teen retreat, the daughter spontaneously gave a testimony to hundreds of teens that drinking doesn't really make life better. And what about the audience who attended the retreat her parents had been leading? They thanked the leaders and told them that watching their calm, authentic, loving demeanor was better than a whole weekend of lectures.

The parent's calm and kind reactions may sound unreal. Remember the EMT who came upon his children in the field? These parents were accustomed to keeping calm heads when hardships hit. They didn't always do the right thing. Yet, they had a family philosophy of treating people well when they mess up. Sometimes it is easier to manage tragedies than it is to mop up spilt milk.

In 1987, Lewis M. Andrews published a remarkable book entitled *To Thine Own Self Be True: The Relationship Between Spiritual Values and Emotional Health*. In it, he presents some of our most difficult emotions—anxiety, guilt, fear, loneliness, and depression—and the particular unethical behaviors that typically cause them. Lewis says:

> [W]hen people begin to approach their psychological problems from a deeper, more spiritual point of view, some remarkable things can happen. Negative feelings that had lasted for years begin to dissipate and social difficulties with friends, colleagues, and family that had always troubled us are resolved in fascinating and unexpected ways. There is a newfound confidence and enthusiasm for living....We learn that the greatest wisdom of all lies not in listening to others but in being true to our deepest

selves....The more I learned to trust my intuitive wisdom, the less I felt I had to judge and manipulate other people.[18]

Our most important work on earth is to grow into an ever-deepening relationship with God. To succeed as Christ defines it is to enter into God's kingdom and be about His business. Whether you make ice cream cones or run a multi-billion dollar business, you can choose to succeed at life by learning about love and spreading it. Your relationship with God will lay the foundation for everything else you hold dear.

---

18 Andrews, Lewis M. To *Thine Own Self Be True*. pp.xiv-xv.

DIGGING DEEPER

AREAS OF CHANGE

Living in a loving environment is no assurance that one will not occasionally make bad decisions. On the other hand, I agree with Dr. Van Horn's poignant observation that we humans rarely go out for dog food if there is steak at home. In *Parenting for Prevention: How to Raise a Child to Say No to Alcohol/Drugs*, author David J. Wilmes describes a family that is too busy to ever eat together. He states that they lack a family spirit of love, belonging, and mutual support so the individuals look for it in other groups. When they connect with the group who is doing drugs and alcohol, these fake highs and relationships *feel* like the real thing. Wilmes then describes a number of techniques that he sees loving, close-knit, united families use to get where they are today: family schedules, activities, events, and meetings as well as house-utilization plan and house/yard work schedule. Sound familiar?

Circle the areas of change you believe are worth buying into:

FAMILY DYNAMICS

- Listening to God
- Learning to wait
- Teaching His ways
- Experiencing Love

STRATEGIC INTERVENTION

- Model
- Mention
- Remind
- Heart to heart
- Consequences

POSITIVE COMMUNICATION

- Positive affirmations
- Positive interests
- Positive invitations

WEEKLY/MONTHLY ACTIVITIES

- One hour of chores
- Couple's date
- Family workday
- One-on-one child/parent dates
- Couple's get away
- Pay off debts

COLLABORATIVE MEETINGS

- Evening updates
- Character/Issue time
- Heart-to-hearts
- Weekly family meetings

PART 4

The Uncommon Sense Lifestyle

MAKE ROOM FOR CHANGE

"Teach me your way, O Lord, and I will walk in Your truth."

—PSALM 86:11

MAKE ROOM FOR CHANGE

"And may you have the power to understand, as all God's people should, how wide, how long, how high, and how deep his love is. May you experience the love of Christ, though it is too great to understand fully."

— EPHESIANS 3:17-18 (NLT)

HOW CAN WE REMEMBER TO be attentive to God and be receptive to what He has for us when He is not visible or audible? We can do extraordinary things throughout the day that remind us of Him and make life different from what it is for most people. Many Christians who love God feel guilty that they don't take the time to read their Bibles in the morning or pray at night. But a wonderful book by Brother Lawrence called *Practicing the Presence of God* makes the point that we can worship God throughout the day as we live life with Him in mind.

The tools of the Uncommon Sense lifestyle are practiced in accordance with the scripture "Owe no one anything except to love one another, for he who loves another has fulfilled the law" (Rom. 13:8 NKJV). Justice is handled predictably and simply. Therefore, safety, integrity, and freedom become inherent for those involved, and our Father's kind magnificence is revealed along with an understanding of free will and the concept of reaping and sowing. All family members are held accountable for unkind and unthinking choices. Children are given a respectful voice. Everyone learns emotionally-intelligent ways of coping with unpleasantness.

If you are ready for a wonderful journey, let this section of the book open your eyes to new possibilities. Jim and I didn't start out with a list of responsibilities. We began with an invitation from an incredible counselor who advised us to wait until the evening to discuss everything that had bothered us during the day. Then, we were to spend no more than 15 minutes telling one another what wasn't working, sorting out the details, and apologizing for any ways we had hurt or offended one another.

When we first began, I couldn't do it. I couldn't keep my mouth shut when someone or something offended me. The kids came to me to referee their squabbles, they left their stuff scattered everywhere, they had more needs than I could handle, and I found myself folding clothes at 10:30 at night while my husband watched baseball. All of the junk that bugged me during the day built up and finally came out of my mouth. No wonder Jim watched the game instead of spending time with me. But thankfully, that all changed.

God tells us that we can do all things with Christ. Yet that's hard to believe when we fail day after day. I can't stand living with someone who nags, reprimands, and releases frustrations on small human beings. And sad, but true, that was me! So, I turned my attention to God and received His invitation. He might as well have spoken out loud. The invitation was penetrating: "I have some ideas for you." It was as if he gave me support beams to stabilize my broken life until I was strong enough to live without them. These tools restricted my movement and kept me from doing more damage. The tools, beginning with Character Tickets, came to me one at a time, and each one supported the others.

Ideally, all of the tools should be used by *both* parents and children. All family members learn to use their words and actions respectfully. That is, the children are encouraged to write their parents Character Tickets, use Potter's Clay for parental bad habits, and reflect a parent's conversation when it is hard to listen because the parent is speaking too emotionally. This may seem incredible, but remember, the tools are designed to teach healthy coping strategies. You wouldn't want to use these yourself and not allow the children to employ them with you. They are respectful alternatives to backtalk, tantrums, and other toxic reactions. The tools teach honest, thoughtful ways to communicate and delay gratification. When you are willing to give and to receive feedback graciously, your children will learn to do the same.

I used the tools as often as I could until my family was able to adopt and apply the philosophies themselves. By the time my girls were teens, they had a rich understanding of how to give feedback respectfully, accept criticism with grace, be honest, recognize that they are not perfect, create healthy relationships, and heal relationships that are hurt. It has been wonderful to watch them reflect one another's words when they are hurting and give one another a hug. They tell me that the powerful words, "I'm sorry, will you forgive me?" and the ability to listen and reflect without defending is like soothing balm when they and their boyfriends don't see eye to eye. They love one another, care about the world, and clearly love and feel loved by me and the dad they lost to leukemia in 2009. Most importantly, they love God, feel loved by Him, and understand His place in their lives.

You might say, "Lots of children grow up feeling loved." I'm glad you pointed that out. The lifestyle was for *me*. I wasn't happy with the way I was going about teaching my children to become Christians. The people who have adopted this lifestyle remind me that the biggest difference it made was that it made *their* lives better. You can live a less chaotic, less inconsiderate, mean-spirited, and anxious life. You wanted to experience God, right? The people around you will experience God through you; that is an added benefit.

CHAPTER 29

TOOL #1: CHARACTER TICKETS

"Above all, love each other deeply, because love covers a multitude of sins."

—I PETER 4:8

C HARACTER TICKETS ARE THE HEART and soul of Uncommon Sense. But how do they help us to follow the soul-soothing teachings of Christ and develop character in ourselves and our children? It is simple; it happens the same way the legal authorities teach us to obey the laws of the road. We agree to certain standards of behavior with the people who are important to us, write tickets when those standards are blatantly and repeatedly violated, and charge the offender for breaking them. A Character Ticket is like a traffic citation for the soul.

Writing the Ticket
This is what it looks like.

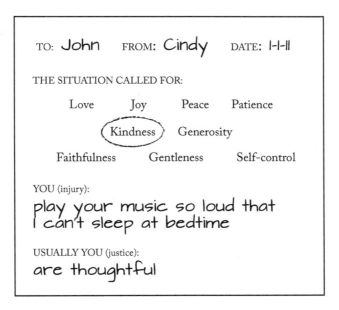

TO: John   FROM: Cindy   DATE: 1-1-11

THE SITUATION CALLED FOR:

Love   Joy   Peace   Patience

(Kindness)   Generosity

Faithfulness   Gentleness   Self-control

YOU (injury):
play your music so loud that I can't sleep at bedtime

USUALLY YOU (justice):
are thoughtful

Now, here's the thing. Character Tickets are not for everyday, mindless mistakes. Most of the time when family members do something that offends you, kindly tell them. Mention it. If they apologize and tend to the correct behavior, move on with life. We all make mistakes and are forgetful of one another's soft spots at times. Injuries that are followed by heartfelt apologies really do tend to take care of the wrong.

Tickets are for times when someone repeatedly does something that offends you and appears not to be interested in your perception of that experience. In other words, he or she doesn't care. Callousness and carelessness do not belong in families, and unchecked, they lead to shallow relationships at best (and lifelong injuries and damage at worst). The Bible refers to this as hardheartedness.

Perhaps you used to run your mouth, give someone the cold shoulder or get back at him or her later in the day. Now, you will go to a gift box, take a ticket, write on it, and put it in an IOU box. Then, you will get on with life. You will continue to be kind and affirming with the person who just offended you. Basically, you are trading out your old response (whatever it has been) for a simple walk to a gift box. Kids love this! When they use Character Tickets, they walk away from the box content that justice will be served at a later time. The change will bless you richly, and by using the box, you remove yourself from the aversive environment for a minute. Character Tickets affect both the giver and the receiver for the better.

Giving the Gift of Feedback

Why are Character Tickets kept in a gift box? Because feedback is a gift. Always keep fresh tickets and a pen or pencil handy.

- Constructive feedback is experienced as a gift when people give it benevolently and learn to love each other even though we frequently fail to live up to others' hopes and expectations.
- Feedback is what people pay professionals to give them when they want to hear the truth.
- Feedback tells us so much about the person who gives it.
- Feedback helps us groom our behaviors so we can more easily love and be loved by the people around us. It helps us to live at peace with those in our country, communities, and families as well as at work and with friends.
- Feedback can help us to consider the condition of the hearts that have driven our reactions to the surface and made them visible.
- Harsh, poorly-timed feedback can do more damage than good if someone is not ready to hear it or hears you say it in a mean, uncaring way. The "gift" is to wait until the right time and place to confront this issue. We don't rehash the experience to prove someone right or wrong. We're just reading matter-of-factly what happened and exchanging forgiveness.

Receiving the Gift of Forgiveness

The IOU box is also a small gift box or bag. Place written tickets upside down in this box, and when the time is right, examine and act on them. For instance, if you gave me a ticket, I will read it out loud to you and ask for forgiveness. Occasionally or daily, a parent should check the box and suggest that IOUs be paid.

For instance, John reads the example ticket shown earlier in this chapter by saying, "Cindy I'm sorry for forgetting to be *kind* when I *play my music loudly at bedtime.* Usually, I am *thoughtful.* Will you forgive me?"

Cindy says, "Yes, I forgive you."

John hands the ticket and one token to Cindy. Cindy tears up the ticket and puts the token in her cup. The ticket is torn up in accordance with the scripture that tells us not to keep a record of offenses (1 Cor. 13:5).

This is important. There will not be a reliving of the incident! All we do is read the ticket and apologize. If you received the ticket, you may feel embarrassed or incredulous, but do not discuss it. If you relive the incident, you will put more trash in your memory bank and dredge up emotional litter. We discussed what a mess that will make of your brain in part two of this book. Do not discuss it, explain it, or tell your side of the story. The only thing to do is read the entire ticket as it is written and apologize. Period. So it is important when you are writing a ticket to write specifically what was said or done, not something general. When you receive a ticket, assume honesty. This will create a sense of integrity and will build a healthy relationship. Believe it. It works.

People will try to make short cuts by not reading the ticket as it is written or by skipping the "Usually you are" part. As an authority figure, don't let that happen. Part of the gift is that the person who wrote the ticket not only mentioned what you did that hurt, but also noticed what you usually do that doesn't hurt the relationship. This balance is important.

Paying the Fine

We have already seen that one cost of receiving a Character Ticket is to face the person who felt hurt by your actions, read the ticket, and ask for forgiveness. Another cost for a Character Ticket is time—Loving time. Use a coin or pebble or any small object to represent five minutes of time. I buy colored pebbles from a craft store so that each family member has a different color and can keep them in separate bowls.

In the example, John owes Cindy five minutes of loving time. Why? Because when a relationship is damaged through repeated carelessness, only an act of love can repair it. Time is our most valuable commodity in life. Loving time is priceless. One of the anchor scriptures for this lifestyle is "Owe no one anything except to love each other, for the one who loves another has fulfilled the law" (Rom. 13:8 NKJ).

Since the cost of each ticket is five minutes, you would spend five minutes of loving time with the person who wrote you the ticket. If you received three tickets from the person, you give them a total of 15 minutes of loving time. Not slave labor, but rather enjoyable time with that person before your focus is back on electronics or other relationships.

A brilliant child psychologist and friend, Judy Wohlman, told me something about consequences I've never forgotten: "It's not the size of the consequence that helps someone change. It's receiving a consequence, so they learn, *When I do this, there is a consequence.*" So please, please keep this simple for yourself. Yelling: 5 minutes. Complaining: 5 minutes. Sneaking: 5 minutes. Tattling: 5 minutes. Fights: 5 minutes. This may seem ridiculous, but this is the miracle I was telling you about. You have opened your heart to a less judgmental and more forgiving way of life. We humans are typically so eager to figure out how much punishment to dish out for any number of given wrongs that we take our eyes off of the human beings who commit them. If you're willing to let God be the judge, He will reward your new philosophy.

Almost everyone I have taught about Character Tickets wants to increase the fine. But I can tell you as one with the gift of mercy, the higher the fine, the fewer tickets you'll write. We don't want to focus on every little behavior, and there is no list in the Bible of which sins get the biggest fines. Give the Holy Spirit room to work. Don't exasperate your children. Scripture tells us to keep our minds on things that are good. So jot a ticket, keep the fine very payable, and get your mind back on what your child is doing right. As Glasser and Easley, authors of *Transforming the Difficult Child* point out, negative attention is junk food. Children who get it keep seeking it because they are starved, but it doesn't satisfy.

This is the only parenting lifestyle I know in which the consequence for doing wrong is spending loving time together. It's not punitive. It's practice. Think about it. If your child wanted to be a great tennis player, would you ask him to talk about it? Would you tell him to go to his room and think about it? Would his skills improve if he was yelled at and told what a bad player he was? No. Your best bet is to put him on the court and ask him to practice. You'd make it a pleasant experience so he would want to try again tomorrow.

Character ticket payoff is time spent with another person sharing a common activity without any conflict. The list of possibilities is endless. Character Tickets help you, the manager of the system, to notice:

- Who is hurting and needs love? If Jessie gets ten tickets from Beth, both Beth and Jessie need your love and encouragement. Is Beth picky or is Jessie filled with angst?
- Which behaviors are causing the most damage for each individual? Name-calling, complaining, tantrums, physical aggression, backtalk, lecturing, selfishness, rude tones—all of these are immature, toxic coping strategies. Over time, your family members will replace them with better, more effective, and healing ways of life. If Jess gets seven tickets for hitting this week and nine the next, she has developed a habit of using hitting as a coping mechanism. Instead of giving her tickets for hitting, you may need to treat it as a bad habit. Too many tickets can

be discouraging and even inspire anger towards the giver. The next tool, Potter's Clay, helps to break bad habits without the tedium of writing tickets. Potter's Clay doesn't take the place of tickets, but is a nice complement.

Remember, Character Tickets are for times when a person knows something is hurtful to someone and doesn't care. They have been asked not to do something, such as take things without asking or badgering others, but continue to do so anyway. You know what your loved ones do. What starts fights and makes your family not like each other? What causes them to tattle, fight, and run to you for retaliation?

If you are sick of it (whatever *it* is) it is time for Character Tickets. They will discourage the old way and help you and your loved ones practice the new. By the way, when you see someone practicing a healthy, more loving response, energize that with a compliment or a hug.

ACT

CHARACTER TICKETS

1. Find two small gift boxes or small gift bags. Label one "tickets" and the other "IOU." Unwritten tickets will be placed in the "ticket" bag/box. Written tickets will be placed in the "IOU" bag/box.

2. Make copies of the tickets found in the appendix of this book or create your own and place them in the ticket box. Place a pen or pencil nearby. (You may want to be sure there are plenty of these around. You'd be surprised how many tickets don't get written because a writing utensil isn't handy.) Remember the symbolism of this being a "gift.

3. Write yourself a ticket today when you catch yourself using an old coping skill that you want to give up. Go to the person and apologize. Offer to do something loving for five minutes to repay the relationship.

4. Present the tool at the next family meeting and listen to people's thoughts about it.

5. Before the meeting, write some pretend tickets to family members and practice reading them together.

Tickets:

John, on Tuesday, I forgot to put a peanut butter sandwich in your lunch, and you were starving. Usually, I make delicious lunches. I'm sorry. Will you please forgive me?

Remember to have your family member practice saying, "Yes, I forgive you."

Susan, on Friday, I tickled you until you couldn't breathe. Usually, I don't tickle you. I'm sorry. Will you please forgive me?

"Yes, I forgive you."

Both parts of the apology are critical. Learn to ask for forgiveness and to give it.

As the person who wrote the ticket says, "Yes, I forgive you," he/she takes the ticket from the person who just read it, tears it up, and is given that person's token worth five minutes of loving time. (This will be explained in greater detail in Chapter 30.)

Tokens:

These can be coins, pebbles, or any small items. Each person should have at least ten in a bowl or container to represent 50 minutes. If you have very small children, think safety with regards to size. The tokens need to be different colors or shapes so you know whose are whose.

What would keep you from utilizing this healing intervention for yourself?

If you need a support person to do this with you, make two sets of ticket boxes or bags and extra token bowls, and invite a friend to try it at his or her house.

CHAPTER 30

Tool #2: Character Time

"If another believer sins against you, go privately and point out the fault."

—Matthew 18:15 (DNLT)

"A truly wise person uses few words; a person with understanding is even-tempered."

— Proverbs 17:27 (DNLT)

CHARACTER TIME IS THE TIME when we pull out our Character Tickets to look at ourselves and take stock of the damage we have done when we let our character slip. Although it doesn't feel good, it creates a sense of justice and harmony in the environment and keeps the rest of the day safe. If your loved ones complain, remind them that these meetings are the reason life is positive the rest of the time. Then, make sure that life is positive the rest of the time! This is an *exchange* for the old way, not an addition to it.

Remind them that they used to have tantrums, but now they walk to a gift box. You used to ground them, take things away, or yell, but now you walk to a gift box. Your old coping strategies have been replaced by these sane, matter-of-fact meetings. If your family members read the tickets, apologize, and trade tokens, the meetings will be over quickly because the injuries are not up for discussion. They happened, or the ticket wouldn't be there. If someone cared enough to walk to the box and give feedback, the recipient is going to learn to apologize and make amends.

Jesus outlines this three-step process for confronting major conflicts among believers: go privately, tell your concern to your brother, and be reconciled through repentance and forgiveness. Nowhere in the New Testament are we told that judging, yelling, or punishing others is a right or a solution. Nowhere. We are actually told repeatedly that these are the actions of fools.

When my children were young, we held these meetings on weeknights after dinner. By the time they were teens, we almost never needed them because each person handled them independently. If you are starting with teens, it will take a while to master this very high-level skill. Their old habits of bickering and defending themselves are deeply ingrained. Let your children help you decide when to hold the meetings. Combining this time with a snack or a pleasant environment can make it seem less harsh. Find a time that is most agreeable to the people involved. This may be decided at a family meeting.

PURPOSE:

1. To show love, value, and respect for each other
2. To focus us on positive communication with each other
3. To learn that our actions and words result in consequences
4. To pay debts for injuries to our relationships
5. To ask for and receive forgiveness
6. To get rid of bad feelings and thoughts about ourselves and others

TOPICS:

1. Character Tickets read/tokens traded
2. Potters Clay may be used (if necessary to decide on a habit to break)

Limits:

1. 15-20 minutes in duration
2. Led by authority figure
3. Assumption of integrity/trustworthiness. Rude responses earn five minute debt per behavior to leader (tallied at the time of the meeting, or tokens taken from bowl upon each occurrence)
4. Led by calm, thoughtful authority figure—must stay safe, no biting dogs. (Remember, a biting dog is one that attacks unexpectedly, or who you can't trust to treat you lovingly.)

Procedure:

1. Go to the IOU box and collect tickets that have been written. Call the people to the table who either wrote or received tickets. Ask them to bring their bowls with their tokens in them. If each person starts out with ten tokens (worth 5 minutes each), everyone will have a total of 50 minutes to share. Hopefully, no one will have ten tickets! (Throughout the week, the bowls will have a mix of tokens in them as your family members pay one another for injuries. As they payoff time, their tokens will be returned.)
2. Start with the person who has the fewest tickets so they can read them, apologize, and put a token in the person's bowl as each ticket is torn up. If others owe them apologies, let them receive the apologies and tokens and then leave. You are attempting not to make mountains out of molehills, not to shame people for relationship mistakes and old, faulty coping strategies. At family meetings, you will be talking about better coping strategies, but not here. Here you will only be reading tickets and exchanging tokens.
3. If one person has the lion's share of tickets, he/she is having a hard week and needs more love from everyone. It is often the most sensitive person in the house who notices that life is not being lived well and

acts out to try and change that. It is not uncommon in therapy for the "identified patient" to be the parent or child who is the most disliked, because they are the most willing to disrupt the family and make a fuss when things aren't healthy. This life-changing perspective can allow everyone to realize that people who make bad decisions are people who need consequences and love, not judgment and shame.

4. When all tickets have been read and tokens have been traded, the meeting is over. If anyone runs out of their own tokens, he or she must pay some time immediately so that some tokens can be put back into his or her bowl. That means no friends can come over and no privileges can be enjoyed until he or she has loving time to spare.

Hint: Let everyone know ahead of the meeting that you refuse to be drawn into negatives during these meetings, and you will be charging a token to anyone who breaks the rules. No one needs to talk while tickets are being read. *You may want a note on the table with these words: No criticism. No story telling. No denial. No tantrums.* With each occurrence, simply take a token from the individual's bowl and put it in yours. They will learn quickly that you mean business. Keep a kind demeanor no matter what because you are teaching them by example. And remember to praise, praise, praise each success.

For individuals who feel cheated or misunderstood, there is heart-to-heart time and reflection (discussed in chapter 33). This is not the time for that.

ACT

CHARACTER TIME

1. Prepare small bowls or containers with 10 pebbles or tokens for each person. They must be different in shape or color.

2. Take the IOU bag and see what tickets have been written since the last meeting.

3. Pray to see the tickets through the Holy Spirit's eyes. That will help you be poised, sensible, and patient rather than angry or discouraged.

4. Who owes apologies? If one person has the lion's share of tickets, they are having a hard week. New coping strategies will take time to acquire. The person who received many tickets needs love and a good role model, not to feel ganged up on. Consider taking him or her aside rather than making a public spectacle in a group setting.

5. Before the character meeting, ask the person who wrote the most tickets if he/she would like to give grace on any of them. Don't let that person throw them away just because he/she is afraid of the other person's anger. But, if you can see this individual is being picky or you feel the number of tickets will

do more harm than good, you may want to adjust the number with grace. If the person says, "No" and doesn't want to give grace, that's fine. Congratulate him or her for using the new coping skill. Loving time spent together is a good thing. So is forgiveness.

6. Hold your first character meeting and remember to take tokens for inappropriate behavior as it goes on. Reread the guidelines to the group including the "Hint" to the leader (given in this chapter) before the meeting starts, and remind them of the consequences. Out with the old, and in with the new!

CHAPTER 31

TOOL #3: POTTER'S CLAY

"Like clay in the hand of the potter, so are you in my hand."

—JEREMIAH 18:6

C AN YOU THINK OF AN unbecoming habit exhibited by one of your friends or loved ones? Have you told him or her about it? Feedback can be a bee sting moment. It is invaluable in relationships and actually longed for by most people, but is hard to give and to receive. As a counselor, I was taught that awareness is the first step toward change, and I witnessed the truth of that statement firsthand. I can remember the wonderful opportunity of being allowed to tell people the truth of how I perceived them and asking them if they were aware of some of their habits.

For example, 1 had a bright, delightful client who was near 30, single, and lonely. As she spoke, she frequently furrowed her brow, sighed, and sat with her elbow rested on the arm of her chair, hand lifted in the air. With each frustrated statement, she let her hand drop with a thud and then lifted it to talk again. "I just don't think I'll ever see eye to eye with my boss." *Thud.* "I don't think David is serious about our relationship." *Thud.* "I spent another weekend wondering why everyone but me is out enjoying life." *Thud.*

Do you know that when I pointed out the thud that punctuated the heaviness of her life, complimented by her furrowed brow and sighs, she laughed and said she had never noticed this about herself. We agreed that anyone could be exhausted by these behaviors at the end of the night. They were chronic. As soon as she became aware of them, she began to give them up.

The summer after Jim and I began the use of Character Tickets, we and the girls were at the beach. We had carried our Character Tickets with us, but, frankly, we were all more interested in the sun and fun than writing the tickets that had been earned. We needed a quick way to address problems and help each person see that some of his or her bad habits were infringing on our joy. So we held a family meeting and agreed on some offensive human behaviors that we were practicing:

- Speaking in a loud, pushy voice
- Having a tantrum
- Complaining
- Interrupting
- Lecturing
- Back-talking
- Paying Lip service

Then we bought some colored toothpicks and assigned the toothpicks to correspond to items on our list. Blue for when someone yelled, red if someone threw a temper tantrum, green if someone complained, and so on. We each took a little piece of clay and fashioned it into a shape we liked. Then, we agreed that if we used one of these unattractive means of expressing ourselves, someone could put a toothpick in our clay. There would be no other consequence. We wouldn't pay time. We wouldn't talk about it. We would only see a toothpick in our sculpture.

You can imagine what happened: the same thing as when I pointed out the thud. The behaviors decreased. There was never any consequence to Potter's Clay other than having the behavior pointed out. Many people who have used this technique have felt a need for a consequence for a given number of toothpicks. But I believe that need for punishment is indicative of our human tendency to believe that vengeance will remove a behavior. (Vengeance is mine, sayeth the toothpick giver.) On the contrary, this is an instrument we are using for habits. The more toothpicks I have for that behavior, the more it shows how enslaved I am to it. Have compassion with me. Remember, Potter's Clay is just designed to say, "You know that bad habit you have? You're doing it again." Give us this day our Potter's Clay and forgive us our trespasses. Put the toothpick in. Have compassion. Realize that you have plenty of your own toothpick behaviors. When someone puts a toothpick into your clay, you'll see it has an "ouch factor" to it. That's enough. The behavior does decrease as the awareness increases. No words are needed with this tool, just time to let the Holy Spirit convict each person. Be silent, and watch God work.

I will say that when the children were young, we learned to work on one habit at a time. For example, if I felt like a child was complaining a lot, I would ask her if I could use toothpicks to see how often it was happening. Sometimes, quite frankly, it was only happening a couple of times a day, and I was exaggerating how bad it was in my own mind. The toothpicks helped keep me honest, and I would compliment the child for not being as whiny as I thought. Other times, for a really challenging habit, I would offer to give the child an inexpensive toy or treat if she reduced the undesirable behavior. It worked, and it gave my children confidence to see that they could succeed.

At the end of the day, all toothpicks should be removed so the family can start fresh the next day. The scripture in Jeremiah says we are clay in the Potter's hands, being molded into the beautiful beings He longs for us to be. The verse also says that God makes all things new every day, so we want to give each other a chance to do just that.

Potter's Clay is a strategy for delivering feedback in a way that is less intrusive and more kind than blurting it out. Complaining, interrupting, speaking loudly to get attention, lecturing, backtalk, and lip service are all common behaviors in an office or home environment. But God has asked us to live without them.

What God has actually asked us to do and told us we are capable of is to rest in His character. When we do this, we will produce fruit. Resting is as easy as breathing in and breathing out. However, learning to rest takes a lot of practice.

We colored some of our toothpicks gold and made sure that each piece of clay that had a colored toothpick in it had at least one gold toothpick as well. Gold is for resting. If we saw people take a deep breath or walk away when it would have been easy to yell, complain, or backtalk, we wanted them to know we noticed the positive gains.

Resting does not mean "do nothing." It means "pause and literally turn your difficulty over to God." Obey God and leave the consequences to Him.

CHILDREN'S CLAY

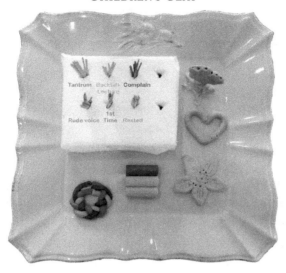

TEEN'S CLAY

Give us this day our "potter's clay" and forgive us our trespasses
as we forgive those who… also are trying to change.
His mercies are new every day.

ACT

Potter's Clay

Sometimes, the best way to convince people that things need to change is to show them in a way they can't ignore. In counseling we call this "taking a baseline." When I taught special education, the way we mapped our students' progress was by taking notes on the current behavior and comparing those notes to the behavior as it began to change. We might see how often or how seldom something happened. Then we would attempt to help them increase or decrease the frequency of the behavior.

For our purposes, if Sam currently lectures his children 15 times a day but then decreases that number to three, you can imagine how much more they will want to see him coming.

To prepare your Potter's Clay for young families:

1. Purchase multi-colored modeling clay, colored toothpicks, and a small box. (I often find this clay for $1-$2 at a discount store in the arts or children's sections.) You may be able to use homemade playdough and create holes for the toothpicks before it dries out.

2. To create a labeled toothpick holder you can use a large pudding box. Fill the box with crumpled paper or floral foam to keep the toothpicks from falling over when they are inserted in the holes.

3. Cover the box with white paper and cut five or six small holes in it.

4. Under each hole, write a toxic (hurtful) coping skill that is currently being used by your family (not just kids) members. Just choose the most frequent ones. We all use some of them at times. Let your family collaborate on this by asking them what they think should be on the box. You can include things such as: having temper tantrums, hitting, yelling, tattling, gossiping, complaining, whining, name-calling, shunning/ignoring, and lecturing/backtalking (both are ways of trying to talk instead of listen when things go wrong).

5. Place toothpicks in each hole so each behavior is assigned a color of toothpick. For example, red toothpicks in the temper tantrum hole, blue toothpicks in the hitting hole, and so on.

6. Give each person a piece of clay and ask him or her to design it.

7. Explain Potter's Clay to your family. Each day during the first week, try giving toothpicks. No words. No meanness. You don't treat the person poorly. You are just "noticing" what coping skills have been chosen by each person. Most parents lecture. Give yourself a toothpick if you catch yourself lecturing, and laugh at yourself so your child will know this is not

mean-spirited. It's hard to change, but this simple process can help you all do just that.

8.   *** Don't forget to buy some fancy toothpicks to add to the others to let them know you noticed something good that day, too. You saw them get it right.

Hint: You can start out with this box for older children, but I have found it is more successful with preteens and teens to use a condensed version and ask them which habit they would like to work on this week. Make a family list, or just suggest the most frequent reasons they are getting tickets. Then just put a tiny piece of paper beside their clay to remind everyone which bad habit they are focused on this week. Choosing the habit for themselves gives them more say and more respect—which they need as they begin to grow in maturity and independence.

CHAPTER 32

TOOL #4: SEEK THE LESSON

"For out of the overflow of the heart the mouth speaks. The good man brings good things out of the good things stored up in him, and the evil man brings evil things out of the evil stored up in him."

—MATTHEW 12:34-35

D O YOU KNOW SOMEONE WHO says, "Do the dishes" more often than they say, "I love you"? Did I hit a nerve? Spiritually, emotionally, and physically, you would be better off to stay up late and do the dishes yourself than to spend your time on earth condemning others for not doing them. There may be a number of preferences you learned growing up that could be done less frequently and no one would care.

"Seek the Lesson" is a tool that helps keep you from focusing on behaviors, actions, physical things (externals) that bother you, and instead helps you focus on attitudes and truths (internals) that soothe you.

When a group of religious leaders were questioning Christ about why His disciples didn't do ritual hand washing, Christ told the religious teachers that they had traded out manmade traditions for God's commandments. "All of you listen," He said, "and try to understand. You are not defiled by what you eat; you are defiled by what you say and do!" (Matt. 15:11 NLT) If you focus on negatives, you will suck the joy out of your life and the lives of those around you. "Seek the Lesson" is simple.

- **Experience a negative trigger.** They happen to each of us throughout the day. Examples include traffic, unmade beds, a too-short skirt, backtalk from a child, a parent yelling, R-rated material on TV, being ignored or berated by someone, or anything that triggers your brain to experience a negative emotion. By the way, unmade beds, traffic, or yelling don't trigger everyone. But if something or someone triggers you, you should…
- **Ask God what attitude you could use to improve the situation.** If you are experiencing a negative trigger, your attitude is probably one of frustration, impatience, selfishness, or judgment. Nothing that is setting you up for health. Memorize the following poem to help you recall nine attitudes that we know reside in our hearts through the Holy Spirit:

> *love, joy, peace,*
> *patience, kindness*
> *generosity,*
> *faithfulness, gentleness, self-control*
> *the fruit of the Spirit in me*

- **Listen.** Don't expect God to talk if you are not going to listen. He is no fool. As you recite the poem, listen for God to stop you on the attitude that will alleviate this trigger.
- **Employ** the attitude from the poem that God expects right then and there.
- **Notice** how much better you feel because you used an attitude chosen by God rather than human tradition and logic to remedy a difficult situation.

This tool produces miracles and is fun because it literally heightens your awareness of an attitude you wouldn't have chosen on your own. When you notice you are stressed, start to slowly recite the poem and stop when you sense you have arrived at the attitude God wants you to use. God always chooses the right attitude for the job because He alone has a view to our hearts. Furthermore, if another person is triggering you, the attitude God chooses for you will also calm them so quickly that you will know you have experienced God's participation.

I plead with you to try this tool. God is willing to interact with you in a supernatural way if you make yourself aware of Him. It is the Spirit of God interacting with your spirit to enable, energize, protect, and make you more like Christ. Over time, this interaction will heal both you and others. You will realize that a lot of the things you used to think you needed to feel peaceful and content are unnecessary. You will gain self-respect and become less dependent on others' respect to be happy.

Human beings often think that standing their ground is the key to respect. The lovely irony is that as we learn to turn challenges over to God and make His desires our own rather than use ineffective and insensitive coping skills, we become easier to respect. Meekness is not wimpiness; it is harnessed power. Jesus tells believers, "Come to me, all you who labor and are burdened, and I will give you rest. Take my yoke upon you and learn from me, for I am meek and humble of heart; and you will find rest for your soul. For my yoke is easy and my burden light" (Matt. 11:28-30). A yoke is actually a piece of equipment that assures two beings will move in unison.

"Seek the Lesson" is a playful tool. Let it teach you to move in synch with God's wise, healing Spirit. You will experience His joyful, life-giving sense of humor and poise. As you model these traits, you will be teaching them to the receiver. Remember, 80 percent of communication is nonverbal. If the other person is all hot and bothered and persists after you have made a wise choice, excuse yourself for a moment. Then go jot a note on your family meeting notepad or write a character ticket.

Encouragement

I can still see myself in the kitchen facing my daughter who was talking loudly and complaining about something she didn't like. I had had a long day and never enjoy hearing people shout when they are complaining. I wanted to tell her to go away, to look on the bright side, or to do something else that I knew would only have made things worse or prolonged our agony.

Thankfully, I remembered to recite the Fruit of the Spirit poem and expected God to stop me on love or patience. He stopped me on *generosity*. *What could that mean?* I wondered. I quickly realized that in this case I needed to be generous, not stingy, with my time. I had wanted to go watch one of my favorite shows. Instead, the moment I gave in to the generosity, my daughter's voice calmed a bit. I remembered to reflect her thoughts rather than adding mine. My attention made her feel better so quickly. Within minutes, she went from a loud, complaining girl to a gentle one who said, "Thanks for listening to me, Mommy. You're so sweet."

Worth every second.

ACT

Seek the Lesson

"This is what the lord says: 'Stand at the crossroads and look; ask for the ancient paths, ask where the good way is, and walk in it, and you will find rest for your souls.'"

—Jeremiah 6:16

Fill in the blank with your name and carry this card in your wallet until you have it memorized:

_____,

This is about you and a lesson God is teaching you. He is pleased with your growth. Seek the lesson.

love, joy, peace
patience, kindness
generosity,
faithfulness, gentleness, self-control,
the fruit of the Spirit in me.

CHAPTER 33

TOOL #5: REFLECTION

"Bless those who persecute you: bless and do not curse. Rejoice with those who rejoice. Mourn with those who mourn. Live in harmony with one another."

—ROMANS 12:14-16

R EFLECTION IS A COPING STRATEGY that is going to help you improve your relationships and save hours of your life. It is a listening strategy that helps the intellectual section of your brain stay alert and available when someone else has retreated to the more habitual, emotional section of his or hers. We learned when we studied the brain that each person appears to have a limited capacity for pain and stress. We learned that only God knows everyone's capacity and how full their cups already are with old wounds and pain. The purpose of reflection is to respond to Christ's teachings on bearing one another's burdens and offering to give others the compassion that has been given to you by God. It is a totally new way of interacting with someone who is either sad or angry. Often people really just need to know that they have been heard. They also need to take the time to hear themselves.

There are two types of effective listening skills, but they are very different. *Active listening* is when you carefully pay attention to what someone else says and then *say it back to them in your own words.*

Reflection, on the other hand, is a very specific type of listening in which you *repeat back what someone says to you word-for-word.* When you do this, two things happen.

1) You understand them better because their exact words are moving through your brain and out of your mouth. That helps you to think like they think—to walk in their shoes so to speak.

2) They better understand themselves and are better able to handle their own problems. Somehow, when our own words come back at us from someone else, we can hear them more clearly and can correct mistakes. "Always" turns into "a lot." Or, at least, we can feel truly heard. That just seems to be the way our Father created us. He wants us to be good listeners and to be able to reflect on what we say.

It's essential that we *learn* this if we're going to help each other. It doesn't come naturally, but it is worth the effort. Reflection creates self-correction and self-discovery. When people feel heard, they become more honest with themselves and usually come up with good solutions to their problems. And when people correct their own thoughts, they often leave feeling more capable and somehow taken care of or finished. Reflection cuts arguments and feuds off at the knees. It doesn't take up more time in your day; it actually reduces the amount people need to get off of their chests.

To introduce this to your family, tell them that you have found a way of paying attention that helps you to be a better listener with someone who is angry, sad, or frustrated. Ask them to let you practice it with them. When someone comes to you with a subject that is stressful and you want to calm him or her down, begin reflection.

Here's an example:

CHILD: *"Mom, Stephen just hit me and told me I'm stupid! I can't stand him! He ruins everything!"*
PARENT: *"Matt, this is one of those times when I want to use reflection, so I can listen to you better, okay?"*
CHILD: *"No, Mom, I want you to spank him! He's so mean!"*
PARENT: *"No, Matt. I'm not going to spank him, and I'm not going to let you dump on me. We can either write a character ticket and be done with this for now, or I can reflect you."*

Your choice. As the mother or father, you can:
a) Move to the Character Ticket box and help the angry person write the ticket
b) Begin reflection
c) Leave the room

As a follower of Christ, you can no longer participate in this destructive habit of gossiping. It may just seem like whining and fussing. But gossip is the act of saying something about someone else—true or false—that makes others think less of him or her. It is devaluing to you, to the speaker, and to the person being spoken of. There is a better way to approach this situation than to stand and talk about someone else back and forth. The result of the old way is negative: you feel dumped on, get angry or grieved, or end up harboring bad feelings for the person speaking or the person being spoken about. This is not what Christ taught.

I recommend you either reflect or write a ticket rather than leave. But if you can't stay and maintain a loving demeanor, just ask them to give you a minute to think. Then go take some deep breaths or get a hug and ask someone to say something loving to you. It will ground you, and remind you that you are intelligent and kind, and you'll be ready to act lovingly again.

This is so important! You match the other person's words, but not the emotion. Your attitude must stay interested and concerned but calm. I said your attitude, not just your tone. This will take practice. So practice it when you are not angry.

CHILD: *"I hate him! And I'm mad at you, too. You always take his side."*
PARENT: *"You hate him, and now you're mad at me. I always take his side. Did I get that right?"*
CHILD: *"Yes. You don't do anything, and the Character Tickets don't work. He's still mean."*
PARENT: *"I don't do anything and the Character Tickets don't work. He's still mean. Did I get that right?"*
CHILD: *"Yes."*
PARENT: *"Tell me more."*
CHILD: *"There is no more."*
PARENT: *"I love you. I'm sorry for whatever part I played in your pain. Do you want to write a ticket on me or Steven?"*
CHILD: *"No."*
PARENT: *"Okay, Matt. I love you. Thank you for letting me listen the new way."*

You don't always apologize for being a part of it. But do say, "I'm sorry" and offer to help use tickets or clay during the next family meeting as a healthy strategy and a way of letting them know you care. It's healing.

You may have noticed that Matt asked his parent not to reflect him, and then he either didn't notice or didn't mind when she did. This is typical. When we are angry it feels insulting to be "psychobabbled," but in the midst of it, it feels good to be heard. If Matt had asked her to stop, she would have. His mom wasn't playing a game. She really cared, and he could tell that. She would not have insisted on her own way, nor would she have stayed and listened to his gossip. Again, gossip is not a lie. It is conversation that is going to make you feel worse about someone. The way Matt's family has agreed to handle hurts is to use Character Tickets. Matt wants to pull his mother back into old toxic patterns. But she is not going to be pulled in because she has a better way. She tries to take the lead and see if he will follow. In this case, he did.

If he had really stayed angry, his mother might have guessed at an emotion like, "That must really be exhausting." Something safe. If she gets it wrong, he'll correct her. Then she'll go back to reflecting. What you will see is that people need to talk a lot less when they are heard more clearly.

Have patience and be persistent. Repeat as many of a person's words and phrases as you can. Ask him to talk more slowly and use fewer sentences so you can really understand why he is so upset. Explain that you really want to be able to see it from his perspective. And let me tell you the miraculous truth—if you are able to do this well, you *will be able to see it from his perspective*, and it will bond you like nothing else could.

Did I get that right? Tell me more.

Speaking like this is affirming, both for you and your loved one. Love does not insist on its own way. You are not going to force Matt to write a Character Ticket or go apologize for the things he just said in anger. You responded in accordance with Scripture, and you healed something in your precious child's brain. If you do this consistently, your family will begin to show more love for one another. And you will be teaching them how it's done. Even my young children could do reflection with only a little guidance from me. Ask them to reflect you and each other when they are not the angry one. Practice makes perfect.

If two people come to you at one time, handle the most upset person first. Separate the two so they don't get more upset by eavesdropping. But see to it that they are both heard. This is not about reality. You are not reflecting reality but perceptions. Don't try to fix it. You'll see, they will move on if you show your willingness to step into their shoes for a moment by reflecting their perceptions.

However, if the other person won't reflect, won't write tickets, and won't leave you alone, use "Three Nice Things," which we're about to discuss.

ACT

REFLECTION

*"Everybody has baggage. Find someone who
loves you enough to help you unpack."*

—Anonymous

Practice this listening strategy often before you need it. Why? It's
nice to make this listening style a habit. Remember what you read
about the body? When your brain is firing, or when someone else's
brain is firing, it can be difficult to remember to pull this out of
your tool chest. Also, remember the story about the emergency
medical technician who had practiced his trade for years? He was
able to tend the victim even though he was in distress.

Remember to ask God for help. Let Him be with you in the
midst of challenging interactions so waiting to speak will be easier.
In my experience, the Holy Spirit will speak to me when I am
diligently seeking, but God seldom barges into my life. He waits
patiently to be invited.

CHAPTER 34

Tool #6: Three Nice Things and Affirmations

*"Let us therefore make every effort to do what leads
to peace and to mutual edification."*

—ROMANS 14:19

Three Nice Things

Purpose: To exchange a good memory for a bad one

IT IS NOT UNCOMMON FOR children to say mean things to one another for no good reason or for them to criticize one another or belittle and devalue their loved ones when they are sad or angry. These are immature coping strategies found in all families. "Three Nice Things" is a fast and easy way to undo damage. Here's how it works.

> Tommy looks at his brother, Joel, his eyes filled with tears and says, *"I hate you. You are a creepy little liar!"*
> **Mom:** *Tommy, say three nice things.*

Tommy: *I don't want to!*
Mom: *You can say three nice things, or you can say six.*
Tommy: *Mom!!*
Mom: *Nine.*
Tommy: *You are a good Lego player. You are funny... you sleep on your stomach.*
Mom: *Keep going.*

If Tommy had said three nice things when he was asked, that's all that would have been required. He created his own consequences when he refused by complaining. Tommy would have to come up with nine descriptions of Sam that were not mean, because for every time he refuses to comply with affirmations, the request grows by three. Of course, by the time he gets to something as goofy as "sleeping on your stomach," everyone is giggling, and the atmosphere is changed anyway. However, if he used a hurtful adjective in the midst of the complimentary ones, you would add an additional three. To be honest, my girls never got beyond six after the first hard lesson, and the time they had to say nine nice qualities, they were well into a laughing fit by the time they got there. I tell you the truth, it's hard to think of nice things when you are angry. My girls soon got around that difficulty by repeating the same three qualities every time they had to use this tool, so it got to be a family joke that "You're nice, positive, and creative," were what they mostly used. For some reason it became a joke among them, disengaged their anger, and did what the tool is meant to do. It replaced a bad memory with a good one.

Perhaps you can only say, "That's a nice belt you have on" or "Your eyes are the prettiest shade of blue." That's okay. The point is it's not mean, and it takes energy to get dressed. Sometimes as a parent, you may need to help an angry child succeed by getting them started. For example, you might say, "You noticed the nice picture she drew, right?" This choice to focus on something positive about the person is disarming. It also just happens to be what the Christian faith tells us to do. "Fix your thoughts on what is true, and honorable, and right. Think about things that are pure, and lovely, and admirable. Think about things that are excellent and worthy of praise" (Phil. 4:8 NLT). This tends to be a favorite tool of many families I have taught.

Affirmations

Tell one another, "Three things I like about you... Three ways you blessed me... Three ways God blessed me..."

This is a passion builder that I learned from Dr. Van Horn. One of my favorites, it reminds both people why they love one another and builds intimacy into the relationship. If you are ever at a loss for words with one of your loved ones, or if a relationship seems damaged or dull, this will spill affection all over it. I strongly recommend it to couples as a daily habit to keep the flame burning.

Not only did I use this with Jim, but also with the children. Can you imagine the difference this makes for the grumpy child when his parent opens his or her mouth and this comes out instead of a lecture? If you had always been told you are valuable and likable and that your parents and siblings trusted you as someone to tell their daily blessings, how might that have changed you? People limit themselves so much by not having the confidence to do the things they want to do. Add this strong cord of affirmations to the weave of your life and watch passion and confidence flourish.

ACT

THREE NICE THINGS

Write down these three sentence stems:

- Three things I like about you…
- Three ways you blessed me…
- Three ways God blessed me…

Take two walks this week, and choose your partner if you have one or a child if you aren't married. First, tell them each of these things. Then, ask them to tell you each of these things. You may find you don't want to stop at three.

If I could encourage every couple to do one thing, it would be make use of these affirmations. I honestly believe it can save marriages because it reminds us of what we are doing correctly with one another and affirms what is going right in our lives.

CHAPTER 35

Tool #7: Baskets — S.O.S.

"Do not store up for yourselves treasures on earth, where moth and rust destroy and where thieves break in and steal. But store up for yourselves treasures in heaven, where moth and rust do not destroy and where thieves do not break in and steal. For where your treasure is, there your heart will be also."

—Matthew 6:19-21

S TUFF. WE HUMANS LIKE ACQUIRING stuff, but we don't like managing it. New clothes are great to wear but tedious to hang up. Toys are great for entertaining a child but frustrating to walk around. Dishes are necessary to cook and serve the food but no one wants to empty the dishwasher. Shoes and keys—where the heck are they when you need them?

At the beginning of this book, we agreed that we were going to simplify our environments and relationships. This is an absolute no brainer. Go to a garage sale or thrift store and buy one basket for each person under your roof. Put the baskets in a place that they pass every day on the way to their rooms. When you find something in your environment that belongs to that person, pick it up and put it in their basket. Then when they say, "Have you seen my wallet?" you can respond, "If I saw it, I put it in your basket."

My husband, Jim, was a gracious, easy-going man. If any of us ever misplaced anything, he said nothing and simply started looking for it. I must say, he was an expert at finding things. We never got a lecture or a reprimand from him. When I went out of town without the family, things didn't get picked up and put away until the afternoon I was going to be home. It didn't bother anyone but me to walk around the mess. No one missed a game or school. So, I'm pretty much the only one who put things in baskets. The rest of the family didn't seem to notice that things were out of place or didn't care. Similarly, I have a friend who has many kids, and they always look put together and are navigating life just fine. But if you could see her laundry room! She doesn't fuss if her kids' rooms are messy, but she keeps the rest of her house neat as a pin.

The point is, there are many acceptable ways to navigate stuff. The best one is don't get too much, and don't blame others for leaving it all over the place if you are the one who keeps buying it. It makes a mess, and we want to manage it without hurting relationships. If you have made a responsibility list, you have a plan for managing most of your material world. For everyday casualties, you now have a basket. Put things in there and move on with life. Tell your children to take it up each day, clean it out, and bring it back. Have an evening once a week when you hang out with your child and chat while they put their stuff in its proper place. Or, if you owe them time, offer to use your time to help them put it away.

SOS — Sack of Stuff

The SOS is one of the best things that happened to me as a young mother. I gave a plastic grocery bag to my oldest daughter, Bentley, who is super organized and asked her to go around the house every day and pick up all the stuff that was out of place. She put it all in the grocery bag and then took it and put it in the rooms where it was supposed to be. Sometimes she put it away. Either way, I could sit in my living room or kitchen and not feel like I had work to do. Later, I used the SOS as a way for the girls to pay off time they owed to me. No one minded this simple chore, because they just sorted it into the baskets and moved on with life. It was quick and easy, and they knew whose stuff was whose better than I did.

ACT

BASKETS

1. If you don't have individual containers where you can toss your own or loved ones' things when they are out of place, make baskets a priority this week.

2. If the idea is offensive to you, ask yourself why and write the reasons here. Discuss it with a trusted and loving friend.

3. Ask each family member individually if they would like you to use a basket for them or not.

4. Remember to use containers you don't mind seeing.

CHAPTER 36

TOOL #8: NO ISSUES OUTSIDE OF ISSUE TIME

*"Everyone enjoys a fitting reply; it is wonder-
ful to say the right thing at the right time!"*

—PROVERBS 15:23 (NLT)

ARLIER WHEN WE DISCUSSED THE initial family meeting, I suggested you might teach your child this tool: to use a pinky finger
to represent "i" for issue. This lifestyle is very much dependent
on your ability to delay gratification so your home environment can be
a pleasure to most people most of the time. The "i" informs you of other
peoples' triggers. Oftentimes, we don't know we are offending others with
what we say or ask.

Remember the process called "bundling" that we discussed in the brain
chapter? We said that the brain is designed to save energy, so it bundles
similar things together to save energy. If every time your family members see
you they can expect a chore or a negative topic to come out of your mouth,
they will avoid you. The sight of you will become associated (bundled) with

displeasure. We are told to take an interest in our children's lives. School and friends are natural topics, but both of those topics are painful for many kids. There are so many reasons why the topic of friends can be painful, including if parents are critical of friends or are constantly trying to choose or fix the child's friendships.

This is an opportunity to experience God. The Holy Spirit in you is able to point out good things to affirm in your child while you avoid issues. If you can't hear the alternative to issues, just give a hug, say "I love you," and be still and know that God "will work all things together for good for those who love Him" (Rom. 8:28). Do you know that my girls have met children whose parents have never said, "I love you" to them? The fathers stopped hugging their daughters when they became teenagers. The girls thought there was something wrong with them, that their fathers stopped liking them. Men, you can still hug your daughters appropriately when they begin to become women. They can still sit beside you and lay their heads on your shoulder and cry. They can take your arm as you walk into church or to a restaurant on a date. You can still hold their hands as you tell them three things you like about them, three ways they blessed you, and three ways God blessed you. If you aren't comfortable showing affection, then at least tell them that you love them so they won't have to wonder.

Some people simply aren't very gifted when it comes to the art of conversation. If that's true of you, you can be an observer. Ask your family about their favorite musicians, TV shows, or movies. Ask them to show you a funny clip on the Internet to give you a lift for the day. Ask them to give you a three-minute demonstration of their gaming technique, piano playing, or some other skill you have been asking them to work on. But watch out. They may raise a pinky finger.

Here's a repeat of what you read during the chapter on the first family meeting. If you learn to use this or some other strategy for realizing how you trigger your loved ones, you will never regret it. Initially, it hurts to get the feedback, but in the long run, you will love being someone they enjoy.

Give me an "i"

A fist with raised pinky finger is an "i" in sign language. At our house, it stands for "issue." That means, "What may be a positive interest for you is an issue for me. I'd rather not talk about it." Remind everyone to keep a pleasant demeanor when they lift their pinkies. No words. No scowls or stiff, angry gestures. Just lift a pinky, and the speaker will respectfully change the topic. Truthfully, this usually makes people laugh, but sometimes, it hurts their feelings. In time, it becomes an effective way to get to know what topics are pleasant and unpleasant to someone else. Of course, they can also tell you, "That's an issue for me."

Remember that in some cases (such as chores and challenges) an "issue" is a subject we set aside for an agreed upon time, not something we ignore and never discuss. Meetings and heart-to-hearts are the times for issues. Just don't forget that too many heart-to-hearts in a relationship can be like too much salt on food. Rather than enhancing the flavor, it is overwhelming and worsens it. You'll know when you've crossed the boundary line because your audience will begin to ignore you.

I-NOTES

An i-note is literally a piece of paper with "issue" written at the top (or a notepad on your phone) where you can jot a few words to remind you to address a topic later at a meeting. If you or someone else thinks of an issue outside of issue time and starts to discuss it, someone could say, "Will you jot that on an i-note so we can talk about it at the meeting?" Then, you'll address it that night if it is time-sensitive, or you will wait until the family meeting. For example, if your son wants to go to a party that you think you don't want him to attend, this allows you to note the request and take time to think and pray about it rather than argue on the spot. It also gives you a chance to go to him at a better time. The best thing about i-notes is that most of the items on them are things you can cross off because you will see they are not worth discussing.

ACT

Issue Time

1. Take some paper, a whiteboard, or the notepad app on your phone. At the top of it, write "Issues" or "i-note."

2. Remind the family that an issue is something that doesn't have to be addressed right away, isn't considered pleasant by both people, or is something both people don't want to talk about right now.

3. Tell the family that the purpose of the i-note is to stay aware of what is important. I-notes teach the art of waiting until the right time to address a thought or need. Each day, ask others which of the issues need to be addressed that night at an update, which ones can wait and be addressed at the family meeting, and which ones can be dropped from the list. Nothing should have to wait for more than a week! The younger a child is, the longer time seems. Stay sensitive to this.

4. Remember that poor communication has been identified as the number one reason for divorce. Don't wait for days to address issues if you don't have to. You may get into the habit of saying, "Can you jot that on an i-note?" When you do, mark things off as quickly as possible so they will feel that putting things on there is worth their while.

CHAPTER 37

TOOL #9: ASK AND ASK AGAIN

"Simply let your 'Yes' be 'Yes' and your 'No' be 'No.'"

—MATTHEW 5:37

THESE TOOLS WERE DEVELOPED AS a direct result of my disappointment in my own erratic behavior and my sadness at what I saw other parents doing. For example, if a group of parents was in a good mood and spending time together, almost anything their children asked for received a resounding "Yes!" If, on the other hand, the parents were in a bad mood, the answer was "no" and was often followed by whining or multiple requests from the child. Sets of "Why nots?" would then be followed by unthinking responses or the meaningless, "Because I said so."

The problem with this behavior is that, as a child moves out of the toddler stage and into childhood and adolescence, social interactions and life events are opportunities for emotional and intellectual growth. Unthinking and uncaring parents can damage their relationships with their children when they don't stop to think or make decisions based on fear or emotions. They can also sabotage the growth they are expecting in their children's lives.

God gave me a wonderfully simple formula for nipping long back-and-forth requests in the bud. This formula will teach the child who participates and who watches you to ask, wait, and let you pray for God's best. It's a winning combination. All of my children learned that this was the way we made decisions. They found comfort in it, and they almost always got a "yes." God is more generous than I am.

If your child asks for something and the answer is "yes," you won't need this, of course. However, if your children ask for something and the answer is "no," here's the five-step process.

1. They ask.
2. You say "no."
3. They ask again. (They have this opportunity to state their case. Teach them to talk, not whine or plead. Give them time to fill in the blanks and explain why it's important to them. This is a step, not a sentence.) When you feel you have the details…
4. You say you want to pray about it. (You pray. They go away and wait.)
5. You give your answer.

ACT

Ask and Ask Again

At one of your family meetings, explain that this is the new way you are going to handle requests. Role-play with them if you need to so you can all get used to this new respectful way of making life choices.

This can turn into extra steps, occasionally, when important details are left out and the child needs extra time for explanations. However, role-play it in five steps.

CHAPTER 38

TOOL #10: PRAYER
AND DEVOTIONS

"Store my commands in your heart, for they will give you a long and sat-
isfying life. Never let loyalty and kindness get away from you! Wear them
like a necklace; write them deep within your heart. Then you will find
favor with both God and people, and you will gain a good reputation.
Trust in the Lord with all your heart; do not depend on your own under-
standing. Seek his will in all you do, and he will direct your paths."

—PROVERBS 3:1-6 (NLT)

GOD ENCOURAGES US TO READ His Word every day and write the
loving wisdoms on the tablets of our hearts. Did you ever have
to write something over and over as a consequence of making a
hurtful decision? *"I will be kind to my brother. I will be kind to my brother. I*
will…" That exercise was designed to make a superhighway in your head that
helped you to do kind things rather than mean things when your brother
annoyed you. We have discovered that most people learn better when they
use both listening and writing in order to learn.

Once I asked Caty, my youngest daughter, to pay off some time to me by typing a worksheet for a class I was going to teach. In it, I was talking about our family's Thursday night room-cleaning and explaining that if the girls' rooms were clean on Thursday, nothing could cause them to lose their freedom on Friday. She called out to me, "Mom! Is this true?!"

It had been a fact for years, but until she typed it (used her body to implant it on her brain), it had not registered! She certainly knew she could *lose* Friday nights, so she understood the down side of not getting the room clean on Thursday. But she failed to realize the up side of cleaning the room on time: freedom! She failed to realize it until she read it and wrote it. This seems to be true of some Christians. We come to church and sit in pews and listen, but we miss so much if we don't hold God's Word in our own hands, read it, write it, and engrave it on the tablets of our hearts.

Are prayer and devotions tools of the lifestyle? It would be more accurate to say that prayer and devotions are standard equipment for those of us who are in love with God. Prayer is conversation with God. Devotions involve learning about and listening to God. Oftentimes, devout Christians will say with regret, "I am forgetting to pray" or "I am not taking the time for my devotions." They are distressed about it because they have taken the time for these activities in the past and know that life is richer and more satisfying when they are a part of the day. Getting to know God is soul soothing. Often, the Scriptures we read in the morning are the principles we need later in the day. They are the antidote to our angst.

MEDITATIVE DEVOTION

Some people think the only way to have devotional time is to read the Bible or books about God and His Word. Although it is not the only way, there is no replacement for God's Word and gaining an understanding of it. To read a passage and then be still and ask God how it applies to you is a wonderful way of learning about Him. I have suggested a number of good books in the resources to get you started. Please find a book and read a page each day to your child to acquaint them with this wonderful faith of ours. There are books for people of all ages. In fewer than five minutes, you can intersect with God in the morning while your family eats their breakfast or use it as a calming event in the evening while you share a little snack. What child doesn't love to be read to?

ACTIVE DEVOTION

A second form of devotion is acting on what you have read. Life itself promotes an understanding of our Father. All of the tools and coping strategies in this lifestyle are designed to teach the user about God. All of them are forms of devotion. For example,

- **Character Tickets** help users exercise self-control and create stillness and kindness in the environment.
  "Be still, and know that I am God...."
      —Psalm 46:10
- **Potter's Clay** encourages both conviction and mercy in the user. It also creates humility in the environment, and helps us to avoid judgmental, negative attitudes toward others.
  "When you bow down before the Lord and admit your dependence on Him, He will lift you up and give you honor."
      —James 4:10 (NLT)
- **Loving time** encourages loving ways in the user; it also creates justice and harmony in the environment.
  "Let no debt remain outstanding except the continuing debt to love one another, for he who loves his fellowman has fulfilled the law."
      —Romans 13:8
- **Reflection** encourages compassion in the user. It also creates sensitivity and healing in the environment.
  "Understand this, my dear brothers and sisters: You must all be quick to listen, slow to speak, and slow to get angry. Human anger does not produce the righteousness God desires."
      —James 1:19-20 (NLT)

- **I-notes** require a user to be patient. They also create order, beauty, and peace in the environment.
  "There is a time for everything, and a season for every activity under heaven."
  —Ecclesiastes 3:1
- **Collaboration** encourages an appreciation for creativity and diversity in the users as well as creates a sense of belonging and unity in the environment.
  "There are different kinds of working, but the same God works all of them in all men."
  —1 Corinthians 12:6

Actions are devotions if they are designed to honor God. The more you exercise the ways of life that Christ prescribes to us, the more your faith will grow. Remember, we are under a new covenant, and as we practice the use of Christian principles, we come to know the God Christ came to give us. A deeper sense of love, joy, peace, patience, kindness, goodness, faithfulness, and gentleness, even humility is ours to embrace. Life as Christ describes it— "Take my yoke upon you. My burden is light"—will become possible. The more we practice resting in Christ's strength and working in union with Him, the better we get at it.

In an Uncommon Sense lifestyle, no matter where the damage begins, the people involved make amends by spending loving time together. The bonds that occur during the loving time lead to a natural positive energy that wouldn't have existed otherwise, and people learn Christian ways of coping with an imperfect world. When we call on a member of the Trinity and say, "Please help me with this" and then behave in a way that is atypically wonderful, we know we have experienced God.

Prayer

The topic of prayer deserves a book, not a paragraph. It covers every aspect of life; it is appropriate at every age and is as global or personal as we like.

My family has witnessed so many miracles as a result of prayer that we are convinced of its efficacy. Many Christians never pray out loud and are uncomfortable talking about Jesus. The remedy for that is to teach your children about prayer at home and model it. Start with simple prayers and pray for personal needs as they come up during the day. In time, talking to God aloud together will be as familiar as talking to Grandma.

We taught our children to give thanks for food, and each of us took a day of the week to be the "prayer warrior." All that meant was that we listened to everyone's needs for the day while we ate breakfast together, and the warrior prayed for God to meet those needs. "God, thank You for this food, thank You for the blessings of this day. Please help Caty with her math test, help Bentley with her audition this afternoon, help me to … help Dad…Mom… the President and all of the leaders of the nations to make good decisions today… in Christ we pray. Amen."

At bedtime during tuck-in, we taught them to say, "Now I lay me down to sleep…" (a prayer that can be found in the appendix) and the Lord's Prayer. Then we offered any other prayer needs that had arisen during the day. If something came up during the day, we would pray aloud with them on the spot. It takes a minute or less and is so soothing.

When someone comes to us with his or her concerns should we just listen? Should we just sit and hope things will change? It makes so much more sense to ask God to promote a change in someone's heart or in a surgeon's hands or in a teacher's demeanor. If God has created it, He can certainly touch it. I believe He will whisper in our ears even if He won't force our hands. Have you ever responded to His whispers? Many people want to believe in God and that He is right here doing loving things for us all of the time. But we are not praying and listening, so we are missing the excitement of the interchange and interaction. Let's speak the requests of our hearts out loud to our Abba Father and notice His participation in our lives.

ACT

PRAYER AND DEVOTIONS

Do at least one of these things.

1. Go to a library, bookstore, or Christian bookstore. (Do make a fieldtrip to a Christian bookstore if you've never been there. They are not odd places, but when I was a common Christian I thought they might be, so I never stepped inside one.) They generally have helpful people behind the counter, and a variety of items including books, posters, gifts, music and family-friendly DVDs and novels that may appeal to you.

2. Pray for the Holy Spirit to help you choose the items that God wants for you.

3. Hang out there as long as you like and read through some of the devotionals and Bibles to see which ones appeal to you. If you aren't familiar with any of the books or authors, check the Internet to learn more about them.

4. Begin to read the Bible or a devotional more often than you do now.

5. See if there are any Christian radio stations in your area that appeal to you. Try them at different times of the day. I have found that some hosts on a particular station do not appeal to me, but a different one at another time of day may be right up my alley.

6. There is good, modern Christian music. Music speaks to some people better than sermons. If you don't know much about Christian music, go to the internet and look up a song by Chris Tomlin called Indescribable. If you check some artists out on the web, you'll be surprised at the variety. Almost every venue is represented there.

CHAPTER 39

TOOL #11: TUCK-IN TIME

"On my bed I remember you; I think of you through the watches of the night."

—PSALM 63:6

A FRIEND TEXTED ME AFTER A playful afternoon with his four-year-old twins. They ran and jumped on him and wore themselves out. "And then," he said, "they both fell asleep on my chest." That text is still on my phone. What a wonderful image.

What do you recall about bedtime in your home? My tuck-in time was playful, soothing, and affectionate. It wasn't until I was ten, though, that I saw a friend get on her knees beside her bed and recite a little prayer. Her parents could drink beer with the best of them and were a lot of fun, *and* they seemed to want her to know about God. It was a life-changing experience for me. I memorized the prayer that night. "Now I lay me down to sleep, I pray the Lord my soul to keep, watch me safely through the night, and wake me with the morning light. God bless Mommy and Daddy...." It was comforting. Special.

Bedtime makes an impression on us. There is that whole darkness thing. And the aloneness of it. And then there is the body and brain that just won't settle down and cooperate with the clock. Or the body that is so tired, but I don't want to go to bed. We know that the age-old saying, "Get some sleep, you will feel better in the morning," is true, but we still have the night to get through. Sometimes all of our worries and fears attack us after dark when we are tired. It's nice to have one last reassurance that someone cares. Maybe even some unexpected laughs.

Tuck-in time is a great opportunity to incorporate three love languages at once: words of affirmation, quality time (uninterrupted one-on-one), and appropriate touch. You can even add acts of service to the mix if you help your child get things in order for the morning (such as putting her shoes by the door or packing items in a backpack). Both anxiety and depression can cause interruptions in the brain's ability to refresh itself, so calm moral support is invaluable. We even know that there are memory benefits from those things that we learn immediately before we sleep. So please don't skimp on this.

How is tuck-in a coping strategy? It reminds us what is important in life—one another—and gives your child a private moment to tell you if anything is bothering him or her. Unless you have more than six children, it takes less than an hour each night to give ten minutes of uninterrupted time to each of your children. If 10 minutes sounds like nothing, consider the fact that most children count on nothing, so 10 minutes a day (50 minutes a week, M-F) of your undivided attention is a lot. If it is 20 minutes a night, all the better. Sing, read, rub shoulders, exchange affirmations, pray for their needs, and let them pray for you. Let them tell you what they want bedtime to look like if you don't know what to do or they seem uncomfortable. You will never regret this.

ACT

Tuck-in Time

Ask each person in your family to give you a _____ minute slot in their evening, and ask what they would like to do with it. Collaborate to decide on something. If a child is older and has lots of studies and extra activities, he or she may stay up later than you do. That's okay. You don't have to literally tuck a teen in. Just let your children know you are glad they are there and ask if there is anything you can pray for. Also, see if you can get them to buy-in to this idea of giving a few minutes each night. Even five minutes will be life changing.

Decide which TV show or daily chores you are willing to give up, in order to improve the quality of your soil. Remember, the soil of your family life is the everyday mix of experiences out of which your souls either starve or thrive. By reading this book and incorporating some of the loving discipline and supportive activities, you are enriching your soil.

CHAPTER 40

TOOL #12: TROUBLESHOOTING YOUR NEW LIFESTYLE

"I am glad to boast about my weaknesses, so that the power of Christ may work through me."

—2 CORINTHIANS 12:9 (NLT)

BOTH MEN AND WOMEN GIVE up on the Christian way of life because it "doesn't seem to work." Oh, my precious brothers and sisters, don't give up! That's a lie. Christ's ways, lived out through us, produce the exact results He wants: health of our souls as well as comfort, courage, and hope.

One week, when I was feeling hopeless as a mom, my best friend gave me a wonderful handout she had received earlier in her life. It was filled with dozens of statements that moms throughout time had said. It made me giggle through my tears. The truth in it is obvious. We have to be told things over, and over, and over; then we still forget. All of us. It's just our nature. Don't get discouraged, and don't take it personally.

When I was consulting in corporate America, we helped the managers of companies realize why their staffs weren't producing quality results. We used a quadrant to look at four areas of need.

Do they *know* what is expected?	Are they *motivated*?
Are they *capable* of meeting the expectations?	Do they have adequate *support*?

The key words are: *knowledge, motivation, capability, and support.*

KNOWLEDGE — ARE THEY AWARE?

Does your family know what is expected of them? There's an easy way to find this out. Ask.

Jim and I decided a long time ago that we didn't want God to take a backseat in our family. Of course, family lifestyles will vary based upon the inspiration of the Holy Spirit. God has different designs for our lives because we all serve different purposes. The goal is to design a lifestyle that is safe and relational and that acquaints your children with Christ, the Holy Spirit, and God.

As our knowledge of our faith evolves, so do our desires and expectations for our children. At first Jim and I just made short lists of daily responsibilities and expectations. As you read my children's answers to some questions, know that they had been several years in the making, but it was worth it. My oldest daughter, Bentley, came to me one day and said, "Mom, in the morning people are sleepy and little things can hit you wrong. I love that we just get to come to the table and get affection and food and that you or Dad read to us. I'm glad you have created a morning that discourages us from complaining or rushing." Say amen and amen. This is the fruit of years of walking with and listening to God. When God inserts Himself into your life because He's been invited to do so, you'll have this incredible, rich, extraordinary outcome.

The first area of troubleshooting is knowledge. You may assume that everyone knows what you expect, but they may not. Rather than getting mad, write it down, and remind your family over and over again. Ask your children these questions and see what they say. What would you like for them to say?

My questions	*My children's answers*
• What do I ask you to do when you wake up?	Say 'Good Morning' to God and thank Him for some of the good things in my life; listen for Him to say, "You're welcome."
• What do I expect from you until breakfast?	Get up, get dressed, listen to Christian music, and be at the table by 7:20.
• What do I expect at the breakfast table?	Say grace, eat, drink our juice, take our vitamins, listen to Dad read the morning devotion, share our prayer needs: the "prayer warrior" prays out loud for us, and take our dishes to the sink.
• What do I expect after breakfast?	Finish getting ready, leave on time with our lunch and school bag, and be in class on time.

My questions	*My children's answers*
• What do I expect after school from 4:00-6:00?	Call and ask if we want to go someplace other than home, be home by 6:00 to help you with dinner, and get our things ready to study.
• What do I expect at dinner?	Eat together at 6:30 or 7:00; the dish person does the dishes with Dad.
• What do I expect after dinner?	Do our homework, get our clothes, shoes, and bookbags ready for the next day, be in bed at 10:00 to read and relax, bring our phones to the kitchen at 10:30 to recharge them, and turn out the lights and sleep.

Their understanding and our expectations weren't perfectly aligned. Sometimes their assumptions were stricter than our reality and other times the opposite was true. But most of the time, they knew. Remember that my home has had many weekly meetings and evening updates, so our family stays pretty well informed. As the children got older and had more studies and activities, we had to forsake some of these clean lines. Realize that in some families trying to get children asleep at 10:30 would create a battle zone—something not conducive to rest. Also, such tidy routines would be all wrong for some parents. I get that. But some sense of rhythms, rituals, and frequent reminders will keep everyone in the know. That's the purpose of "Evening Updates"—you're checking in a family setting for needs, calendar updates, and friendly invitations and to review the rituals and rhythms of the home you share. You're praising them for following through on agreements. Speaking of praise, let's look at the next condition necessary for living a lifestyle of love.

MOTIVATION — ARE THEY INSPIRED?

It is amazing how many of us who consider ourselves to be "devout Christians" forget to apply the following scripture to our lives:

> *"Let everything you say be good and helpful, so that your words will be an encouragement to those who hear them."*
> —EPHESIANS 4:29 (DNLT)

Let's look at three key motivators: praise, collaboration, and consequences.

PRAISE

The first thing your family should hear from you at evening updates is what they're doing right. It's very motivating to be noticed and praised. We each participate in and promote the well-being of our family members in many ways each day. From a very young age, my children have been able to respond to my discouraging complaints with a list of "Mom, Let-Me-Tell-You-What-I-Did-Rights." In other words, they would use my affirmations from earlier in the day to remind me of what they had done right when I came up and criticized them for what they did wrong. It's good for you to be told if you are being too picky. I thank God for their being courageous enough to set me straight. It is humbling and balancing. It brings peace.

If you live in an environment where condemnation outweighs praise, don't expect our Abba Father to give you peace until you've changed the system. God's way is to impart wisdom, and Christ has shown us how:

> *"Fix your thoughts on what is true and honorable and right. Think about things that are pure and lovely and admirable. Think about things that are excellent and worthy of praise. Keep putting into*

*practice all you learned from me and heard from me and saw me
doing, and the God of peace will be with you."*
—Philippians 4:8-9 (DNLT)

God created us in such a way that when we focus on negatives, we become sour, and people don't want to be around us. There are helpful and kind ways to turn things around when they are headed in the wrong direction. Complaining is something we have been warned against in the Bible because it's offensive.

COLLABORATION

My sweet parents taught me to collaborate. I watched them do it all of my life. Not until it was not happening one day did I realize how demotivating it is to be told that there is only one way to do something when there is clearly more than one option. For example, we were trimming trees one day, and the person I was trimming with wanted me to bag the limbs a certain way. He is capable. When I did it my way, he corrected me. If he had shown me and given me a choice, that would have been okay, I guess. But it was obvious that he wanted it done his way. You know what I thought? I thought, "Who cares how the darn limbs are bagged?" I was enjoying the task until he insisted that I do it his way. Then it became work.

There is no right way to do dishes, make a bed, cook, or clean. There are hundreds of ways. If you don't believe this, go to a college campus and visit for a week. Young adults demonstrate many ways to accomplish domestic chores when no one is there to correct them. Yet it's not unusual for me to say to my children, "This is the way to do it." Tasks are more pleasant when we are allowed to dress them up a bit with our own personality. Whenever possible, let others do that, please. It brings peace.

Meal times, free time, study habits, and many other details of our lives have come about through collaboration. Proverbs 12:15 says, "The way of a fool seems right to him, but a wise man listens to advice." If we align our lifestyles with the preferences of our family members (when possible), they will be much more motivated to align themselves with our agreements. For example, once-a-week bedroom cleaning is an example of collaboration at our house. I prefer daily tidying and bed-making; they prefer to clean up only when the feeling hits. We collaborated and created a new system for keeping life in order. I find that if their rooms are tidy and cleaned weekly, our lives run smoothly enough. After years of this compromise, I still don't like "messy" and they still don't like cleaning, but we all like the benefits that come with it. I don't nag about their rooms, and they tidy them more often than once a week without a word from me. We are all thankful for the beauty and order in our lives.

Consequences

As you might expect, this is the toughest condition to provide in a loving Christian way. So let's look at it:

When you set a boundary like "Do this by this time," there must be a consequence that makes it inspiring, or the doer won't be motivated to do it. Sometimes praise and collaboration are simply not enough.

As was mentioned earlier, if our child's room was clean by 9:00 on Thursday night, she could not have Friday night privileges taken away. A clean room was a ticket to Friday freedom. What? Yes, it's true. I have had audacious behavior occur after Thursday night at 9:00 and have still given the child Friday off. Do you think that's crazy? If so, you have forgotten the scripture that says: "Simply let your yes be yes, and your no be no" (Matt. 5:37). This amazes our children, and they are thankful for our constancy. We will not take away their Friday when we have promised it.

At the same time, we will keep them home with us and enjoy their company on Friday night if they don't get their room cleaned by the agreed upon time on Thursday. That doesn't mean, "You're grounded. You can sit in your room alone with your computer." It means you'll spend time (giving and receiving love) with at least one family member until it's done. No electronics. No friends.

Your children may choose not to clean it at all some weekends. They may want to spend the weekend with you. Other times, you won't believe how fast a room can be cleaned! As soon as it is, they are free. And, yes, now and then Jim and I did have a commitment, so we did give grace and let the girls go out even if they hadn't cleaned their rooms, but they never knew when that would be. Grace is something that you don't deserve but are given anyway. Grace is what Christ gave to us. Exceptions like this are a nice way to teach grace without words.

Another big motivator is the Character Tickets and loving payoff system. This is the replacement for punishment. God has told us not to punish, but He certainly expects us to discipline (Eph. 6:4). Family members have been told which behaviors are offensive and that if they hardheartedly continue to do the behavior, they may receive a ticket. The cost for each ticket is an apology and a five-minute fine. They know what the risk is. Just like we know the risk when we speed or run a stop sign. Sometimes we take the risk. If we get a ticket, we pay it. Receiving and paying off an occasional ticket motivates us to think about our driving and slow down.

You may decide that each family member will have ten tokens. When they are out of tokens, friends and electronics are not allowed. Their decisions, not their parent's mood, determine the loss of and the return of their privileges. Also, family comes first. That means they cannot owe the family more than 50 minutes without paying someone off and getting some tokens back. You may decide that by the end of the week, they have to have all ten tokens back in their container before they can use electronics or spend time with friends. Is it really so much to ask to give siblings or parents 50 minutes of loving time while watching TV, playing cards, or shooting baskets? Surprisingly, according to the families I have taught, the answer is "yes." In our hectic culture, it is hard to give up one's precious time and requires discipline.

When you play together, compliment one another. Notice one another's improvements, or if you are not athletic, be willing to keep a good attitude, have a sense of humor, or be persistent. Thirty minutes returns six tokens. That's motivating.

If you have a mercy heart or a busy life, you may have a hard time following through on tough consequences, so be careful when you set up your family's system. Sometimes less is more. We teach others to keep their word by keeping ours. Isn't that what faithfulness is about?

Capability — Are They Able?

Our God-given intelligence, personality, preferences, and physical make-up are all factors that determine our capability of living life by the rules. Our man-given training, role models, environments, and spiritual maturity add to or subtract from that capability. This is the area in which embracing the Scripture "do not judge" is so critical.

When you are addressing another person's capacity to accomplish and abide by the standards, it is time to ponder some things:

1. Is it possible that he can't see this the way I do?
2. Is it possible that this isn't worth fighting for right now? When she is older, more mature, we'll revisit this.
3. Is his personality too laid back or too intense to accomplish this task in my way at my pace?
4. Have I asked which task she prefers, rather than assuming my preferences are better for everyone?

For some people, the human brain is simply not capable of certain tasks at certain ages, and no two brains are alike. One child's brain may have strength in themes or creativity and low electrical activity. One family member may have a brain and personal style that makes acquiring rhythms and rituals a breeze. Do not despair, and do not judge. You may never know for certain when it comes to capacity. Only God knows, and for now, He's not telling.

When you have tried everything else to help a family member succeed and nothing seems to be working, you may need a professional counselor or physician's input. In the meantime, allow this pondering to keep you humble, curious, and kind. All brains function better when they are well rested, well fed, and watered—literally. And all humans function better when they believe they have some control over their stressors.

If you've never seen them do it, there is a possibility that they can't. If you have seen them do it, but they don't, consider offering a hand.

Support — Can They Do It if You Add Tools or Manpower?

Spiritual Support

I'm going to start this off with fireworks, so get ready. Christianity teaches that we are eternal beings housed temporarily in these human bodies. These bodies need air, food, liquids, rest, and at times, protection from the environment. The spiritual being inside this body needs energy that comes from:

1. Hearing and understanding God's Word
2. Prayer, so we know God can make happen what we can't do alone
3. Love from God and others around us
4. Quiet time to meditate on these truths

We function best when all our spirit, soul and body get support. Did it ever occur to you that you may not be fully functioning because you are not fully fed? Do not forget to feed those precious spirits around you with spiritual food. They may simply be feeling tired and sickly because there is too little spiritual food in their homes. Remember that God asks us to seek Him daily. Many of His promises depend on this. And that, precious ones, is the point of this book: to make God the vertical weave in the fabric of our lives.

Relational and Physical Support

If you are taking the few minutes a day to remind your family to walk with God through reading and prayer, are you also supporting them physically?

Relational and physical support means you work alongside of them to help lighten their loads. You bring a helping hand, tools, and emotional encouragement to the activity. Here are some examples:

Kim: I always go to wake the boys up. Today, in fact, before they left for school I walked into their rooms and said, "This looks like a college dorm" and laughed at their perfectly made beds.[19]

Mary Helen: At our house, a parent helps with dishes. It's a relational opportunity.

Joanna: I'll do one of their chores (put away their laundry, clean their closet, etc.) as a surprise so they don't have to do it when I see them really busy with school and other activities.

Jill: We write notes on the children's napkins in their lunchboxes, and I send affirmation texts (ex..."You have a beautiful heart" filled with emojis, of course:) to them before school every day and whenever they leave the house.

Paula: Since my girls are still in grade school they love the Fruit of the Spirit song. We sing it before they get out of the car at carpool to remind us of the way to handle difficult people during the day.

Judy: I picked up Jake for the doctors and went to Taco Bell on the way back even though it made him late for class. It makes going to the doctor a treat.

How do you give support to make the chores of life more enjoyable and energizing?

If you are doing evening updates, you are more likely to have poster boards, school paper, soccer shoes, and other physical equipment ready

---

19 Most high school kids awaken to their alarms. The point here is a cheery and welcoming presence first thing in the day. If your child is an introvert, he or she may prefer silence and solitude.

when it is needed because you've looked at the calendar ahead of time. If they watch you do this for years, they will know how to do it when they can drive.

Troubleshooting Supernaturally

For the person who wants to experience God and live fully in the midst of His kingdom, there is a supernatural force field that sits atop these four quadrants. As you motivate, inform, support, and consider capacity, you do it all with a thought for God. First Peter 4:9-10 contains one of the most meaningful keys to troubleshooting your lifestyle and to experiencing God: "God has given gifts to each of you from His great variety of spiritual gifts. Manage them well so that God's generosity can flow through you." (NLT)

It is God's energy flowing through you that transforms and heals over time. He is patient. Consciously give your difficult situations to Him. As you walk into your son's room, tell God to speak for you. As you face the mess in your living room, ask Jesus to help you put it in the baskets. As you walk up to your son's room on Thursday night to check it at 8:30 and are longing for him (and you!) to have Friday night off, say, "Holy Spirit, spread your cheer and give me the energy to support this effort to tidy this room with positive conversation and respect." Whichever person of the Trinity you are comfortable asking to help, ask, and then allow.

Christ asked us to take on His yoke. That means we work with Him, power under control and without feelings of entitlement. Ask yourself what you can change in your life to make it better. For instance, do you drink too much alcohol? Watch too much junk on TV? Get too little exercise? Hang out with whiny friends? No wonder you are tired. Listen to your conscience, and little by little, act on it. You'll change! It is your built-in coach. Just remember the qualities of God from 1 Corinthians 13. If it is God talking to you, the words you hear won't be mean-spirited.

There's one last thing about troubleshooting this lifestyle that I want to share with you—Don't give up. The victory is worth every tear. More than once, I looked at my family and said, "I seem to be the only one who believes in this. None of you are writing tickets or using Potter's Clay for habits. I'm going to scrap this whole thing." Then, all of my tools would be (carefully) set outside in the trashcan. I never had the heart to just demolish them. One of the girls would go and get them. They would hug me and offer to try again. The truth is that once we became accustomed to this more loving, temperate, respectful, healing way of life, we didn't want to go back. In truth, we couldn't go back. Thank God for that. It is one of Christianity's new opportunities to tell the world what Jesus came to teach us. Look what Peter wrote to scattered Jewish Christians who were undergoing intense persecution for their faith:

> *"Finally, all of you should be of one mind, full of sympathy toward each other, loving one another with tender hearts and humble minds. Don't repay evil for evil. Don't retaliate when people say unkind things about you. Instead, pay them back with a blessing. That is what God wants you to do, and He will bless you for it....So don't be afraid and don't worry. Instead, you must worship Christ as Lord of your life. And if you are asked about your Christian hope, always be ready to explain it. But you must do this in a gentle and respectful way. Keep your conscience clear. Then if people speak evil against you, they will be ashamed when they see what a good life you live because you belong to Christ. Remember, it is better to suffer for doing good, if that is what God wants, than to suffer for doing wrong!"*
>
> —I Peter 3: 8-9, 14-17

ACT

Troubleshooting Your New Lifestyle

Some of us know what our weakest link is, and some of us don't. Do you?

Look at each of the four areas we have discussed in this chapter on troubleshooting.

Knowledge   Motivation   Capability   Support

What do you think is your weakest area?

Why do you think it is weak?

What do you expect of yourself and others? Too much? Too little? According to whom? What do people tell you about yourself? That you are laid-back? That you have it all together? Do you think that makes you easier or harder to live with? Why?

Now, breathe a sigh of relief. Spiritually, all you have to do is learn to love God, yourself, and others and leave the consequences and details to God. Are you listening? Which details are really important?

PART 5

Tips and Tales for a Simpler Life

LIVING IN GOD'S KINGDOM

"For it is not mere words that nourish the soul, but God Himself, and unless and until the hearers find God in personal experience they are not the better for having heard the truth. The Bible is not an end in itself, but a means to bring men to an intimate and satisfying knowledge of God, that they may enter into Him, that they may delight in His Presence, may taste and know the inner sweetness of the very God Himself in the core and center of their hearts."

—A.W. TOZER, THE PURSUIT OF GOD

A Day in the Life — Common vs. Uncommon

A Common Morning

Wife to husband: Did you wake Suzie up?

Husband: I thought you were gonna wake her. I'll start breakfast.

Wife: No. You need to walk the dog because I have an early meeting. I wish you would listen when we talk, honey. I'm tired of feeling like everything everybody doesn't do has to fall on me.

Husband: What do you want me to do? Make breakfast or walk the dog?

Chelsea: No one woke me up! I can't find my shoes or my geography book!

Wife: I get so tired of you guys telling me at the last minute that you can't find something. You're supposed to...

Breakfast may or may not be eaten together. We may never say, "Good morning" to one another. We forget to kiss or hug one another good-bye and rarely affirm what's going right.

AN UNCOMMON MORNING

No one asks who's doing what because that was decided weeks ago at a family meeting. Morning is calm and kind and predictable. There may be light or cheery music, but probably not TV. Morning is about us and God.

Each individual knows his or her job, so conversations can be interesting and fun rather than focused on minutia. We know what each person's morning schedule and needs are because we discussed it the night before at a quick family "evening update."

If Joe forgot to organize his belongings last night, we respond to his needs by helping him to find his things. No lecturing or complaining occurs. If we are angry with Chelsea because her lack of organization put a wrench in the morning, we can write her a character ticket or jot a note on the "issue" pad and get on with the day. The anger or frustration that comes from one human's failure does not lead to more disappointment.

The family sits together at an agreed upon time to eat breakfast, hear a quick devotion, and pray for the day's needs. As each person leaves for the day, he or she receives a hug or kiss and affirmation.

A Simple and Safe Home

I N ORDER TO LIVE A newer, simpler life, we must choose to leave the old life behind. That is what Christ asks of His disciples. Sometimes we forget to do that. We are not supposed to add this new, uncommon lifestyle to old parenting habits that attempt to manipulate and insist. Rather, we use the tools to plant the seeds of forgiveness, love, consequences, collaboration, contribution, and mutual support into the hearts of those under our care. Then we trust God to grow those qualities—even when we cannot see.

Families that have chosen this lifestyle say the philosophies of love, mutual respect, and simplicity create a framework for approaching almost any topic. Having a support system (friends outside the family) creates an energy and diversity that allows us to think big. Recently, a room full of men in my church community group said they were thankful they had displayed love for their children during some rebellious phases of life or else they would have had little relationship with them when the rebellion was over. (These were strong men who had parented their children through many of the typical cultural challenges including addictions to drugs and alcohol.)

When we feel hurt, angered, embarrassed, or insulted by someone, we may instinctively want to fall back on old ways. But if we're willing to lean on Him, the Holy Spirit will tug at our souls and remind us that we are made to love and be loved. When we change direction and take the high road, sometimes we will write a ticket and pay consequences. Sometimes we won't. Rather than strike out in anger, we may gently stroke the person's hair. We complement our child's work. We remain silent when little disappointments come and are thankful that our spouse doesn't make a habit of coming home drunk or something worse. We try to recall what everyone does well. We like them—and ourselves—more because of it.

One of your jobs as a parent is to make your home simple and sensible. This will stand as a stark contrast to life outside your four walls. In the world, plenty of unforeseen consequences will teach the young that life's not fair. Out there, they will find unpredictability, hurriedness, and disappointments. There is unending work to be done from the time children leave home until they return. They are constantly pressured to perform for authority figures, with peers, and in extracurricular settings. They don't need those things doled out by their loving family members. They need simple, sensible, windows of belonging, purpose, and love. This section is an offering of support to you, to aid you as you come to embrace the lifestyle that can provide your children something they desperately need.

A necessarily short index of topics has been provided here. After reading these, you can begin to think ahead of time and discuss how your family might handle certain situations in a way that supports one another. Oftentimes, people parent like they were parented because they never think to do things any other way. However, Christ came to this planet and shook up a lot of people's notions about life. He invites us to free ourselves from rules that endanger relationships and try new ways that make life more healing. Perhaps some of the things you have read so far have had that effect on you.

As you read on, pray. Find peace.

Look up. Lighten up. Live up.

Kitchen Counter Tools

THE TOOLS IN PART 4 are meant to train you to energize positives all day and save negatives for one short meeting, so they need to stay visible so you will remember to use them. Remember, you are training your heart, mind, and brain. Place the tools together on a kitchen table or shelf where they are easily noticed.

- Bible
- Potter's Clay & toothpicks
- Family devotional
- Bowls of ten tokens for each family member
- Gift box of tickets
- Pad & pen to jot issues/ needs for meetings
- IOU box or bag

There is nothing more important on your kitchen counters than this! And most of it can be prepared at home or purchased for about ten dollars. I actually had women tell me that they reorganized their kitchen counters so that their basket of tools was convenient and cute. (Some of them even had to purchase something extra—a dome to protect the clay from hungry dogs!)

GETTING STARTED

SOME MOMS THINK USING CHARACTER Tickets, payoff with time, and Potter's Clay is a piece of cake. "What's hard?" they say. For them, it's a huge relief from traditional discipline and self-expression. When life starts to spin out of order, they bring on the tickets and clay. And for those moments when life is more peaceful, they live mostly by the meetings and principles of the lifestyle, using baskets and the other tools as staples.

Other parents find the tools to be a little challenging, simply because it is hard to change! The longer you have been parenting traditionally, the harder it may be to break old habits and activate new ones. You may need to encourage at least one friend to try the lifestyle with you so you'll have a companion on the journey. Your friend can remind you how good it feels when you banish acts of anger and replace them with acts of love. Below is a testimony from Kelly and Peg who quickly began to use tickets, payoff, and meetings. Following their testimonies are comments from a few moms who had to work Uncommon Sense into their homes more slowly. I hope these will encourage you.

TESTIMONIES

Kelly's Testimony: I love the Uncommon Sense lifestyle. It gave me the freedom to parent differently and much more effectively than the traditional parenting of yelling, consequences, grounding, or other ways that don't really work. I have three daughters who grew up using it. When my oldest was in high school, she thanked me for not taking her phone away or grounding her out of the blue "like all her friends' parents did." She is in college now and loves coming home to visit. Our relationship has stayed intact. All of my children are making good decisions. They are genuinely a joy to have in the house.

We've gained so many different things from the lifestyle. The family meetings provide a way for our children to address issues I would have never known they were dealing with otherwise. They love knowing we are there to help support them in whatever they need. I love it that I can apologize for my wrongdoing and teach by example. I learned quickly how much a ticket can sting; it's no fun to be called out on ugliness. I also love that the consequence for the ticket is always time spent together which genuinely helps to rebuild the broken relationship.

The tickets helped me not to lecture, but they also regulate my brain. I know the issues will be addressed at a later time, so I can focus on what really matters. They also help the kids because they know that they can write it down and not retaliate.

Our mornings are calm and help provide the support my family needs to get out the door; it changed everyone for the better. I saw miracles happen. For instance, when my youngest was in grade school. She didn't want to go to school some days, but I stayed in a calm place, which helped her become peaceful and to talk about her reasons. We always got to the bottom of it and out the door on time. She was *never* late to school, and that is a miracle. I had told myself that it would be okay if she was a little late, which helped me to stay calm and in turn diminished the entire meltdown.

I would love to say that I had meetings every week and always wrote tickets, but that simply is not the case. We would do the meetings and tickets really well for a few weeks and then the house would be running so smoothly that we just wouldn't make the time to do it. Eventually, the house would crumble, and we had to break out the tickets again. They were something that I loved having in my back pocket. I am here to say that Uncommon Sense worked wonders in my house.

Peg's Testimony: When Carroll first asked me to join the original Uncommon Sense group and try these strategies in my own family, I thought to myself, *What a wonderful way to give everyone in the family a voice! Perhaps this will stop some of the bickering and manipulation that is frequent in our family and driving a wedge between any hope for peace and tranquility.*

We were a small nuclear family by the time we incorporated Uncommon Sense into our lives. With one 13-year-old son, Walker, left at home and the two older boys on their own, arranging family meetings once a week was easy. Getting through them at first was not! We adopted the "talking stick"[20] out of necessity at these meetings, which stopped the persistent

---

20 This "talking stick" is any object you choose, and is held by the person speaking. If you aren't holding it, you don't speak. This teaches the art of listening without interrupting. It doesn't need to be used during the entire meeting, but is very helpful when topics make everyone want to speak at the same time. My team came up with this brilliant idea. Be careful not to hold the "talking stick" for too long.

interruptions from others and gave our son the "voice" he needed to make his own hopes and desires known.

Character Tickets became our way to communicate that damage had been done to another family member instead of picking a fight or shouting at each other. Payback became a time of treasured companionship when we spent thoughtful loving time with one another. Our morning routines became just that—routine. Finished homework was stashed in the backpack and shoes placed at the door rather than lost under the bed or, well, just lost. And reflection often stopped grievances within the first or second complaint.

Most importantly, Uncommon Sense reminded us to live with Jesus under our roof and build relationships on love, trust, and respect—the stepping stones of 1 Corinthians 13:4-7. Love is patient, love is kind, love never gives up. We have a version of that verse hanging in the office as a constant reminder of what true love should look like.

So what began as a ploy to change everyone else in my family became my own undoing. I gradually gave up my attempts to control my household and everyone in it, and my yelling repetitive demands up the stairs became less and less frequent until it finally disappeared. Little did I know that I would be the one to whom the Holy Spirit spoke the loudest or that it would be me who changed the most. I like who I have become.

I thank God for the friendships and strong support system I found with the other women in the first Uncommon Sense families. I believe that, without them to hold me accountable, I may have given up. My admiration and respect for the families who have lived this, through all our hardships and trials, has grown into a sisterhood of support and encouragement. I cannot imagine where we would be now and what our lives would have been like without one another or Uncommon Sense. Go God!

Sabrina's Testimony: A dramatic difference I saw in our home is that the principles caused Ken and me to stop calling up the stairs at the children for things we needed them to do, and we began to support them more and spend more loving time together. It has been wonderful for all of us. We realized that when things weren't going the way we wanted them to go, all we needed to do is keep our cool, address things calmly, and have the children spend time with us. It really did make such a difference and, hopefully, they learned some good ways of handling life from us.

One time, my children, Jimmy and Hannah, were at the park with me. When it was time to go, Jimmy didn't want to leave and began to resist. In the past, this would have escalated and led to a fuss between us. This time I stayed calm and decided I would just write him a ticket when we got home. After a few minutes, he got into the car, and we rode home. I stayed really sweet, and we had a nice ride. When we got home, I told him that I was writing him a ticket for his actions. I asked him if he wanted to go ahead and pay his time to me. He thanked me and said, "Yes." Later, I was unloading the dishwasher, and he asked if he could help me. He did, and we had a wonderful talk while we did it. It was great! What a difference.

Lisa's Testimony: The thing that held me back was feeling like my husband had to be on board. He didn't understand it and thought it fell in my camp of grace and mercy. He didn't get the boundaries, discipline, accountability, and consequences. I realize now that he doesn't have to be in sync with me. Unless he witnesses it, he will never embrace it. Today he doesn't think of our lifestyle as Uncommon Sense, but has become a regular part of weekly family meetings and other aspects of the lifestyle as we have integrated them into our lives.

Jill's Testimony: We need to be patient with ourselves. As one of our moms stated, "You may not be able to change too much all at one time, or you might feel off balance." You need to remember why you wanted a change. I just knew some of the things we were doing weren't right.

Liz's Testimony: With young children, it is easier to change your ways because you haven't been practicing your parenting style for long. The kids like trying new things, and these forms of discipline are more predictable and seem less mean-spirited than some that they have had in the past.

An Anonymous Testimony: I once showed Character Tickets and Potter's Clay to a friend who is a parent. She is an atheist, so I was curious what she would think of this faith-based lifestyle. She said, "You know what leaps right out at me? It teaches unconditional love. You can do something really bad or stupid and still be treated like you deserve to be loved." She called me several times to tell me how our discussion that day had changed her interactions with her son for the better.

TOPICAL INDEX

THE FOLLOWING ARE SIMPLE PATTERNS for handling a variety of circumstances and topics that come up in family life. Remember that God calls us to live by principles over preferences. His two most important principles are 1.) Deeply love Him and 2.) Deeply love yourself and others. He defines love in 1 Corinthians 13 and says that it, "does not insist on its own way." We know that Christ kept His word. So, in this day of fickle and sometimes cruel relationships, Uncommon Sense invites us to learn from Christ: to be uncommonly predictable. Choose some loving ways and trust God to bless them.

AFFECTION—*Nothing* tops affection for pulling sunshine into a gloomy relationship. I recall a day when I was disappointed with one of my daughters for something she hadn't done. She walked in the door, and as she was about to pass me on the steps I opened my mouth to complain. But instead, I caught myself and stroked her hair. I said, "You have the most beautiful hair." She said, "Awww, Mommy. You are the most wonderful mom in the world." What forgotten task could have been more important than that?

Another form of affection we traded in our family was ten-minute backrubs. Touch is so important to human beings that babies literally cannot flourish without it. Can we offer too much affection to one another? Only if one person is offended by the form. Early on, let your family members know that you want them to tell you if there is ever any touch that they don't like. Some people love tickles. Some people hate them. Find what works for your loved ones. Just an affectionate attitude or word while watching your child or spouse or friend tells them so much about who they are to you.

AFFIRMATIONS—A person with the gift of encouragement will always find the silver lining, even in behaviors that annoy you. One year, we were giving affirmation rocks to each second grader for a keepsake. It was just a common rock with a word written on it that captured his or her personality. I asked the teacher to define each child with one word. For some, she was stumped. When she told me one little boy never sat still and was hard to manage, I put "energetic" on his rock. A girl who "talked all the time" got the word "engaging." I assure you there is a positive slant that can be given to any behavior. Many multimillionaire philanthropists had rocky starts in life, but they typically had at least one person who believed in them. (I said "multimillionaire philanthropists" because so many parents fear that their children's negative qualities will keep them from making a living or being a good person. Those fears are often unfounded.)

If affirmations are hard for you, write down some of the following words and put them beside your character ticket box. People do positive things every day. Take the time to notice and remark on them.

- Clever
- Bold
- Determined
- Generous
- Loving
- Patient

- Respectful
- Responsible
- Funny
- Honest
- Spunky
- Flexible

- Humble
- Creative
- Positive
- Good
- Fair
- Caring

- Helpful
- Faithful

- Kind
- Tender

- The list goes on and on!

ALLOWANCE — Give your children a dollar a week for every year they are old. (Four dollars a week when they are four. Five dollars a week when they are five. Eighteen dollars when they are eighteen.) For the parent, it is money that would have been spent on children anyway. You are just trusting them with it and teaching them to use it wisely. It actually saves money in the long run because less of it is spent on spontaneous purchases, and it saves all that bickering at the stores. Have them put ten percent in savings and give ten percent to God's work. Then, when your child says, "Can I have this toy?" or "Can I have this candy?" you can reply, "Do you want to spend your money on it?" They will say "yes" or "no." No arguments, just choice.

This financial arrangement teaches children so much about money. One of our daughters bought the family a porch swing when she was nine. She also had expensive hobbies, including photography, and was able to buy nice camera equipment because she hadn't spent it on frivolous items. Another daughter saved and was able to add money to the car we bought for her. A third child had enough saved to travel to Europe by the time she enrolled in college because she was very frugal. All of them had money in savings for their first fender bender. None of them ever got paid for helping around the house. Our philosophy was that it was a family home and caring for it was a form of thankfulness. Allowance was guaranteed, never threatened. God has never taken my food when I've had a bad attitude, so I never took their allowance when they had a bad attitude. It is something they could count on.

APOLOGIES — In all of my years as a counselor, I have never heard anyone say, "My parents apologized too much." The words "I'm sorry" are invaluable. Practice them. Say them over and over again out loud until they slide easily off of your tongue. We will never know all of the underlying reasons why people are touchy about a given subject, but if they are, they are. When their posture, behavior, or words tell you that you have hurt them, apologize and see what can be done to reconcile yourself to them. Many of us did not come from homes where reconciliation was taught. Or, we may have been taught to reconcile but preferred to defend, debate, disparage, or walk away. Now, as our children choose denial or debate when they fight with one another, we see how it keeps both parties from feeling heard. We don't want to pass destructive coping strategies down to our children, so we can't model them. After you apologize for a bad habit you have developed, consider using Potter's Clay on the habit for the week. It will show your family that you really are sorry and you want to change.

ARCHITECTURE OF THE BRAIN— You influence the physical design of your brain and the brains of those around you. We are born with over 100 billion brain cells. Each moment of life results in the creation and redesign of your brain cells and the pathways between these cells. Each moment determines the architecture of our brains. Some of those designs become our best memories and problem-solving strategies.

Genetics, talents and gifts, health, education, and our interactions with others all influence our brains. And let's not forget that, especially in childhood, our brains will clean themselves out from time to time and discard billions of cells that seem to be getting in the way or are seldom used. Our caregivers will play a dramatic role in the cells we keep versus the ones that are pruned.

In the face of stress, do you choose to get curious or furious? Think of the difference in the chemicals and cells that come together for the curious mind and brain rather than the furious one. Specific cells will connect repeatedly until it is second nature for your brain to respond to stress with either curiosity or condemnation. Which structure do you want to build? Our construction has already begun. Are we more kind or blind? We are handing down our inclinations to our children.

BASKETS — For as many homes as have acquired baskets, there are different ways to use them with your family. Most people put them on the stairs on the way to the bedrooms, but yours may end up by the back door. Whatever size you need for the clutter, buy it. Your goal is to remedy the bad feelings and maintain the flow of God's love, so make it happen.

Most people start out wanting the baskets to be emptied frequently with some kind of fine (5 minutes of loving time per day) for not emptying them. As the love grows in the family, the condition moves to letting baskets be emptied occasionally with a fine for ridiculous abuse. And by the time the children are teens, everyone is just thrilled to know the phone, keys, and billfold are in the basket. Trust me, by then you'll have bigger fish to fry, and they won't be misplacing their important stuff very often anyway.

BEDTIME PRAYERS — Reading God's thoughts is such a wonderful way to tuck ourselves in at night. Some Bible verses that are hard for adults to memorize can be learned by a child in no time at all.

Because fear often accompanies darkness, a verse you can give your children is, "Whenever I am afraid, I will trust in you" (Ps. 56:3). Let them look up simple prayers or verses to help you find a favorite if you don't know one. You can use The Lord's Prayer (Matthew 6:9-13) or Psalm 23. This little prayer is also popular, but not found in the Bible:

> *Now I lay me down to sleep,*
> *I pray the Lord my soul to keep.*
> *Watch me safely through the night,*
> *and wake me with the morning light.*
> *God bless Mommy and ....*

Continue until the child has mentioned the people who are most important to him or her, and consider praying "for our leaders and for peace on earth."

Bias — To be biased is to prefer one thing or perspective to another. Everyone has a life story, so all of us are biased and view the world differently. One day while teaching, I presented a story of two children who were having a difficulty. One parent said, "The older child had it right."

Another parent said, "Oh, no, the younger child was in the right. I would have written the ticket on the older child."

"I would have written it on the younger child," a third mom chimed in, "because I was the older child growing up. I can see why he felt the way he did."

The whole group laughed and talked about how our position in a family colors the way we look at life.

That day, we learned that we see life through our own biases. That's why God tells us not to judge and not to seek vengeance. We may think we have things figured out when we really have it all wrong. If you need to write a ticket because no one else will, it may be best to write a ticket on both people involved in the disagreement (or counsel or hug both of them.) Since we have limited knowledge, our biases can fan the flames of sibling rivalry. Be careful about taking sides. Remember Paul's advice, "Live in harmony with each other… and don't think you know it all!" (Rom. 12:16 NLT).

Bickering — In our home, if two people started yelling, we would ask them to "stop littering our airspace." If they wouldn't stop, we could warn them that we were going to charge them time for littering. If they still didn't stop, we were allowed to take a token from each of their bowls. Sometimes, they were asked to tell one another three nice things to repair damage. Why? Because "Avoiding a fight is a mark of honor; only fools insist on quarreling" (Prov. 20:3 NLT).

When people start arguing or bickering loudly, ask them to stop for 60 seconds and try to let the feeling pass. Give them an egg timer. Just focusing on time causes them to use a different part of the brain and takes some energy away from the emotional center. There are some colorful, small hourglasses on the market. Since they are antiquated and uncommon, children like them. We found a little timer actually in the shape of an egg. We called it the "good egg award." If you could avoid talking until the sand ran out, you got to put it in front of your plate at the table. Praise success of any length by giving a thumbs up, smile, nod, or hug. This competes with the negative situation. Especially praise each person later behind closed doors. Private praise is powerful. It feels especially honest and meaningful.

Brainstorm—At family meetings and other times when you are trying to solve problems or make family decisions, invite your children to brainstorm with you. Allow ideas to come without interruption.

Think of a storm. It is not controlled. That is what it means to brainstorm. It means invite and temporarily accept all solutions. Once you have them on paper, eliminate those that won't work. For example, a parent might ask:

"How shall we clean the house?"

"Open all the doors and see if the wind will just blow it out!"

"Okay, Sue. Write down, 'wind blows through house.'"

Now, we all know that wind is going to be eliminated, but the person who said it feels free to continue to contribute his or her thoughts, and sometimes these creative thinkers are the ones who eventually come up with million dollar ideas. Don't be afraid to collaborate. It allows you to see the bounty God has given.

Car Fights—After I was introduced to the healing effects of love, I stopped yelling at my kids or threatening them when they fought in the car. I learned to stop when a skirmish broke out. I would pull over as soon as it was safe, take the angriest child out of the car and ask to hug her. I'd tell her things I loved about her. If she was still upset, I would reflect her and hug and affirm her some more. While I was embracing her, I'd think, "Christ, embrace her through me because it is Your touch that heals." Then, if I needed to, I would put that child back in the car and do the same with the other. These embraces and affirmations calm a child so quickly. A friend riding home from church with me one day saw me do this. She was so taken aback by the beauty of it that more than ten years later, she still tells the story.

A quicker version of this healing fix for car frustrations is to offer the angry person your hand. Ask Christ to love the hurting person through you. Say, "Take my hand." Let him or her squeeze or hold it for as long as it takes to give the other person the calm resolve and strength to overcome the stressor. If another person in the car was the stressor, you may have to give him or her your hand after you have finished calming the first unhappy camper.

A loving touch is so much better for our souls than a raised voice or ignoring the situation by asking them to be quiet and watch the movie. Watching the movie may sweep the dirt under the rug, but the mold will grow. A loving response is sunlight.

CAR RIDES — Most families have plenty of electronics to keep everyone entertained, but this strategy kept our car a peaceful place even before electronics were available. Write four simple expectations on a piece of paper such as "quiet voices, kind hands, keep belongings in your own space, ask before taking others' things." Review these with the children and explain that if they follow the rules, they will receive continuous rewards. Then every so many minutes (based on the age of the children and length of the trip) give a tiny treat for success. Have the children go to the store with you before the trip and buy a cheap treat or two to earn for successful behavior. (I'm talking tiny pieces of candy or clay or a coloring book you might have bought anyway). Praise them occasionally to let them know they are on their way to success. As they grow older, they will succeed without the treat, and you will have learned to tell them intermittently that you enjoy riding with them. The time flies as you dole out the treats. This really works! Be sure to help them succeed at first, and do not be too zealous for perfection. If they are in the ballpark, give them credit. Every teacher knows this is a key to success.

There are also many car games a family can play that require no tools or toys. These include but aren't limited to I Spy, 20 Questions, The Picnic Game, Count the Cows, Geography Lesson, Name that Tune, License Plates, Where's the Alphabet, and Tunnels.

Character Tickets — Moms who have used them say:

- It has been fun to have my friends in an Uncommon Sense group with me. Our children are in preschool and elementary school and are all using the same discipline style, so we laugh about it. It works! The other day I saw two of my friends' kids talking to each other. One said, "Hey, that was mean. You should get a character ticket." The other replied, "We do that, too. I'll help you."
- Our kids know the other families who are using Uncommon Sense, so they want to do it with them.
- Tickets allow the children and their friends to handle the problem without you. When you say, "Go get a ticket," the problem feels finished. They know what to do from there, and it is a Christian response to stress.
- Just writing the tickets is healing for me because I typically avoid stressful things. When I have to write them down, I have to face them. I don't pretend the elephant isn't in the room anymore. I realize I have a problem and need to respond to it.
- Initially, just writing the ticket feels good because it lets the person who is hurt or angry know he or she is going to be heard. But it is important to follow through on at least some of the tickets. If no one pays their fines, people stop writing tickets. It doesn't take a lot to see things change. No one likes to get them or to lose free time, but once they have paid each other, they do seem to feel good about it. It is so much better than the old way and settling arguments when both people are upset.

- Sometimes, I feel like I have to lie to write something good at the bottom of the character ticket, so I wait until my brain isn't overloaded. Then, when I go back to the ticket to finish it, I can write something nice. When I do that, I tend to realize that although they were not patient at the time, for example, usually they are patient.

- It's almost always true that the quality you are asking them to use is something that they use often but just didn't this time. So, I can usually put the same quality under "Usually you..." that I circle at the top. Sometimes, I put something funny to break the tension during character time, but I try to make sure it won't hurt.

CHILDHOOD DEVELOPMENT — As a young mother I recall feeling reassured by a little book titled *Your Three Year Old: Friend or Enemy* by Louise Bates Ames and Frances Ilg. My first child, Bentley, had been such a calm two-year-old that I wondered why people talked about the terrible twos. But at three, she began to have a mind of her own. The authors explained that a surge of independence was common and healthy for children her age. They titled their chapters things like, "Your Six Year Old: Loving and Defiant" and "Your Four Year Old: Wild and Wonderful." The descriptions may not perfectly fit for your child. What's important is familiarizing yourself with stages and ages because it makes it easier to let life flow. Educate yourself with these or other highly respected and easy-to-read books. They will eliminate needless fretting and hurtful comparisons.

CHORES — Jim used to say I underestimated how long it took to do something. He was often right. I'd say, "It will only take a few hours to clean out the space under the house." The family would start the "three hour" project with me in the morning and by 10:00 that night, I'd be closing the lid on the last box — either alone or with one very good sport. The good sport would not be Jim. He was loving and had good boundaries, so he set himself and the girls free after a reasonable amount of time and left me to my own preferences.

Think back to the animal descriptions in chapter 17. Do not torture your family if you are a beaver. Be honest with yourself. If you like to finish a project, finish it without resentment or bad feelings. If you consistently underestimate the time or energy that will need to go into a chore, be a good sport and support those doing it or complete it yourself.

Remember that perfectionism and pickiness are big stressors. They drain the energy needed to keep people engaged and positive. Always comment on what people are doing right. When possible, let them choose their tasks. Smart managers give people breaks and room to breathe. So state expectations up front, check with each person for understanding, and then avoid micromanagement.

COUPLE GETAWAYS — Nothing will be a more overt statement to your children, your family, and those around you of your commitment to your marriage.

Conversation ideas for bi-monthly couple getaways:

February	Passion builders for our marriage
April	Wise use of our money
June	Ways we can bring play to our lives
August	A look at our lifestyle for the new school/work year
October	Plan for the holidays
December	Giving ourselves to God and the world

This is a delicious time for a woman and man to set aside all of their other roles as mother, father, daughter, son, friend, boss, employee, or volunteer and just be husband and wife. Nothing tops intimate time alone for inspiring passion. Play, laugh, love, dream together. Read to one another. Once, Jim and I read all of *Sacred Romance* by John Eldridge out loud to one another while we relaxed on the beach. We never forgot how rich an experience it was.

Take walks. Watch romantic movies. Pray. Have individual devotions in the morning and share what you learned. Review your blessings. The setting is so much less important than the activities and your dedication to one another. And always remember to affirm, affirm, affirm.

One wife told me, "My husband surprised me, and we went to a hotel two miles away for two days. He packed hors d'oeuvres and a list of loving activities and called my parents to babysit. All of this is working to change my father. Watching our marriage and my spiritual growth is affecting him. For the first time ever, I'm hearing my father pray the prayers in church. Last time we went to service, Dad put his arm around me. All the stuff we're doing is giving my dad a new sense of fatherhood and a sense that there's someone bigger up there. I've been telling him about this lifestyle and its connection to God, and it is transforming my life in every way."

COVERT PAYOFF — What can you do if your child is angry at you and doesn't want to write a ticket because he doesn't want to spend time with you? Spend loving time with the child, and afterwards, point out to the child how painless it was. Label the time after the fact, and give the tokens back. Sometimes, it is easier to *experience* how good it is rather than to be talked into it.

Also, if your child spends good time with you and asks if he or she can count the time as payoff, say, "Yes". Remember, the goal is not punishment, the goal is repair and learning how to love.

DATE IDEAS — What is a date? It is one-on-one time without distractions. It makes people feel special. Invite each member of your family to spend time away from the house with you. Put your commitment on the calendar, keep your word, and be on time. If you begin this habit while your children are young, you can help them understand that some of the best dates they will ever have will be free. Spending an hour or two at the park or festival, window shopping, exploring the countryside, starting a collection of nature's bounty—all free. By the way, there are no issues during dates. No performing. No lectures. If you are playing a game or sport, resist the temptation to teach. A date is a time of enjoyment and getting to know one another. Also, if you want to have a heart-to-heart, do it another time. Don't disguise it as a "date."

You may agree that the two of you need to use your date time to do something constructive: shop for something specific, build something, collect materials for a project. If so, put it on the calendar and add lunch or dinner to it. Or simply invite your child to a meal and take turns telling one another about your lives. Humans like ritual, so a particular spot may make the date all the more appealing and memorable. Just be careful not to go to a "kid" spot where they will leave you and join other children. The point is to spend time together.

I have a friend who is in his fifties and came from a large Catholic family. He was a sensitive boy, and his father's harsh and dismissive parenting style was devastating for him. Recently, after watching an old movie he remarked, "My dad had me go to that movie with him when I was 15, just him and me. I still don't know why he did that." Forty years later, my friend still ponders it. It inspired us to talk about some of his father's gentler characteristics. Can you see how powerful this is? Whatever else you do in your Uncommon Sense lifestyle, don't skimp on this.

DIET—If you want people to eat healthy, put healthy food on the fridge shelves prepared, at eye level, not in the drawers hidden. If they don't like what you like, keep searching. Also, people have an easier time choosing between two things rather than among many. I know almost no adults who still eat only chicken nuggets and macaroni. This too shall pass. Do your best and just keep the amounts reasonable.

Discouragement — Who do you suppose loves to bring us down? Not God. He told us to build one another up. Listen to this story I heard on Christian radio some years ago:

One day, a tool collector saw a room full of shiny and dull tools of varying prices. He became curious when he came across a very old, worn tool because the price on it was astronomical. The collector looked at the owner, Lucifer, and asked, "This tool looks more worn than any of the others, and yet you are charging the most for it. Why is that?" The owner replied, "It is worth the most to me. It is very effective. It does just what I want it to do." "What is it?" the man inquired. "Discouragement," Lucifer answered.

Discouragement sickens the heart. But you don't have to let it sicken yours. Perseverance is a muscle that is strengthened by standing up to discouragement and pain. It is a wonderful character quality that gets you through an experience and gives you hope. If you've done something before, you believe you can do it again (or that others can do it.) In the Bible, our heroes are typically supported and encouraged by friends or family. When you feel discouraged, call on your support system. If you can't find them, read your Bible. Find a book that discusses the topic in a positive or even humorous way. God will always support and encourage us. Are you noticing the ways He is doing that for you? Are you giving encouragement to others?

Family Meetings — Karen, one of my initial family participants, told me, "This is my favorite thing to do, but unless we are held accountable, we don't carve out the time, especially when life is so busy with activities. My kids really get energized by hearing the positive feedback first. They like to know what's on the week's agenda, get only one thing that they could improve on, and tell us what one thing we could improve on as parents. They enjoy the times when we all sit on our bedroom floor. Even if they are brief, these meetings keep everyone on the same page."

Remember that you want the time everyone puts into the family to be meaningful. This is their opportunity to make sense of life and feel a sense of ownership. For the first year or so of family meetings I would frequently ask these questions:

Why are we here?
They might answer:
- To flow in love
- To grow our relationships
- To practice healthy communication
- To remember our commitments
- To dream together

What have we decided we are going to do in our home when someone messes up?
- Write tickets
- Use clay for habits
- Listen with reflection
- Energize positives
- Give up hurtful coping skills and use healthy ones

How can we be respectful and use our time well during this meeting?
- Let parents lead
- Someone take notes
- Take turns talking
- No pile-ons

Speaking of pile-ons, it can be hard to sit on the sidelines and watch two people discuss difficult topics. We may have an urge to put our two cents in even if it's not about us. For example, Karen is taking Sue's iPod without asking. Sue wants to talk about it. This has nothing to do with Mark. But Mark takes this opportunity to criticize Sue for being stingy.

This form of group condemnation might be convicting if it happens a few times a year, but it will be debilitating when it happens several times a month.

We developed some little abbreviations, all said in a quiet and respectful way, *to keep people from interrupting and taking sides during the meetings.*

- "MYOB": Mind Your Own Business
- "TYOG": Tend Your Own Garden
- Hold up three fingers. It forms a "W" that stands for "Wait, please."

So, we might say, "Mark, TYOG for a minute." That means, leave your sister alone while she is working on this. The shorthand lets the authority figure do most of the facilitation without hurtful remarks being made. However, always encourage people to comment if their words and thoughts are edifying.

Some families have also made use of something we've come to call "The Talking Stick." It helps people take turns talking during these meetings because only the person holding the object can speak. Abbey (my friend's daughter) and her college roommates were having a heated debate over the state of their apartment. Things were getting out of hand and Abbey said, "Okay, everyone, let's go in the living room and sit down. We are going to have a meeting and set up responsibilities. See this football? If you are holding it, you can talk. If not, you gotta listen." They ended up having a great conversation. What makes the story amusing for us is that Abbey is definitely an otter, but she clearly learned from her family meetings how to take control, coordinate a crowd, and quickly replace confusion with clarity. Of course, she also found a way to make it fun.

If you choose to use this idea, remember to make it as fun as possible. What is a fun symbol for your family? Do you love baseball? The beach? Summer vacation? Maybe it's just a stick with sparkles. If you can't make the experience somewhat pleasant, try to live without it.

Family Notebook — Use this to keep notes on tools, agreements, values, and responsibilities. This will be one of your favorite family keepsakes. Use a one-inch binder or small notebook with pocket dividers. In the front section, write notes from the first meeting about toxic coping skills that everyone wants to give up and healthier behaviors that people want to adopt or use more frequently. Responsibilities with initials can be kept on a sheet in the front pocket of the book and changed frequently as you discover what is and is not successful. It is not helpful to assign responsibilities if they are being done unsuccessfully. Offer alternatives to your family until they are older or have better support. Also, use this book to keep a copy of some of the anchor scriptures that you believe will be helpful to refer to as well as notes about your family values.

Also, let each family member have a section with his or her personal commitments to refer to when he or she has initialed agreements. For example, "When I am given permission to do A, I will not do B without asking" or "If Mom says I can go to dinner and soccer with Joe, I won't assume I can also spend the night. I will call and ask permission." *Let the agreements be ones they help come up with as much as possible. Otherwise, it will feel like forced signatures on contracts.* Authority figures each should have a section and should encourage children to use the notebook to help remind them of their good intentions. This book is ultimately for you. You want to grow. You notice God more when you reach for the light.

FAMILY PROJECT—It is essential for a family to work together. Even if you can only do this during the early years, it will be life changing as well as practical and rewarding. It creates a sense of purpose, belonging, and accomplishment. This is an extended amount of time once a month to invest the whole family in something that is important to us. We would put it on the calendar a month ahead of time and treat it like a business meeting. It allowed us to care for our home, cars, people, and other gifts from God. Big jobs are accomplished so much more quickly with a group than if one or two people attempt to do it. These projects tell the family that they are all needed and wanted, and promote home and community improvement.

One of our family physicians says she creates an annual theme, and her family thinks about life from that angle for 12 months. For example, one year, the theme was "Less is more." One month, they cleaned out the basement and gave their goods to a charity. During another, they scaled back on electronics, and in a third they took a hard look at their diet. If you set your family up for these connections with one another, you will create strong common bonds, especially if you remember to keep stressors and pickiness to a minimum.

FEAR — Almost all of my mistakes as a parent come from fear: *If they aren't dressed right, they'll be mistreated. If they aren't respectful in the classroom, they won't get the teacher's favor. If they act out in the neighborhood, they'll embarrass their dad and me, and we'll all be shunned. If they act this way now, they'll grow up and be that way as an adult.* Sometimes these things may be true, yet our own lives testify that many fears are unwarranted. Be honest. How hard are you on other people's kids in a given day?

If you are controlling your kids or are parenting with fear, you are missing the point of Christianity. Christ came to free us from that. Sheila, a wise grandmother, told us this about her son: "I have an adopted son. The doctor who arranged the adoption told me that he chose Carey and me as parents because he knew we would handle any challenges that came our way. As a result of this comment, I chose to over-parent. I regret it. Our son did have some challenges, but I can tell you that if you just get your children through school, and give them confidence, they don't have to be good students. My son is dyslexic and really struggled with school and now he is COO (chief operating officer) of his company."

Scripture says this so clearly that I cannot help but quote it. "And so we know and rely on the love God has for us. God is love. Whoever lives in love lives in God, and God in him. In this way, love is made complete among us so that we will have confidence on the day of judgment, because in this world we are like him. *There is no fear in love.* But perfect love drives out fear, because fear has to do with punishment. The one who fears is not made perfect in love" (1 John 4:16-18, emphasis added).

IHR Intimate Healthy Relationship—An intimate, healthy relationship is one you have with a person who:

- Has heard the good, bad, and ugly about you and still loves and admires you for the beautiful creation you are
- Will not lie to you when he/she is asked an honest question
- Will gently and respectfully identify distortions in your thinking and try to guide you back to a healing path
- Will give you time to talk through your emotions
- Will love other people involved just as much after they hear a painful story as he/she did before they heard the story. This takes a lot of character. I have to be able to tell you that someone I love failed, and know that you can still see them as the whole person they are.

Let me tell you how my IHR's did this for me one night. I got a call from one of Caty's teachers. She recognized Caty's potential, but said that she had failed to turn in her homework assignments which negatively impacted her grade. Fortunately, Caty was not here when I received the call or else, out of old habit, I might have called her in and scolded her. Instead, I called my IHR, Lisa, and she just happened to be with two of my other IHRs, Alison and Mary Helen.

Mary Helen explained some things about her children's experience with school that were soothing to me; Alison reminded me not to move toward the old "I'm not a good enough parent" guilt; and Lisa reminded me that God has a plan for Caty and did not need straight A's to get her there. I'm grateful that our God is so big, loving, and wise. The wisdom I received that night about God, fear, and false guilt has helped throughout the years.

On another occasion, one of my IHRs called and said, "Can you come over? I'm trying not to jeopardize my relationship with Jesse, but there are dishes in the sink he won't do. It's been two days, and dishes are his responsibility." I came over to calm her. I looked at the sink and began to laugh. I had to stand over it to find the dishes. They sat, well-rinsed, in one small corner. I pulled out my phone and took a picture so I could relay it to our friends. We began to giggle together. She was living by the letter of the law, and her son saw this as nothing to worry about. Once she saw the dishes through my eyes, she was able to let go of them and her frustration with her grown son.

Jesse was honoring their agreement. He was just handling it his way. He is an adult, and it was time for him to choose his own ways. Healthy adults are adaptable, so both Jesse and Mary Helen will need to adjust to one another, which will take time and effort.

Christ said a shocking thing to his friend, Martha, one day. She wanted help from Mary who was sitting at Christ's feet, listening. A woman's place in their culture was to serve, not to sit. So Martha asked Jesus to tell her sister to give her a hand, and Jesus told Martha that she was concerned about too many things. No matter what translation of the Bible you use, Jesus told Martha that Mary was making a better use of her time. Martha was "distracted by all of the preparations that had to be made" (concerned about rules, tasks, and stuff) when it was more important to focus on one another and being Christlike (Luke 10:38-42). In certain situations, we actually have to let go of our preferences and concerns if we are going to be able to hear what Christ has to say about them. IHRs can help with that.

LEADERSHIP—True leadership is guidance by direction or example. There are several ways parents can demonstrate leadership:

- Ask children to write tickets. Write tickets yourself.
- Help children to apologize and pay time. Do that yourself.

- Know your responsibilities and keep them. Don't make excuses.
- Open and close family meetings. Limit yourself by covering essential topics only.
- Facilitate family meetings. Manage behaviors respectfully, but decisively. Allow some laughs.
- Support people when they are failing. Review the trouble-shooting chart and brainstorm with people who want to come up with new ways of managing life.
- Read family devotions, read God's Word, pray out loud for the family and others.
- Stay upbeat during family meetings so that children have an opportunity to see their parents doing something important with a pleasant demeanor.

Many spouses are disappointed if their partner doesn't do all of these. I encourage you to be thankful if your spouse does one of them. Be thankful if you do one of them. See if you can add a second and then a third. In time, you may be good at several.

Both parents do not have to be involved, but a tree with only half of a root system will not be as sturdy as one that's fully formed. If you are a single parent or have an uninvolved spouse, let me assure you that God knows what you are up against and is standing beside you. He will enable you to bend with the strong winds and remain standing after the storm. If two parents are available, the parent who has the mercy heart can see to it that the tickets get written, and the other parent can be there to hold people accountable for paying time and making sure discipline is truly taking place. Typically, parents naturally take turns playing good cop and bad cop.

As a leader, remember that you are not looking for perfection. You will never find it in others or yourself. You are a leader who is seeking to keep the flow of God's love moving among the members of your family. You are helping them to make deposits back into relationships when they have carelessly hurt one another and to learn to solve problems in respectful ways. An environment that enables people to give and receive esteem produces kind, productive people rather than cruel, uncaring ones.

Love Languages — These are all common ways to show love, so take the time to figure out which one makes each member of your family feel special (Words of Affirmation, Acts of Service, Quality Time, Physical Touch, and Gifts) The more children feel loved, the easier it is to discipline them.

Jim's uncle is a Brigadier General who also happens to be a powerfully loving man. There is no doubt in my mind that the men and women who served under him knew that he meant business when he spoke and also that he loved them deeply. The combination of those traits make it more likely that people will both trust and follow us.

Ask each family member what makes him or her feel loved, and attempt to give that gift as often as possible. Ask the individual to help you find creative ways to do it. Someone who loves acts of service probably has ideas about that because we are usually good at giving the gift we like to receive. Someone who loves affirmations may be able to tell you five things that make people feel special. Write the answers down in the front of your notebook so you won't forget. And remember that gifts are important to all of us.

Check out Gary Chapman's and other books on The Five Love Languages. Take the quiz.

Loving Time — This is kind time spent with one another to repair a relationship that has suffered damage. Find easy ways to make loving time happen. Imagine what your car would look like if you had fender benders every day and never got repairs. That is the shape some relationships are in when regular repair does not take place.

Loving time is any activity that increases feelings of safety or positive regard with one another. Since only God can see a heart, only God knows how both people are contributing to the problem, so positive time spent together will give something good back to the relationship. Possibilities are endless and include things like playing games or sports, watching shows both people like, baking a snack, helping one another with a task, and exercising. This will not be an activity that only one person likes. If you make humans do something they don't like, they are not likely to flow in love. And since love — not just time — heals, love needs to be at the heart of this.

It may be helpful to make lists of these loving activities ahead of time so that when someone owes you, he or she can choose something from your list. At family meetings, give out pieces of paper and help one another come up with ideas. What does each of you like or need to do?

Sometimes when life feels busy or someone earned a large debt, you may choose to help one another with chores. You could mow the grass while your child trims it, but you'll be in the yard together with a sense of camaraderie — just the two of you. Stop for water breaks together and chat, no bossiness. You may address holiday cards together, or clean out a closet or walk the dog together. This takes a little more effort, but the payoff is worth it.

Also, remember that the human mind is like the software of a computer. The brain is programmable. Sometimes when my children owed a lot of time, I asked them to watch old TV shows. Choose to watch ones where good manners and healthier lifestyles are the norm. As they watch these heroes and heroines, their brains and yours will create new maps. Your children may grumble when they are young and make fun of you for having them watch *The Andy Griffith Show*, *Leave It to Beaver*, *Little House on the Prairie*, *The Cosby Show* or other shows with wholesome and moral examples. However, as you all grow older the laughs will become sweet, and your children will thank you.

This technique can even work in complex circumstances. For instance, one Friday, it was homecoming. Our daughter had done something audacious the week before and owed three hours. She had cleaned her room, so she had the night free, but she had not paid off the time from the week before, and we had told her there would be no friends or electronics during the weekend until that debt was paid. For some reason, she did not get the time paid off even though we offered several opportunities. So, on that homecoming Friday, she said, "I'm going to Sara's house to make t-shirts for the game. Then we are going to tailgate."

"Oh," I responded in a concerned but pleasant tone, "I'm sorry, but you still owe three hours. You could make it to the game, but you can't make it to the t-shirt or tailgate gatherings because you still owe three hours. I'm going to take your sister to soccer practice. Why don't you go get a shirt to decorate on the way? If you spend the next three hours helping me carpool and make team snacks, you will have paid your time. You can't go to your pregame activities, but a good attitude will get you the rest of the night."

This child is a passionate kid who, like the rest of humanity, knows how to fly off the handle! Yet she accepted this with complete poise. During our car ride, she cheerily told me things about herself and her friends I would never have known if I hadn't had this time with her. She made a t-shirt that was different from her friends' creations, but it was one she was proud of. And she tucked the day away as a pleasant memory. I am so thankful for this uncommon, positive life.

MANNERS AND MEALS — A voluminous body of research supports the critical importance of family meals. Families that eat three or more meals a week together increase the chance that the children will have a better diet, a greater sense of family, and will place less value on drugs and alcohol. The findings even suggest that this is true if the television is on. Because smaller meals can be just as good for us as three large ones, we have more opportunities to find a good time to sit and eat together. Even if you just have a drink or a snack, come together.

Some families make dinnertime miserable by trying to teach manners. Parents who eat with their children regularly can model good manners every time they eat. I noticed, for example, that if I straighten my posture at the table, my daughters automatically straighten theirs. (Of course, if the TV is on or we don't sit with them, they are not likely to see what we do.) Children love to make their parents proud. Remember the pattern for instruction as we discussed intervention strategies in chapter 26? First model, then mention, and finally, remind.

Occasionally, have a "good manners meal." Tell your children that this is the meal when you want them to show you that they know their etiquette. You might even put a written piece of paper on the table with the ten manners that are the most important to you so they'll know what you're looking for. (You can even have them help you research what constitutes good table manners as a way of paying off time.) What you want is to know that they can use etiquette when they need it, not browbeat them with rules. Home is meant to be the one place we can relax, not where we are required to continue to perform.

MISSION ACCOMPLISHED BOARD — Make a daily "to do" list and watch it disappear. It's energizing. Write a list of your day's tasks then ask the Holy Spirit to order them in such a way that they can be accomplished most effectively. Since God is not limited by time, He knows what will come up and what will be most expeditious. Pray for God to help you accomplish what He wants to be accomplished and assume He will. Your children will learn from your model. All of my children are list makers, and we have had some great laughs at some of the miraculous lists we have accomplished with God's help. It has been faith building.

MODELING — One of Christ's favorite training tools.

Our family rescued a cute little poodle terrier from the humane society, and to our delight she came fully trained. At one-year-old she could do all kinds of tricks and would heel, sit, and stay upon command. She was a delight. During her 15 years with us she almost never got scolded. Why? She was trained early. Yet we often wait until our children are several years old to begin training. The time when our children's brains could absorb so many little housekeeping tricks from us, we are separated from them during the day, and too tired to teach at night.

In fairness, we are working parents in a technologically distracted environment, and can't focus on all things at all times. Boy, do I get it. So, remember, you are only called to teach the children God gives you. Look honestly and pray earnestly about what God wants to be the important things in your child's life and then stick to that list. For the little things, like wiping off a sink after you use it or which utensil to put to the right of the plate, start **very** early by cheerily asking your child to "help me do this" when they are with you. Make it pleasant. Reward them with high 5's, praise, or a kiss on the head. Puppies get treats when they do things right. That's why they are inspired to do them again. By the time a child is two or three you'd be surprised what they have learned!

If you didn't start early, don't be plagued with guilt or resentment. Major on the majors and ask God to put good role models in their lives. He will.

PERSPECTIVE — Victor Kiam, the former owner of the New England Patriots, once said, "Even if you fall on your face, you are still moving forward." Funny, but also very true. A correct perspective is critical to helping people adjust their attitudes toward themselves, one another, and life. Recently, some of the nation's greatest companies have stopped heavy recruiting solely from Ivy League schools. They have branched out to include diverse schools from across the nation. Why? They have found that the synergy from the combined perspectives achieves a better product. The combination of skills and perspectives that your family members possess can strengthen your team, too. God has not put that diversity there by mistake.

POSITIVE COMMUNICATIONS ALL DAY — You know what we learned by communicating positives all day and saving issues for a small meeting time?

- Life was 100% more wonderful with each other.
- Little things we had been asking one another to do out of our own laziness stopped.
- Life became much more respectful.

- It was impossible to pull off, unless we cleared up minutia, assigned responsibilities, and then kept our word. That level of ownership felt good. Integrity is its own reward.

Jim and I had grown up watching TV dads who sat in easy chairs in homes where no one ever made a mess. Our marriage was self-destructing because I never stopped working, and Jim resented being asked to help after a long day at the office. We realized that putting shoes by the door, getting book bags and homework ready, and even grooming are chores if you are a child. Those activities require support, so those were their chores. We didn't add much to them on weeknights.

Jim and I made ourselves a responsibilities list, and once we assigned and initialed responsibilities, we no longer suffered the I-thought-you-were-going-to-do-it syndrome. Jim could knock out a list like it was going out of style and seemed to take pride in it. He had helped create it. Remember? That's buy-in. I felt supported and loved and realized how much he was doing for all of us while he was home.

If you are a single parent or your spouse won't participate, remember you have the Holy Spirit. God gives abundant grace in life. The Spirit will help us keep our thoughts on whatever is going right, things that are worthy of praise. In this case I mean God's grace allows us to feel okay when people would expect us to feel bad due to our circumstances. Calling on the Holy Spirit rather than the people around you is one of the mainstays of this lifestyle. This God-reliant attitude is your responsibility. It will help you listen to God, delay gratification, share His ways, and experience His love.

POTTER'S CLAY—Here are a few tips for supporting change.

1. Let the child help you decide *which coping skills or habits he/she needs to change.* People generally change what they want to change, so this will help everyone see more success.

2. Help decide on a *new coping strategy to use in place of the one he/she is giving up*. For example, "Instead of complaining, you are going to just ask" or "Instead of interrupting, you are going to wait or say, 'Excuse me.'" With an older child, the sentence would be, "Instead of tattling, what could you do?" If he or she suggests another toxic option, say, "Yes, but is there something that would be better for you?" The purpose of Potter's Clay is to help shift us from hurtful coping strategies to healing ones.

3. When you witness the toxic coping skill, put in the toothpick and move on with life. You may say "uh oh" gently to heighten your child's awareness, but your voice should stay pleasant. If mentioning it bothers the child, then don't. Just put a toothpick in the clay and move on.

I was amazed at how refreshing it was to put a toothpick into clay rather than trying to talk someone out of the behavior. It works better! The people who are using Potter's Clay are willing to honestly look at the frequency of a bad habit and receive support for change. Don't revert to the old way of talking. Instead, say something honest like "It's hard to change," or "It takes time to change," or lovingly remind them of the new behavior with a word. For example, if they come to you complaining, put the toothpick in the clay. Then in a kind tone say, "Ask" or "Write a ticket" or "Write an i-note." This means, instead of complaining, think of what you want, and find a tone, time, and way that is more effective and attractive to handle your need. Some things that can keep this tool encouraging include:

- Awarding small prizes when skills improve. Be aware of each individual's love languages as you seek to motivate and reward improvements
- Temporarily changing friends or environments to kick a habit
- Making sure that a lack of sleep, food, and water or an illness are not a part of the problem

- Occasionally trying not to notice mistakes. The confidence that comes with success and praise will help children conquer other habits in the future.

- Always put a fancy toothpick in their clay along with the others to let them know that you noticed something unusually good that they did that day. Try to remember what it was, or jot a note with a one-word reminder. If you forget, ask them to tell you something while they are removing it. If you don't do this frequently, this tool will lose its effectiveness. It hurts to see only toothpicks in your clay that represent failure. Balance it out with one that represents a success.

QUIET TIME/QUIET SPOT—No matter how small a house is, there is a room or corner that is seldom used. This space can become your quiet spot. Put favorite spiritual books, pictures, music, blankies, pictures of happy memories, stuffed animals, and other comforting belongings there. When someone is confused or angry and needs to take time to think, let him or her go there alone or with someone who loves them. Remind them that Christ left the crowds so He could come back refreshed from having time with God. Associate quiet time with wisdom, but remember not to reject people if they come to you there. It should be a place of mutual affection. Remember, Christ said, "let the children come to me" even when the disciples thought He was too busy.

REQUESTS—"Ask & Ask Again" is a five-step negotiation system designed to limit your children's tendency to plead and beg until they wear you down. It is also designed to help you think before you answer "no" for no good reason. Remember that Uncommon Sense is not designed to be legalistic. If your child comes up with a good point of discussion that goes beyond the five-step concept, of course you would respond sensibly to it. Here's how it works:

1. The child asks for something.
2. You say "no."
3. The child fills in the details.
4. You ponder and pray.
5. You give your spiritually informed answer.
6. Sometimes, the child will remember pertinent details he or she forgot to share. Of course there will be times when you give additional opportunities to "add to" the original request.

Throughout this process, reflect, listen, and continue to let the Holy Spirit flow in you. The extra debate shouldn't happen every time, but occasionally all of us leave out important details and want to be heard in full. Your God-given "no" may turn into a God-given "yes." It happens in the Bible. (See Luke 18:1-8.)

REFUSAL TO WRITE TICKETS — A common dilemma with Character Tickets is that some children, and even some adults, will choose not to write them. Why? They don't want to stop what they are doing to write them or to reserve time for the person they are writing them on. Yet this is what we know: it is not healthy to hurt people. Nor is it healthy to walk away and pretend damage didn't happen. Doing nothing and coping poorly are not options in a family that wants God's best.

If two people are using destructive coping skills and won't write tickets, a parent can write tickets on both people. It will cost them twice as much time because both people are getting a ticket and they have to pay one another. Be sure to write some of their exact words and actions on the ticket. When we see/hear what our overwhelmed brains lead our bodies to do, it's often convicting and embarrassing.

Don't ask your older child to triangulate by writing a ticket on two younger siblings. Triangulation is the habit of a third party managing a relationship for two other people who need to be learning the skills themselves.

We can help one another, but we don't want to become a necessary part of the transaction.

However, do allow children to write a ticket on you and your spouse if they see you quarrel. It gives them a healthy outlet for a very uncomfortable condition and reassures them that you want your relationship to be healthy and good. Let them know that you are paying off the tickets. For example, you can tell them, "Your mom and I are going to go running together to pay off our time."

REFLECTION—People are willing to pay counselors big bucks for this skill. That tells us people feel being heard is important. So when someone has a strong negative reaction to life and needs to talk about it, you can listen traditionally or you can listen effectively—purely for the sake of the other person.

Imagine a child says, "I hate Cindy! She always takes my things."

You reply in a matter-of-fact tone, "You hate Cindy. She always takes your things. Did I get that right?" Once your reflection is going well, you can change your phrase from "Did I get that right?" to "Tell me more." Pretty soon the person will say, "That's all."

After five more sentences or paragraphs of this reflection, the child will admit he doesn't hate Cindy and she doesn't always take things. All you've done is reflect him word for word. No advice. No input. Just letting him hear himself. It's like confronting my foolish self with my wise self at a better time and place.

What do you do if the child goes on and on without giving you a chance to reflect them? That's easy. Say, "I don't want to miss anything. Will you let me stop you every so often and make sure I understand?" Then repeat as many of the sentences as you can piece together. He will correct it as you go.

If a child attacks you and makes it hard for you to listen, it becomes more complicated. It is human nature to defend yourself when you or your character is being attacked. If this happens, explain that if he says something negative or untrue about you, you will need a turn to be reflected, and make it clear that he needs to focus on the circumstance and himself, not you.

When reflection doesn't seem to be effective, the child can end the conversation and go write a ticket, or you can get a neutral third party. The Bible suggests we go to someone one-on-one when we have a grievance, but if the other person won't listen, it suggests we bring in another. Remember, if you bring another person in, make sure it's someone who loves you both.

RESPONSIBILITIES AND JOBS—Many people are not accustomed to keeping their word with friends and family and doing what they say they will do. Text messaging has made quick changes of plans more acceptable than ever, but over time, your new lifestyle will change that somewhat. Put your responsibility list in a front pocket of your notebook and ask family members to sign their initials beside their responsibilities. Remind them that initialing something is a sign of acceptance. Persevere. Tweak it until you find success. Einstein is credited for sayings that if a fish were asked to climb a tree it would feel stupid and assume it could never succeed at life. The same concept applies to people. So do your best to assign jobs that work for everyone.

SEEK THE LESSON—This entire lifestyle is about you and lessons God is teaching you, so seek the lessons.

I'm sure God gave *me* this lifestyle to help me relax a little and stop being a control freak. I could way over-parent at times. When I felt myself getting uptight I would say, "What attitude do you want me to take on, Lord? I would sing my "love, joy, peace, patience, kindness, generosity, faithfulness, gentleness, self-control" song and find a positive attitude. That exercise—and the single word that came from it—swept away the tension.

When my daughter was a sophomore in high school, she had a big art project due midweek. She needed to take pictures of all different kinds of signs. It was a stressful, busy time of year, and she had a lot of other activities on her plate. I was frustrated with her lackadaisical attitude toward this important project. I didn't want to nag or stuff my emotions down only to have them come spewing out. I remembered to seek the lesson.

As I went through the fruit of the Spirit, God stopped me on "joy." I didn't know what that had to do with this situation, but tucked the word into my heart and mind. Over the next hour, I asked several questions that challenged the fine line between positive invitations and issues:

"You only have an hour before the play, are you going to study?" I asked.

"I can't right now," she replied.

Joy my heart said. I felt almost giggly rather than dismayed. *Thanks, God. I needed that.*

"Where do you want to eat?" I asked.

"I'm not hungry," she replied.

Joy

"Shall we go take some pictures?"

"I don't feel like it."

Joy

No progress was made on the project and no healthy dinner was eaten, yet no hard feelings were created between us. Joy was certainly feeling better than frustration. Thank you, God.

To make a long story short, the very next night, we were invited to a restaurant in another city. We decided to go. Guess what we saw as we walked in the door of the restaurant? Dozens of extraordinary neon signs, and my daughter had her camera with her. Can you imagine our joy? Had I nagged and insisted on my own way the night before instead of seeking God, we would have spent hours taking pictures of boring signs and then scrapped them after seeing these. God is good. He is always good.

SIMPLICITY—With Uncommon Sense people have thought through life ahead of time and simplified it. The hope is that you will no longer have to say, "What shall we do about this?" at every turn. Constant wondering and planning and problem-solving can make parenting and being a child exhausting.

All tickets are five minutes. At home, the worst you will suffer when you mess up is either a natural consequence or a few hours of loving, constructive time. We will have meetings and this is when they will be. We eat one meal a day together as a family, even if "the meal" is a cup of juice while we go over tomorrow's agenda and dreams.

More simplicity can come in the form of: "Three things I like about you…Three ways you blessed me… Three ways God blessed me…." If you share these with someone instead of the usual "blah blah blah" or "How was your day," you will be amazed by the ways the Holy Spirit takes over your tongue. Jim and I often took walks when we did this, and it was a flood spilling over for both of us. I could have continued the praise during the whole walk, but Jim would stop me so he could have a turn. As the Bible says, "Give, and it will be given to you. A good measure, pressed down, shaken together and running over, will be poured into your lap. For with the measure you use, it will be measured to you" (Luke 6:38). What's surprising is that occasionally when I started, I wasn't pumped up for it. Sometimes, I wondered what I was going to say, but I opened my mouth and out it came. There are two benefits to this practice. First, the more you talk about honest positives, the more you notice them. Second, the more you hear honest positives about yourself, the better you become at giving and receiving them.

THREE NICE THINGS — This is the consequence for saying unkind words to someone. It is an immediate, in-the-moment correction for careless, hurtful speech. For instance:

> **TOMMY:** Sam's fat and stupid.
> **DAD:** Tommy, say three nice things.
> **TOMMY:** Sam is friendly, funny, and a good baseball player.

The positives may or may not be true! In the moment, when someone's brain is firing, it will be hard to come up with positives. You being picky will not make the job easier. (Picky is a stressor, remember?) If you want to be picky, help out.

Remember, if the person refuses, add to the consequence by increasing it to six nice things right there on the spot. Then with each refusal, the number grows by three. Other activities do not continue until they comply, and the number of positives required keeps going up. *However,* if your kids are out of control and you can't get them to do it, write Character Tickets and move on with life. You may not have a strong enough relationship with your children to influence them for the better until you spend more loving time with them. Acting like a dictator won't change that.

Try Another Way—When I was working on my master's degree in special education, we studied the work of Marc Gold. His concept was simple: take developmentally challenged students and assume that they can do a task. Then allow them to keep attempting the task in different ways until they arrive at the correct solution. They try. If they fail, you say, "Try another way." Support them as they move closer and closer to the correct behavior—the one necessary to accomplish the task. When they achieve the correct behavior, offer them praise or a reinforcer that lets them know they have succeeded.

The challenge Gold gave to students with IQs as low as 11 (an average human IQ is 100) was to put together a bike brake. His strategy works. I began to use the phrase, "Try another way" with my profoundly and severely mentally disabled students. We taught them to dress themselves, use sign language, make beds, write their names, and perform many other tasks using this system.

With Uncommon Sense, I have taught parents to use this phrase when they want their children to change their approach to a situation. For example, your child comes into the kitchen whining about a sibling. You are willing to listen for a moment, but you dislike his tone of voice and the victim-like posture he has assumed in order to get you on his side. You say, "Try another way," which means you want him to change his tone of voice or use the new loving lifestyle rather than the old, ineffective coping skills.

You should explain this request in a family meeting and model it often. If they aren't trying or don't know what to do, demonstrate it for them. *If your child is not finding a solution to a problem when you tell him to "Try another way," help him succeed before he gives up, otherwise he may grow to hate the phrase.*

VALUES LISTS — This is a short list of principles to guide family choices and give life a sense of stability and integrity.

God designed me for my children and you for yours. There are familial curses that you know need to be broken, not handed down to the next generation. Perhaps your grandfather and mother were critical and perfectionistic, and now you are. One of your family values may be, "We will make room for individuality." Or maybe you came from a secretive and suspicious family and longed for intimacy and transparency. What family value can you create to counter that? How about "We will not punish others for telling the truth and showing their feelings"?

You don't want to hand destructive values from the past down to your children. God gave you a child who is ready to learn. What values can you put into place so that your child can move into the world as a man or woman with confidence, capability, and compassion? How can you model those? What values will allow you to show your children that success comes in many forms? If you are stumped, talk to a counselor or wise friend and get help, and pray before you go.

Here are some comments from some real moms as they worked to find values for their homes.

M: I came to Uncommon Sense with a big hole in my heart. My daughter moved out in high school because home didn't feel like a respectful place to her. I want to respect my kids. I want my children to have a voice, a respectful way to address us when we treat them in disrespectful or exasperating ways. Otherwise, we are doomed to repeat the failures of the past.

L: One of the hard lessons I learned from conflict with my parents was that I did not know that whatever I did, I was still loved. I made it a point to be sure my children heard me say, "There is nothing you could ever do that would make me stop loving you." My husband and I never sat down and said, "How will we raise our kids? What standards do we want to live by? If our kids don't want to go to college, what will we say? What values are important to us? So I decided to write rules that we have to abide by so we can hand them down to them. One standard is to build up rather than tear down. I also want my kids to know that God is first. I want them to wake up and say, "Good morning, God." Beauty, order, and simplicity are important. That philosophy will turn our lives upside down but we will be right side up for the first time.

N: Create a life that makes room for human error. We all plan for the ideal day, but human error comes in, and life happens. Keep life simple enough that you can most always keep your word. If you make a commitment, keep it.

K: I want us to be open in our communications and aware of relationships. Uncommon Sense strategies have helped me teach my children to communicate, to relate to positives in others, and know that it's not all about them. I want our values to reflect that.

P: Being patient, faithful, self-controlled, and having deep, rich relationships is important to our family. Nothing is more important than relationships that build you up and help you to pursue what is best for your family and community.

WEEKLY CHORES — These are tasks done to contribute to the maintenance of the home. We found that an hour of concentrated work once a week is such a reasonable and thoughtful request that we rarely had a word of protest. We got this buy-in at family meetings.

Saturday was the workday at our house, and I would cheerily say, "Where are you going to fit in your hour today between your activities?" Our children weren't expected to do extracurricular activities that kept them away from home all day. That is a form of work itself. Also, although the house is important to parents, social activities are more important to the child. That shouldn't make us angry or indignant. We need to guide them, not jerk them back, to the realization that mutual contribution at home is necessary. Stay calm if they protest.

If a family member will be gone on Saturday, on which day should you expect the hour? It is essential that a parent has the job lined up, makes materials for the job available, explains thoroughly what is expected, and demonstrates the task (or works alongside the child) until the work behavior is established or the task is completed. If the job can be done in less than an hour and no other job is ready to be done, the service is complete. Don't punish a child for working quickly. He or she works until the job is completed or one hour has passed.

Remember that you have the monthly family project time for big chores like washing windows, painting, cleaning out a garage, or major yard jobs.

Most of the families that have chosen an Uncommon Sense lifestyle have allowed their children to clean their rooms once a week. And we all know a one-week mess can look like a five-month job. Most of us have given our children a day and time as well as a checklist of expectations. Once the day and time arrive, the parents check the room and then decide whether the child has earned the privilege of going out with friends and having electronics or if those will be withheld until the room is cleaned. When you check the room, try to notice what *has* been done as well as what hasn't.

Once their friends realize that your children's freedom is dependent upon this condition, they will learn to do without them, come and help them clean their room, give them a pep talk to inspire them to hurry and finish, or be clueless why you are so mean. Never fear. There are many ways of dealing with this lovingly. Sometimes, your child may want to stay in because there is an event that he or she needs an excuse to miss. Other times, they may have an exhausting schedule and need your support to get the job done. Occasionally, you may need to give grace as God often does, and let them go out even though they didn't earn it. Please remember to listen to the Holy Spirit and seek wisdom as you assess each week's complexities with wisdom, courage, and humility.

WOUNDS— Do you have sore spots? These are sensitivities that come from real or imagined emotional injuries in our past. They are bundled together in the brain and sit dormant waiting (more or less) to be triggered by a current circumstance. Heaven help the people who tap into them. Emotions (conscious or subconscious) quickly and automatically flood our thoughts and we react. If we have learned to avoid pain, we will withdraw. If we have learned to confront, we may attack. Some of us have learned to combine attacks with strategic withdrawals. Sometimes childlike feelings tumble out when we think we have been overlooked, disrespected, betrayed, abandoned, intruded upon.... We may even react in ways that are out of proportion to the current event and later wonder why. What sets you off? Do you withdraw, attack, or both? If you think you do neither, ask your family. They'll keep you honest.

Triggers (the circumstances that tap into the pain) and wounds begin to become less powerful as we work on them. They stay powerful if we fight them or ignore them.

How can we help someone heal from a wound? We can become a safe person in their life.

Realize that anger is a mask for sadness and pain. When someone is angry or aloof and is willing to share, we can

1. listen to what causes the person's strong emotions;
2. reflect the words so he or she can modify the story and calm down;

3. say "I'm sorry" (that this circumstance triggered that pain) and give the person a hug or a kiss on the head; -- THIS IS HARD. FEW PEOPLE CAN DO THIS, BUT IT'S HUGE.

4. try to get to know them better so we don't unnecessarily cause the problem again.

Listen carefully. You'll hear their themes. "I'm not special to anyone." "I'm sick of being used." "I'm tired of trying to be perfect." These hurts started *long* ago. It doesn't matter if it seems silly or ridiculous to you. Our brains are a complex mix of relationships and life events. You can never begin to imagine what another person has witnessed and experienced in life. If the emotion is there, the wound is there. If you are a trigger, you have an opportunity to heal the wound. My friend, that is an honor, even though it is mighty inconvenient sometimes!

As you listen and hug, remember to pause for a second and remember who is really in control, and say, "God, listen and speak through me, hug through me." If you say it *and mean it,* you'll be surprised what you experience. God is in our midst and loves to transform us with His companionship and miracles.

If the wounds are yours and you've had a tough past, remember this. It's not what happened that makes the difference in the remainder of our lives. It's what we do with it. Decide to live with love, faith and freedom.

APPENDIX

⪘

A HANDFUL OF KEY SCRIPTURES, ENLIGHTENING books, and regular responsibility lists were essential ingredients to keep us on track as our family created a path. As children grow, their routines must loosen up, but having things in writing can keep life clear and uncomplicated.

SCRIPTURAL ANCHORS

These verses were the ones that kept my actions in line when I wanted to do something foolish. If we remember these words and act in accordance with them, we will make good decisions. Key phrases within each verse may be especially helpful.

"Love is patient and kind. Love is not jealous or boastful or proud or rude. Love does not demand its own way. Love is not irritable, and it keeps no record of when it has been wronged. It is never glad about injustice but rejoices whenever the truth wins out. Love never gives up, never loses faith, is always hopeful, and endures through every circumstance.….There are three things that will endure—faith, hope, and love—and the greatest of these is love."

—I COR. 13:4-7, 13

"But when the Holy Spirit controls our lives, he will produce this kind of fruit in us: love, joy, peace, patience, kindness, goodness, faithfulness, gentleness, and self-control."

— GAL. 5:22-23

"Let everything you say be good and helpful, so that your words will be an encouragement to those who hear them."

— EPH. 4:29

"Fix your thoughts on what is true and honorable and right. Think about things that are pure and lovely and admirable. Think about things that are excellent and worthy or praise."

— PHIL. 4:8

"In everything you do, stay away from complaining and arguing, so that no one can speak a word of blame against you."

— PHIL. 2:14-15

"It is better to trust in the Lord than to put confidence in people."

— PS. 118:8

"Trust in the Lord with all your heart; do not depend on your own understanding. Seek his will in all you do, and he will direct your paths."

— PROV. 3:5-6

"A gentle answer turns away wrath, but harsh words stir up anger. The wise person makes learning a joy."

– PROV. 15:1-2

"And don't sin by lettering anger gain control over you. Don't let the sun go down while you are still angry."

— EPH. 4:26

"Stop judging others and you will not be judged. For others will treat you as you treat them."

— Matt. 7:1

"God alone, who made the law, can rightly judge among us. He alone has the power to save or to destroy. So what right do you have to condemn your neighbor?"

— James 4:12

"Don't make your children angry by the way you treat them. Rather, bring them up with the discipline and instruction approved by the Lord."

— Eph. 6:4

If another believer sins against you, or is caught in any transgression:
> *Go privately and point out the fault*
>> — Matt. 18:15
> *Gently and humbly help that person onto the right path*
>> — Gal. 6:1
> *Forgive them always*
>> — Matt. 19:21

Never pay back evil for evil to anyone. Instead:
> *Do things in such a way that everyone can see you are honorable. Do your part to live in peace with everyone as much as possible*
>> — Rom. 12:17.
> *Don't retaliate when people say unkind things about you. Instead pay them back with a blessing*
>> — 1 Peter 4:9

"Your anger can never make things right in God's sight."

—James 1:20

"Your own soul is nourished when you are kind, but you destroy yourself when you are cruel."
——Prov. 11:17

"Let no debt remain outstanding except the continuing debt to love one another, for he who loves his fellowman has fulfilled the law."
——Rom. 13:8

Books From My Shelf

There are so many excellent works about God and parenting that a short list is impossible unless I just grab a few from the shelf to get you started. This list includes both modern and classic authors, lofty thoughts as well as simple. I encourage you to begin with this list and discover new ones for your own library.

Getting to Know God and Adapting Your Lifestyle

A.W. Tozer——*The Knowledge of the Holy* and *The Pursuit of God*
Andrew Murray——*Humility*
Andy Stanley——*The Grace of God*
Brother Lawrence——*The Practice of the Presence of God with Spiritual*
C.S. Lewis——*Mere Christianity*
Charles Stanley——*The Blessings of Brokenness*
David Gregory——*Dinner with a Perfect Stranger*
Eknath Easwaran——*Love Never Faileth*
Gordan MacDonald——*The Life God Blesses*
Gregory Frizzell——*Returning to Holiness*
Jim Cymbala——*When God's People Pray*
John Eldridge——*Sacred Romance* and *The Utter Relief of Holiness*
John Lynch, Bruce McNicol, and Bill Thrall——*The Cure*
Kay Warren——*Choose Joy*
Ken Boa——*Face to Face: Praying the Scriptures for Intimate Worship*

Michael Belk—*Journeys with the Messiah*
Rick Warren—*The Purpose-Driven Life*
Sarah Young—*Jesus Calling*
Stan Telchin—*Betrayed*

DVDs
Jim Cymbala—*When God's People Pray*[21]
The Visual Bible: Matthew[22]

COUPLES BOOKS
Harville Hendrix—*Getting the Love You Want*
Henry Cloud and John Townsend—*Boundaries in Marriage*
Jeff Auerbach—*Irritating the Ones You Love: The Down and Dirty Guide to Better Relationships*
Lee Strobel and Leslie Strobel—*Surviving A Spiritual Mismatch*
Milan and Kay Yerkovich—*How We Love*
William Van Horn—*7 Steps to Passionate Love*

PARENTING BOOKS
Adele Forber and Elaine Mazlish—*How to Talk So Kids Will Listen and Listen So Kids Will Talk*
Daniel J. Siegel and Tina Payne Bryson—*The Whole-Brain Child*
David J. Wilmes—*Parenting for Prevention* and *How To Raise a Child to Say No to Alcohol/Drugs*
Gary Chapman and Ross Campbell—*5 Love Languages of Children*
Howard Glasser and Jennifer Easley—*Transforming the Difficult Child: The Nurtured Heart Approach*
Dr. Laura Markham—*Peaceful Parent, Happy Kids*

---

21 http://www.zondervan.com/when-god-s-people-pray Inspiring. The story of the creation of Brooklyn Tabernacle

22 This is Christ with a wide range of emotions, likely to be meaningful to today's Christian who likes faith talk to be realistic. You will hardly notice you are being read the Gospel of Matthew word for word. Richard Kiley narrates as the grandfatherly disciple, Matthew.

CHILDREN'S BOOKS

Fred Rogers — *The World According to Mister Rogers: Important Things to Remember*

Josh McDowell — *Family Devotions*[23]

Max Lucado — *You Are Special* (Also a DVD)

One Year Bible for Kids, New Living Translation, Tyndale Publishers, 1997.

Holy Bible, NIV, Children's Edition, Zondervan Kids, Zondervan, 1988.

The Beginner's Bible, Timeless Children's Stories, Gold 'n' Honey Books, James R. Leininger — 1989

The Children's Daily Devotional Bible, Contemporary English Version, Thomas Nelson, 1996.

MUSIC

If you have a genre, there are artists for you today. These are just a few ideas to get you started.

Amy Grant — *Better Than a Hallelujah*

Casting Crowns — *Thrive*

Chris Tomlin — *Indescribable* and *Whom Shall I Fear*

Mandisa — *Overcomer*

Matthew West — *Do Something*

Mercy Me — *Greater* and *I Can Only Imagine*

Smokie Norful — *No Greater Love*

SIMPLE PRAYERS

If you are not accustomed to praying out loud, let these little prayers get you started. Eventually, add on some sentences about specifics to go with them, and before you know it, you will be talking aloud to God as if He were another person in the room. By the way — He is.

---

23 Family devotionals come in so many forms. Most can be read in 5 minutes or less. Find one by an author that fits the perspective you want for your family. If some of the days don't seem to agree with your take on life, skip them. You will find that children and teens will prefer to be read to rather than lectured to. Some mornings our whole family laughed or had stimulating conversations inspired by these simple offerings.

Also, some people tell me they don't know to whom they should pray. Pray to whomever you choose. God, Jesus Christ, Holy Spirit, Father, Abba (which is a more intimate term for "father"). Speak to the person who makes you feel most understood and reassured. For me, it changes according to my need.

And remember to encourage others to say "Amen" at the end of a prayer. When they do, it's like saying "I agree" or "confirmed."

MEALTIME

Come, Lord Jesus, be our guest, let this food to us be blessed.

Lord, we thank you for this food, we thank you for the blessings of this day.

God is great, God is good, let us thank Him for our food,
By his hands we are fed. Thank you, Lord, for our daily bread.

BEDTIME

Now I lay me down to sleep, I pray the Lord my soul to keep. Watch me safely through the night, and wake me with the morning light.

Father, we thank thee for the night,
and for the pleasant morning light.
For rest and food and loving care,
and all that makes the day so fair.
Help us to do the things we should,
to be to others kind and good.
In all we do, in work or play,
to grow more loving every day.

RESPONSIBILITY LISTS

Each family member has a simple list of individual expectations that resonates with his or her needs and abilities. For the children, make the list cute or allow each child to decorate it. Instead of talking and nagging, this physical aide allows people to make checks in boxes and hold themselves accountable. This becomes a life skill. Don't forget to support each person with affirmations and boundaries, hold meetings, and troubleshoot when needed.

Here's an example of our lists long ago. Before you read them remember, they are simply a guideline, an alternative to talk. A goal of 100% can become a constant stressor, so in some homes, partial completion will provide a sense of accomplishment.

Daily Routine — Bentley (Age 8)

Bentley arrived home from school at 2:30.

To be completed before 4:30 PM:
- Eat snack
- Empty bookbag at table
- Begin homework
- Reload bookbag (restock school supplies and snacks)
- Practice jumping rope at 4:00 PM
- Practice piano at 4:15 PM

To be completed before 6:00 PM:
- Bathe
- Wash hair and face
- Lay out clothes
- Comb hair
- Lay shoes at door

To be completed before 7:40 PM:
- Finish homework if needed
- Put book bag by the door
- Brush teeth
- Tidy room

Daily Routine — Carroll

- Be in the kitchen at 6:00 AM
- Family devotions at 6:15 AM
- Prepare lunch for Jim by 7:00 AM
- Help pack snacks and bookbags at 3:00 PM
- Watch kids jump rope at 4:10 PM (to let them know I appreciate their progress)
- Help children practice piano at 4:25 PM
- Have dinner on the table at 6:00 PM
- Handle family issues and conduct Bible study between 6:30-7:30 PM
- Share individual time with girls from 7:30-8:30 PM
- Time with Jim from 8:30-9:30 PM
- Complete couple prayer time with Jim before going to sleep

Character Ticket

TO: FROM: DATE:

THE SITUATION CALLED FOR:

Love   Joy   Peace   Patience

Kindness   Generosity

Faithfulness   Gentleness   Self-control

YOU (injury):

USUALLY YOU (justice):

ACKNOWLEDGMENTS

I am blessed to have many wonderful people in my life who made this book possible and helped bring it to fruition.

First, I would like to thank my parents, Richard and Gloria Rose. Because you lived a fun, sensible, respectful life, I knew when I wasn't. You *ignited* my belief in Christ. You also gave me Sher, Jeanne, and Dave who, beyond being siblings, are among my best friends. Oh, how I love you all.

I am also thankful for my wise, easygoing husband of 23 years, Jim, and his loving family. Jim told and *showed* us that he loved us with an everlasting love. I'm grateful for his sense of humor and the kind but solid ways he brought wisdom and logic into our home. And I am touched by the enduring patience of my precious daughters, Bentley, Caty, and Laine. Thank you for teaching, loving, and encouraging me and putting up with some real nonsense in the middle of it all! I'm so proud of the women you are.

I cannot say enough about my team — Peggy Blount, Kim Steuterman, Mary Helen Thompson, Lisa Stalica, Alison MacDonell, Sheila Barnes, Judy Davis, and Kelly Merritt — and their husbands and children. Our weekly lunches over the past ten years have been a treasure chest of laughter, (and a few tears), ingenuity, problem-solving and support. Together we created this book and an honest respect for the different ways families will live into its messages.

Sincere thanks are also due to Bridget, Jill, Kristin, Liz, Sabrina, Sophia, and Sue and their families. They have been fun-loving explorers who tested out the philosophies and tools of this lifestyle and kept me honest as an author and teacher.

I am blessed that Sharron Vogelhuber, Pam Reimann and Katherine and Taylor Huskey read my *long* first draft and convinced me I had a book and a lifestyle worth sharing. Thank you for this generous gift.

I will be forever grateful to Bill Van Horn who introduced me to a level of love *for* others and *from* others that was life changing. His willingness to let me use any of his material "without acknowledgment" is a level of generosity that people seldom see in life.

Finally, I want to thank the artists who crafted the final product. I am blessed for the work of my wonderful editor, Jamie Hughes, whose skills and insights grace every page; Caty Coplin, my artistic director and photographer; Liz Cox, my dedicated illustrator. And this book could not have been finalized without the talents of Jera Publishing team, including Kimberly Martin and Stephanie Anderson.

ABOUT THE AUTHOR

CARROLL ROSE COPLIN, M.ED., M.S., LPC

Carroll is a Licensed Professional Counselor and founder of Uncommon Sense, LLC, a business dedicated to understanding human nature, and to the practical and spiritual ways we can teach people to love. Carroll has a master's degree in special education, and taught in public schools for ten years. She followed her teaching with a master's degree in counseling and psychology and a private practice specializing in stress reduction, high performance living, and team management. Her work has included corporate and church settings as well as families and individuals. Carroll was married for twenty-three years prior to widowhood, and is a mother to three grown children. You can contact Carroll through her website at www.uncommonsenseliving.com.

Photo Credit: Shanon Bell

SCRIPTURAL INDEX

Index